POINTS OF DEPARTURE

POINTS OF DEPARTURE

ERNECE B. KELLY
Loop City College,
Chicago

JOHN WILEY & SONS, INC.
New York • London • Sydney • Toronto

Library of Congress Catalogue Card Number: 79-180271

ISBN 0-471-46805-3

Printed in the United States of America.

10 9 8 7 6 5 4 3 2 1

To J.K. and V.S.
who have helped both
this book and me to
become.

FACES

By Ted Joans

I want to see faces
of all races/winning faces/grinning faces/happy faces/faces that face East in prayer/faces covered & uncovered with hair/faces uplifted & proud/ faces of joy of being in love/faces of yesterday,today,Now & tomorrow faces/faces that erased war/faces that destroyed ignorance, disease, & hunger/faces that face the tasks & won/freedom faces/freedom faces/faces of one nation and that nation is the human being congregation of faces/freedom faces/I want to see faces/I want to see faces/I want to see faces/I want to face me

Declan Haun/Black Star

PREFACE

The frontispiece, "Faces," suggests the comprehensiveness of this textbook. The book deals with many sides of the American experience and includes writings by and about minority-group Americans. It also includes writings by members of the larger Anglo-Saxon population.

The selections portray the diversity of our nation: the suburbanite and the rural family; the impoverished and the middle-class American; the conformist and the maverick. They help the student (regardless of his ethnic, economic, or behavioral pattern) to find, define, and understand his own "face." Just as the frontispiece poem moves through a jumble of faces to a final self-confrontation, the reader (I hope) will follow the same route.

I have been guided by two assumptions in the selection and arrangement of the literature. First, many teachers realize the value of quasi-personal materials in the classroom. The poems, short stories, and audio-visual materials (films and recordings are recommended for about 50 percent of the readings) presented here relate to the things that students talk about. Thus the book is designed for the teacher who considers students as whole persons, not just as "students who sit in the classroom." As whole persons, students have problems, concerns, and preferences. If their work at school overlaps the very concerns that hold their attention, the work is likely to be more interesting and meaningful. Therefore, I divided the book into four areas of student interest: self-identity, love and marriage, employment, and community.

My second assumption is that many students consider a textbook more relevant if it includes the experiences and expectations of nonwhite and nonmiddle-class Americans. Some textbooks have portrayed America as lily-white and uniclass. This is a false picture, and I think it is a potentially dangerous one. In this volume I depict the American experience as it is: variegated, difficult to adjust to, and sometimes difficult to survive within. In order to give a balanced picture, I include literature that spans socioeconomic classes and racial groups.

For example, "The Happiest Man on Earth" is about Jesse Fulton who is driven to a desperate act by poverty; he is white. "We Real Cool" depicts young Afro-Americans in the city who maintain a special life style in order to "live." "Long Night's Journey" describes the sights and sounds of summer in a Puerto Rican neighborhood in New York City.

The cartoons, comic strips, song lyrics, and photographs are an integral part of the development of the four themes of the text. These illustrative materials present a vivid facet of the experiences described in each of those sections or reflect the mood or message of the overall theme.

Black and brown people are discussed frequently throughout the text. For this reason the selections will have a special meaning for the Chicano, the Afro-American, the Puerto Rican, and the American Indian student. But the material will also be of interest to white students. The realism and drama in the selections reflect the basic needs of all of us: the need to feel worthwhile, to feel loved, and to identify with a physical location.

Finally, my purpose is to help the student to improve his reading and writing skill. But, in doing this, he will learn that even though people differ in color, culture, and ethical heritage, there are some cultural, social, and fundamentally human characteristics that are shared by all of us.

NOTE TO THE INSTRUCTOR

I cannot (and would *not* if I could) tell instructors how to use this text. I can only be explicit about the audiences for whom it was designed and the goals I had in mind in developing it.

Insofar as audiences are concerned, the text was designed with English and social science classrooms in mind. The feature which most works it into the framework of the general social science classroom is one of a consistent questioning of the personhood and the general social surroundings of the reader. The reader is asked again and again to examine and understand himself and his surroundings in terms of the queries raised in the materials of the book.

The same kinds of questions and directions are useful in English classes. But in addition to them, there are questions of style, language appropriateness, problems of explication, and other literary considerations raised by the materials also. This focus would probably be of equal interest to the teacher of English.

The text is designed primarily for students' use; teachers were conceived to be an adjunct to the students' experience of the materials. The three main suggestions for uses of the text which follow will bear this out, for two of them suggest that students work without the instructor. In other words, this text is a self-contained instrument, in that students can use it with only minimal assistance from their instructor. The instructor would probably be needed in the role of discussion facilitator or as an identifier of resource materials in the library or of other kinds of research materials. Other than these kinds of marginal roles, I believe the instructor can step back and allow the student to move about and discover more about himself, society, literature, and other media within the boundaries of this book.

The book lends itself to classroom use in three different ways: (a) as the major textbook in a reading-composition class; (b) as a controlled-supplementary reader similar to a group casebook; and (c) as a supplementary text in much the same way that periodicals are used in some classrooms.

As a major textbook: There are questions which require verbal responses following each selection. More complex questions are also included which require written analysis or discussion. Through these kinds of questions, the student is invited into discussion and writing experiences which grow out of the very materials he has read.

A third category of questions suggests materials for the student who is going to write a more elaborate paper (such as a research paper) and who needs to familiarize himself with the resources of the library. However, it is not necessary to assign a research topic in order to guide students to the library. Throughout the book I have suggested that students use library resources to check the meaning of terms or to gather additional information on a certain topic.

As a controlled-supplementary reader: There are the four major themes around which the text is organized. Students may select one which interests them and meet with other members of the class who have selected the same topic. Discussion and analysis of the materials provided in the text as well as those referred to which are available in libraries can proceed independent of the instructor.

Writing skills may be improved by these same students selecting that writing topic which most appeals to them. Although each student will be writing his own paper, those in a given group will be free to confer with one another. Thus, the usual solitary reading experience may be broadened into a group in which students can draw upon the supportive cooperation of their colleagues.

As a supplementary text: Students can be instructed to use the text as either a reading or writing source. The semipersonal nature of the selections and the liberal use of illustrative materials should motivate students to read and use the book, not so much because it has been assigned, but because they are enjoying it. Their progress through the text can be tested at intervals by requiring them to submit a written assignment or an oral report.

Ernece B. Kelly

CONTENTS

POINTS OF DEPARTURE

Learning made me painfully aware of life and me. I began to dig what was inside of me. What had I been? How had I become that way? What could I be? How could I make it?

from Down These Mean Streets by Piri Thomas, 1967. Reprinted by permission of Alfred A. Knopf, Inc.

PART 1

"I BEGAN TO DIG WHAT WAS INSIDE OF ME. . ."

An American college counselor has commented that today's young people have an intensity in their concern for the questions of human existence that is probably unrivaled in any other American historical period. Their questions—which are perennial human ones: "Who am I?" "Where do I belong?" "What am I worth?"—often go unasked, and consequently unanswered, in our classrooms.

But these are among the fundamental and basic questions raised by the selections of this section. Dramatically different responses are offered here.

For example, in "The Store" a young boy instinctively senses the significance of the older men who witness the pain his father inflicts on him and tries to be *the man* his father wants. The fellows in the poem, "We Real Cool," seem, at first, miles away from the father's act in the country store. And geographically they are, but their bravado is similar to the small boy's. They participate in different rituals, but they share the same end: proving who and what you are.

The poem, "Ex-Basketball Player," examines the crucial role that crowds—anonymous but adoring—can play in the development of an individual's self-concept. This approach is radically different from the independent spirit of the fellow who defiantly wears the yellow flower in E. E. Cummings' poem, "Nobody wears a yellow rose." For he seems to be certain of who he is and anxious to flaunt it.

This section deals with the revelation or rediscovery of the variety of ways we Americans have of testing our worth and of analyzing our own makeup and that of others. The mere discovery that there are others who hold on tenaciously to their sense of self and still others who are looking for it (in their peers, their parents, or their fans) may make it easier for the reader to see and to accept himself.

MISS PEACH

Mell Lazarus

Mell Lazarus. Courtesy of Publishers-Hall Syndicate

What do you think?

1. What exactly is Arthur doing? What is causing him to go from person to person testing these ideas about himself?
2. Should Arthur listen more to himself and his own perceptions or more to other people's opinions of him? Why?
3. What differences would you expect to find between your own opinions of yourself and those of your friends and associates? Explain your answer in some detail.
4. Most of Arthur's friends make reference to what are "desirable traits" *today.* Do standards for evaluating a person's worth change from generation to generation? If so, can you name one or two changes that you have observed or have heard about from older persons? (In addition to talking about this, you might wish to write a short paper in which you describe a change in standards.)

Suggestions for writing and drawing

1. Obtain from the library a copy of the poem "Richard Cory" by Edwin Arlington Robinson. Write a short paper of two or three paragraphs in which you describe the difference between what is apparent about Richard Cory and what was actually going on inside him. Note carefully the differences between the consequences of the opinions of others in this comic strip and in the poem.
2. Draw four more cartoon boxes on a sheet of plain paper. Show by drawing figures what Arthur does with his last description "Very nice person." Include whatever words you need by putting them in the balloons that are drawn above his head.

Wayne Miller/Magnum Photos

THE POOL PLAYERS SEVEN AT THE GOLDEN SHOVEL

Gwendolyn Brooks

We real cool. We
left school. We

Lurk late. We
Strike straight. We

Sing sin. We
Thin gin. We

Jazz June. We
Die soon.

What do you think?

1. From the information given, what does being "real cool" mean in this poem?
2. Is there any way of detecting whether the speakers in the poem are happy or unhappy about the pattern of their lives? Are they bent on enjoying or destroying themselves? Give reasons for your answer.
3. Are the pool players conforming to what society expects of them? Support your answer. In whose view are they "real cool"?
4. What explanation can you offer for the fact that the lines in the poem are short and staccatolike? Would the poem best be read slowly or rapidly? Why?

Suggestions for writing and drawing and listening

1. In a paper of moderate length (100 words), describe one of the pool players who is speaking in the poem. Give a detailed account of the style of clothing he wears, the color, and apparent cost. Or, draw a picture that shows clearly his taste in clothes and that gives a vivid picture of what his surroundings are like.
2. In a short paper (500 words), go behind this poem to explain why the pool players behave as they do.
3. Listen to the 45 rpm recording of "Elegy" by Shelley Fisher (Aries label: #A 5002). This is another poem by Gwendolyn Brooks, which was set to music by Oscar Brown, Jr. Does the description of the young boy in this song contrast or compare with the lives of the pool players? Does the recording help you to find reasons for the living patterns of either subject? Does the flavor of the music make the story happy or unhappy?

"ESPONTANEO–SPONTANEOUS . . ."

nuestros cantos–
gemidos del alma–
    aguitarrados y volantes,
cautivan
    el chicanismo . . .

yo soy AZTLÁN,
  fuego encendidor
de
  mundos
y de ideas. . . .

yo soy Bronce
y gitano:
    un dia y dos noches,
    cuauhtemoc y quetzalcóatl,
    el templo y la fuerza . . .

yo soy sánchez
suspendido en el pecho
de mi raza

hierro y coraje,
caló, pachuco, y barrio,
el paso, san anto, y los,
denver, el valle, y el burque,
el bato de la vida loca,
de grifa, prisión, y llanto,

con alm pa revolucion . . .

yo soy Chicano

y mis nubes son coloradas
como mi sangre;
soy
    azteca de verano,
    hispano de invierno,
pero
    Chicano todo el año . . .

Ricardo Sanchez, mi raza es . . .

our chants
soul emanations–
    like guitar strains flying,
enthralling
    chicano sensitivity . . .

i am AZTLÁN,
  blaze igniting
worlds
  of realities
and ideas. . . .

i am bronze
and gypsy:
    a day and two nights,
    cuauhtemoc and quetzalcóatl
    temple and strength . . .

i am sánchez
caught in the context
of my people

iron and rage,
mestizo-ness, hoodlum, and ghetto,
el paso, san antonio, los angeles,
denver, texas valley, albuquerque,
lowriding cat from the jailing life,
pot cultist, prisons, and life-wail,

inwardly breeding my revolution . . .

i am Mexican-American

and my skies are sanguine
like the juice in my veins;
i am
    summer aztec burnished,
    wintry spaniard white,
but
    mestizo all year-long . . .

What do you think?

1. In your own words, explain the central thought of the poem.
2. This poem is similar to the preceding one, "We Real Cool," in that it is descriptive of the feelings of a person belonging to a minority group. Explain how it differs in language, in rhythms, and in imagery.
3. Explain what the poet means in the line

   "i am sanchez
   caught in the context
   of my people"

   In what ways are most, if not all, humans caught in the context of their racial or ethnic group?
4. Explain how the cities, places, and roles that the poet names can "inwardly" breed his revolution. What kind of revolution is he talking about? Be prepared to defend your response by making reference to the poem itself.
5. Although there is little description here, an image of the speaker is conveyed through his statements. Describe the impression you get of the speaker.

Suggestions for writing and viewing

1. Write 6 to 8 lines describing the prominent cultural and social associations of the racial, ethnic, or cultural group you most closely identify with. Open your verse with the lines:

   i am ______________
   caught in the context
   of my people
2. *Very Nice, Very Nice* (National Film Board of Canada, black and white, 8 min.) is a film made up of rapid images suggestive of the flavor of American culture and society. It is recommended for use with students having difficulty identifying what aspects of their wider surroundings most likely affect their sense of selfhood.

THE STORE

John Yount

John Yount "The Store" from *Southern Writing in the Sixties* (1966) by Louisiana State University Press. Reprinted by permission of Louisiana State University Press, Baton Rouge.

He remembered walking down the road with his father to the store. He remembered it the way it was in the early fall. When the sun had been hot during the day, the tar on the blacktop road would melt and stick to his feet, and occasionally a piece of gravel would stick to his foot, and he would have to hop along and pick it off, and then run to catch up with his father again. Someone would be chopping wood somewhere, a satisfying whapping sound that could come from a long way off. A cow would be bawling. And down at Daltey's Store, where he and his father would be going to get some staple, the smoke would be rising almost straight up from the chimney in the still, clear air.

The store was always cool and dark, and if by some chance his father should give him a nickel to spend, he would always come away feeling cheated because what he bought was always less than what he wanted, and what he wanted, though he didn't know it, was the old and pungent atmosphere of that place. He wanted the combined smells of candy and soda pop, and even the cool, watery, cankered smell of the cooler where the soda pop was kept. He wanted the smell of saddles and harnesses, of tobacco chewed and spat on the stove where it sizzled and steamed, the smells of feed and fertilizer that drifted in from the feed room, combined with the smells of cow and horse dung tracked in on the feet of farmers, mingled with the odors of new guns and used ones, the close sweet smell of the yellow flypaper spiraling down from the ceiling; he wanted it all, and he'd hold the nickel so fiercely that his palm would sweat, but what he bought was only a soda pop, or a piece of candy, and as soon as he had taken the first bite or sip, he knew it was not the right thing; it wasn't what he wanted at all.

But going to the store was one of his biggest pleasures because he could watch and listen to the men there. He could almost always find a box or something to sit on just outside their circle, and he could listen to them talk and watch them spit on the stove. And always he felt a kind of sneaky complicity and pride in manhood when he was in Daltey's Store with his father.

But there was one time when things changed and weren't ever quite the same again. His father had gone off into the feed room with Glen Wilcox, who had a bottle. He had cleared his throat and given Tom the sideways look that bound the two of them in secrecy against Tom's mother and given him a nickel which made the pact complete and said, "Here, boy, getcha somethin."

Tom had crossed the dark oily floor to the candy case, his hand immediately warm and sweaty around the nickel, and Daltey came to wait on him, patient as the earth, while Tom scrutinized every kind of candy through the greenish, flyspecked glass. He turned the little wheel of money in his palm and puzzled.

"Hey, boy, you gettin any gravel fer yer goose?" he heard someone ask. He turned and saw Dallas Ayres grinning at him. Dallas Ayres lived on the ridge above Tom's father's place in a shack that had only hard-packed mud for a yard. Tom searched his face for some hint of meaning, something that would let him know how he should reply, but he saw in an instant that no reply was expected. The man laughed at him before he could say anything, even if he'd had something to say. Tom's face began to warm, but Dallas Ayres's flat grey eyes would not let him go.

"Come'ere, boy," he said, and when Tom came closer, he caught him by the arm. He had been leaning back in the split-bottom chair, but when he drew Tom to him, he let the two front legs of his chair plop down on the floor, narrowly missing Tom's bare feet. The clumsiness and violence of the man frightened him, and he tried to pull away, but Dallas said in a cajoling voice: "Aww, come on now, I ain't gonna hurt ya." And he winked at Tom with his mirthless flat grey eyes. "See these here hands?" He shoved one of his broad callused hands under Tom's nose. "You gotta split a few rails and shell a little corn and dig ya some postholes so's you kin git hands like thet. See them horny ole calluses?"

Tom shook his head yes. The muscles of his face felt paralyzed because he didn't know what expression to put on.

"You know why you want calluses like that?"

Tom shook his head no.

"Well, boy, when you git hands like them and ya run em up inside a gal's pretty little step-ins, they'll pee like puppies." He squeezed Tom's arm so hard his lips began to tremble. Tom was leaning away from him, looking for his father and trying not to cry, when he saw he had come in from the feed room and was standing close behind him. He could see in an instant that he had drunk quite a bit. The effect of whisky on his father was always immediate. Not that he was drunk; his father stood steady on his feet, but his eyes already looked a little glassy, as if a thin film had been drawn over them. Though while Tom looked, his father's eyes seemed to clear, and his face lost its color. His father laughed a funny, short, brittle laugh that seemed to put an end to something. Dallas released Tom's arm then and laughed too, winking one of his mirthless grey eyes at Tom's father.

"Reckon, he'll ever amount to anything?" Dallas asked.

"Oh, I think he might. I think he'd do to cross the river with." There was the nasal tone in his father's voice that was only there when he was mad, though Tom didn't know exactly who he was mad at. "Come here son," he said, and Tom went to stand beside him, close enough to feel his father's body heat and smell his sweat, and he felt safe and thought to himself, "You come over here and try to grab me, Dallas Ayres."

Then he heard his father asking, "You ever see anybody get picked up by the hair?" At first he didn't realize what his father was planning to do. He didn't realize it until he saw that Dallas Ayres was looking at him with curiosity, and even then he didn't realize it fully, standing, as he was, so near his father, in a space warmed by his father's body. Even when his father's blunt hard fingers grappled in his hair, trying to get a good grip close to the scalp, he felt secure. It was his father's hand. When the thick fingers closed and made a fist, sharp pains shot across the top of his head and made his eyes water, and when his father started up with his hand, he felt his eyes draw up at the corners like a cat's. But he thought to himself, we'll show him. There was a moment as his toes swung clear of the floor when he thought he couldn't stand it, and he started up with his hands. But it was okay; his head was warm and tight with pain, and he couldn't see what Dallas looked like now, but it was okay; he could stand it. He waited for his feet to come down again, but they didn't, and he heard his father say, "Look at that!" Then it happened. His scalp popped loose with a wet sucking sound he was sure everyone could hear. His skull felt bathed in fire and a red light burst in his head and filled his eyes. When his feet touched the floor, there was no strength in his legs, and for a moment his father was supporting him still by the hair. He didn't know when he had begun to cry, but he had no control over it; he heard his own sobbing as if it too came from inside his head and was a part of the red light that filled his eyes. Little by little his father's voice came to him, "Whoa boy, whoa son, whoa now." And he realized that he was standing on his feet and his father was kneeling beside him. His hands went up to his scalp, and he was surprised to find that he still had it, that the top of his head still had its hair. When he rubbed his head, his scalp felt wrinkled and much too large for his skull and seemed to slide around wetly. He couldn't see anything clearly. His eyes were so full of tears, the world looked melted, and he walked clumsily across the oily floor and out through the blurred doorway. He heard his father talking behind him, and he heard the men laugh.

They walked most of the way home without speaking a word to each other. Tom had smoothed the wrinkles out of his scalp which seemed to fit his skull again the way it should, but rage had taken the place of weeping, and it burned in his throat. It was almost dark when they turned off the blacktop onto the dirt road that led to their house, and Tom walked through the soft dust, mild as face powder.

"Son," Tom's father began. "When I was a youngun, my poppa could pick me up by the hair and I wouldn't make a sound."

"My scalp come loose," Tom said. The rage in his throat ripped his voice. He was very close to crying again.

"Aww, a man's scalp don't come loose," his father said, and there was the nasal quality in his voice again.

"My scalp come loose!" Tom bawled. Tears sprang to his eyes, and he stopped walking and glared at his father with his fists clenched at his sides. He hated himself for the steady half-moan, half-growl of weeping that escaped between his clenched teeth. Tears were tickling his cheeks and seemed to mock his anger. He slapped them away and watched his father's broad back swaying slowly up the dark road ahead of him.

His father's voice drifted back, sad and nasal, "Come on, boy."

Tom stood still, seeming to sink down into the soft, dusty road. He felt too heavy and too tired to walk. He watched the darkness swallow up the figure of his father who kept his regular pace up the road. The dark sky spread out above with a wilderness of stars in it, and when he looked up at it, he felt he was falling back into a well. Because there were so many stars, because the night was soft, and because he felt suddenly clean, as if something had been washed out of him, the pain seemed a little thing now. Maybe I could have stood it, he thought. If he had just put me down in time, or if I had known it was going to happen. He wished he hadn't cried. He picked up his feet then and started home.

When he got to the smokehouse, which was only fifteen feet from his back door, he sat down just outside the shaft of light coming from the kitchen window. He could hear his mother sliding pans across the stove, the oven door squeak, his father's low monotone. He knew his father would not tell her about it. Though he didn't exactly know why, he knew it was between the two of them. The more he thought about it, the more he felt he should have let his father pull the top of his head off, if that's what he wanted to do, and he shouldn't have made a sound. Someone passed the kitchen window, and he started and drew back into the shadow of the smokehouse. He did not want to face his mother and father. He didn't want to walk in that lighted kitchen where they could see him and talk to him. He saw his mother bend down to the window and look out, but he knew she couldn't see him.

"Tom?" she called. "Tom! You come in to supper!"

He drew up into the shadow and did not answer.

"Tom! Are you out there?" She rolled her eyes listening for him to answer.

"Find me," he whispered fiercely, but not loud enough for her to hear. "Come out and find me."

"Tom, do you hear me?"

"Yes um," he said, and he went in to supper.

What do you think?

1. Tom remembers that after this particular trip to Daltey's Store, "things changed and weren't ever quite the same again." Explain, in your own words exactly what happened to bring this dramatic change about? Did Dallas Ayres' treatment of Tom have anything to do with how his father treats him?
2. Tom enters into three pacts with his father: not to reveal his drinking to his mother; to "show" Dallas; and not to tell his mother about the incident at the store. Why does he so willingly enter into these pacts? Since he is angry at his father, why doesn't he tell his mother about the incident?
3. Why didn't Tom reach up and force his father's hand out of his hair? And why did Tom think to himself, "We'll show him" when his father starts lifting him? Why does he want to "show" Dallas? And what does he want to "show" Dallas?
4. What is the significance of Tom's father shifting from the term "man" to "boy" in the talk they have on the walk home? (Lines 113 and 121, page 11).
5. What has been "washed out" of Tom by this incident? (Line 126, page 11).
6. What is Tom's meaning when he challenges his mother to "come out and find me" when he is only sitting outside the back door?
7. In your own words, what are the most important ideas about becoming a man which this story suggests?

Suggestions for writing

1. Tom's father states that he supposes his son would "do to cross the river with" (page 10). List as many other sayings that you're familiar with which describe a person's character or attitude in a similar indirect fashion. If you don't know of any sayings, choose 6 to 10, from a reference book, such as *The Macmillan Book of Proverbs, Maxims, Famous Phrases* that seem most accurate to you.
2. Write a short paper in which you analyze a saying such as the one Tom's father states on page 10. In your paper determine *exactly* what the saying means and comment on whether you accept the saying as being sensible or true.
3. Write a short paper (500 words) about an experience of your own that changed your self-concept and your relationship with a parent or another close relative.

THE GAS STATION

George Segal

The Gas Station by George Segal. 1964.

Collection of the National Gallery of Canada, Courtesy of Sidney Janis Gallery, New York

What do you think?

1. Imagine that each of the following changes were made in the sculpture, The Gas Station. How would the feeling change?
   (a) That the man on the right were standing straight and drinking his Coke.
   (b) That the garage were messy and dirty.
   (c) That the picture were in brilliant and flashy colors.
2. Name all the ways in which this sculpture is suited to the feelings and the matters mentioned in the poem, "Ex-Basketball Player." Name all the ways in which it contrasts with the poem.

Suggestions for writing and drawing

1. Imagine that the sculpture, The Gas Station, is an advertisement for Coca-Cola. List 3 to 5 captions that you would draw under the picture. Or, if you don't think this would make a good advertisement, write out or draw a Before and After advertisement using this picture as the Before. (You will have to write captions under each picture if you draw.)
2. A pictogram is a certain kind of drawing in which you use sentences or phrases rather than lines to draw your picture. Take any verse from the poem, "Ex-Basketball Player," which follows, and use the lines from it to illustrate the poem.

EX-BASKETBALL PLAYER

John Updike

Pearl Avenue runs past the high school lot,
Bends with the trolley tracks, and stops, cut off
Before it has a chance to go two blocks,
At Colonel McComsky Plaza. Berth's Garage
Is on the corner facing west, and there,
Most days, you'll find Flick Webb, who helps Berth out.

Flick stands tall among the idiot pumps—
Five on a side, the old bubble-head style,
Their rubber elbows hanging loose and low.
One's nostrils are two S's, and his eyes
An E and O. And one is squat, without
A head at all—more of a football type.

Once, Flick played for the high school team, the Wizards.
He was good: in fact, the best. In '46,
He bucketed three hundred ninety points,
A county record still. The ball loved Flick.
I saw him rack up thirty-eight or forty
In one home game. His hands were like wild birds.

He never learned a trade; he just sells gas,
Checks oil, and changes flats. Once in a while,
As a gag, he dribbles an inner tube,
But most of us remember anyway.
His hands are fine and nervous on the lug wrench.
It makes no difference to the lug wrench, though.

Off work, he hangs around Mae's Luncheonette.
Grease-grey and kind of coiled, he plays pinball,
Sips lemon cokes, and smokes those thin cigars;
Flick seldom speaks to Mae, just sits and nods
Beyond her face towards bright applauding tiers
Of Necco Wafers, Nibs, and Juju Beads.

What do you think?

1. Do you get the feeling from this poem that Flick Webb lives in the city or a small town? What are some concrete clues which help support your impression?
2. The narrator says "the ball loved Flick." This can't be literally true. What does he mean? What evidence do you think he has for the remark?
3. By your standards is Flick a success or a failure? As you explain your answer, examine what your own standards for success are.
4. The last three lines of the poem suggest that Flick became accustomed to being a "star." Can such a relationship between an individual and a group be harmful? Beneficial? Or both? Give reasons for your answer.

Suggestions for writing, drawing, and viewing

1. Draw sketches of the gas pumps just as John Updike describes them. Is it appropriate to describe them as "idiot pumps"?
2. There is no explanation for why Flick didn't either learn a trade or go on to play professional basketball. There are some hints in the poem, however, which might explain why. Write a short paper in which you provide reasons why he didn't take either of these alternatives. (Be certain that you remain consistent with the tone and information in the poem.)
3. Listen to the song, "The Statue," by Rod McKuen (RCA Victor #LPM-3635). It is about a war hero who, though dead, talks to a statue that has been erected to him. He sings about the ways in which heroes are "created." Compare the relationship between the crowd and the hero in this song and in the poem above. What are the differences and similarities? What significance do you make of these?
4. The film, "The Day Manolete Was Killed," presents a poignant story of the manner in which the life and violent death of a famous Spanish matador was fashioned by the intense demands of his admirers (19 min). It is highly recommended as a catalyst for discussion of the relationship between popular "stars" and their audiences.

Lucille Cunningham

THE UNKNOWN CITIZEN

W. H. Auden

To JS/07/M/378
This Marble Monument Is Erected by the State

He was found by the Bureau of Statistics to be
One against whom there was no official complaint,
And all the reports on his conduct agree
That, in the modern sense of an old-fashioned word, he was a saint,
For in everything he did he served the Greater Community.
Except for the War till the day he retired
He worked in a factory and never got fired,
But satisfied his employers, Fudge Motors Inc.
Yet he wasn't a scab or odd in his views,
For his Union reports that he paid his dues,
(Our report on his Union shows it was sound)
And our Social Psychology workers found
That he was popular with his mates and liked a drink.
The Press are convinced that he bought a paper every day
And that his reactions to advertisements were normal in every way.
Policies taken out in his name prove that he was fully insured,
And his Health-card shows he was once in hospital but left it cured.
Both Producers Research and High-Grade Living declare
He was fully sensible to the advantages of the Installment Plan
And had everything necessary to the Modern Man,
A gramophone, a radio, a car and a frigidaire.
Our researchers into Public Opinion are content
That he held the proper opinions for the time of year;
When there was peace, he was for peace; when there was war, he went.
He was married and added five children to the population,
Which our Eugenist says was the right number for a parent of his generation,
And our teachers report that he never interfered with their education.
Was he free? Was he happy? The question is absurd:
Had anything been wrong, we should certainly have heard.

What do you think?

1. An everyday definition for the word "saint" is a person who is exceptionally charitable or meek. What does Auden have in mind when he describes the Citizen as being a saint, but "in the modern sense"?
2. What does Auden have in mind when he mentions the Greater Community? Is it a good thing to serve it? Why or why not? Is it good to serve it *in everything one does,* as the Citizen does? Give reasons for your answer.
3. One line of the poem is in parentheses. Why? What new insight do we gain about the speaker from that line? Exactly who is the speaker and what organization does he belong to?
4. Double check the items that are "necessary to the Modern Man." Do they seem *necessary* to you? What kinds of things are omitted from that list? Why do you think Auden omitted those items?
5. Could you justify the consideration of questions of one's freedom or happiness as being absurd? How? What point is Auden making in labeling such questions as absurd?
6. Describe, in your own words, the process of depersonalization that has taken place in this poem. What aspects of our own society have approached this?
7. Explain why an individual in the society Auden describes would find it more difficult or easier to maintain a sense of self than is the case in American society today.

Suggestions for writing and reading

1. One way of looking at this poem is to consider it a portrait of a conformist How does the dictionary define the conformist? Write a short paper in which you use a dictionary definition to open the paper and then explain why a society or community goes about encouraging its members to conform.
2. Write a short paper in which you describe yourself in terms of conformity or nonconformity. Carefully select two aspects of yourself: the way you dress or speak or walk—any two which seem harmonious. After describing these two, go on to describe yourself as a whole person. Do you think you are a conformist or a nonconformist?
3. If you are interested in reading some other material about persons who conformed or others who consistently did not, you might be interested in these paperbacks: *End of the Road* by John Barth; *Rabbit Run* by John Updike; *Catch-22* by Joseph Heller; and *Been Down So Long, It Looks Like Up to Me* by Richard Farina.

LETTERS TO A BLACK BOY

Bob Teague

Dear Adam, in trying to paint a portrait of Mister Charlie for you, I have neglected one of his more flattering characteristics. Underneath that white mask he is often a great deal like you and me—quite human.

I would estimate that in 15 percent of my face-to-face dealings with Mister Charlie, he impresses me as being just another individual. Who happens to be white, not a hunky.

I try to remember that 15 percent whenever I meet Mister Charlie. And until he says or does something that reflects the other 85 percent, I forget that he is a descendant of Simon Legree and perhaps a distant cousin of a modern-day Alabaman named George C. Wallace.

The 85 percent often shows up in subtle ways. For example, some of the whites I have worked with over the years felt free to tell me their most sacred secrets, things that should be told only to their psychiatrists. My guess is that they did so—and still do so—because deep in their bones is an unshakable belief that a black man is not a part of their reality, that the chances of my repeating their confidences to anyone who counts in their world is zero.

Other 85 percenters, I have found, are anxious to assure me how liberal they are, that they belong to black organizations such as the N.A.A.C.P. Or that they don't hate blacks at all. Just southern whites, or Jews or Italians or Puerto Ricans. Or that they have nothing but admiration for "good" Negroes.

While waiting to pick up my little red station wagon this evening at the public garage near my office, I was recognized, as often happens, by perhaps a dozen men and women clustered around the cashier. Television fans. All white. One of them was much more candid than the rest. A handsome, well-dressed chap around my age. There was a fuzziness in his voice suggesting that his candor had been poured minutes before from a bottle. If asked to describe his attitude on the race question, I am positive he would say, "A very liberal white liberal."

Well, there in the garage—after joining the enthusiastic chorus of "I watch you every night"—he delivered what he clearly regarded as the compliment supreme:

"If the rest of them were all like you," he said cheerfully, "everything would be all right. No problem at all."

Luckily, I had the presence of mind to short-circuit my automatic response to compliments of almost any sort—as gracious a "thank you" as I can manage. In this case, I clamped my jaws tight, looked away and said nothing. I did not erase my smile, however. A concession I often make in situations like that. Anyone's television career depends on alienating as few viewers as possible. My excuse for not telling that very liberal white liberal what I thought is this: I need the money I am making to maintain that wall of dollars I have built around my family to protect us as much as possible from the whims of Mister Charlie's society.

Had I been facing another "liberal," one who was not one of my fans, I would have told him that the reason "the rest of them" are not like me is that they never get anything like the almost-equal opportunities I have had, that perhaps only a thousand black men in the entire country receive comparable opportunities in a given year, that the other 21,999,000 blacks are virtually locked out of this society, that they are outside looking in. With bitterness, anger and hate.

I wish I could tell you, my son, that the "very liberal white liberal" I met at the garage represents the last breed of tasteless white that is likely to set your teeth on edge. The uncomfortable fact is that the 85 percenters are masters of self-deception; they are also resourceful, coming up periodically with disguises so clever that you are forced to admire their inventiveness. Because of my long experience, however, I am not fooled for a moment by such innocent-sounding gambits as "Some of my best friends are Negroes" or "Frankly, we've never had a Negro guest at our yacht club, but we'd be proud to have you and your wife come out for the weekend."

I also recognize 85 percenters among my closest white associates by their inability to recognize me in an unfamiliar setting. In the office, I am an individual, of course. But elsewhere—even on the street immediately outside the office—I become, in their eyes, just another animated blob of black protoplasm. Which couldn't possibly have any connection with them. It is not that they refuse to see me; their minds simply won't let them if I am not where they expect.

So how do I respond to their snubs, their impersonal confidences, their N.A.A.C.P. cards, their condescension, their insults to nonblack minorities?

I don't.

I let them go their way without challenge; I let them rave on and on without comment. Sometimes they get the point. In any event, I have come to believe that any man who behaves in any of those fashions is a hunky, and well beyond repair. I try to spend as little time as possible in his presence.

What do you think?

1. Does use of the phrase "Mister Charlie" tell you something about the author's attitude toward whites? What exactly?
2. The author distinguishes between a white man and a hunky. What characteristics make one different from the other? Can you think of other racial names that carry different meanings even though they refer to the same racial or ethnic group?
3. List the ways in which the white man treats Bob Teague which show that he doesn't think he's a worthwhile individual. Do you agree with Teague's interpretation of these incidents or is he being overly sensitive? What would you do if you were in his place?
4. How much of a person's sense of value comes from the way in which others treat him? Do you think Teague thinks highly of himself? If so, on what grounds? If not, why not?
5. What do you think of the comment, "If the rest of them were all like you everything would be all right"? Would that sameness in Afro-Americans be desirable for them? For whites whom they dealt with? And would all racial problems go away if every Afro-American were like Bob Tague? Give reasons for your answer.
6. Is Teague correct in thinking he can protect his family within a "wall of dollars"? Why or why not? What are the implications of that goal for the Afro-American man who is poor?
7. Teague calls the 85 percenters "masters of self-deception." How do they deceive themselves? Is anything wrong with doing so? Explain.
8. Is Teague an Uncle Tom? Militant? Or something else? Defend your answer by citing passages from the letter and by carefully defining whatever term you use to describe him.
9. Allusions are references in a piece of writing (or speech) that point to persons, places, or events that rest outside the immediate piece. Usually they have historical, religious, or mythical significance. There are allusions to Simon Legree and George C. Wallace here. Who are they? What do the allusions add to the thought or feeling of the letter?

Suggestions for writing and reading

1. List as many of the gambits you've either heard or read (or even said) which are intended to conceal feelings of prejudice against certain kinds of people, even though the statement is an assurance of a lack of prejudice. You might start with, "But some of my best friends are Mexicans."
2. Write a letter of response to some friend of a different race or social class who has sent a warm note to you saying, "If the rest of them were like you, everything would be all right."
3. The paperback, *The Nature of Prejudice,* offers an interesting discussion of how prejudice against certain racial and ethnic groups develops and its effects on both parties.

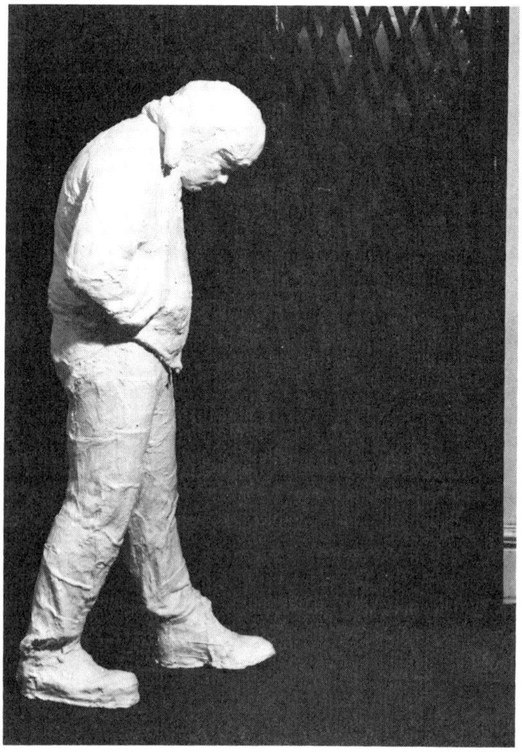

Walking Man by George Segal. Collection of the City Art Museum, St. Louis, Courtesy of Sidney Janis Gallery, New York

NOBODY WEARS A YELLOW ROSE

e. e. cummings

Nobody wears a yellow
flower in his buttonhole
he is altogether a queer fellow
as young as he is old

when autumn comes,
who twiddles his white thumbs
and frisks down the boulevards

without his coat and hat

—(and i wonder just why that
should please him or i wonder what he does)

and why (at the bottom of this trunk,
under some dirty collars) only a
moment
(or
was it perhaps a year) ago i found staring
me in the face a dead yellow small rose

What do you think?

1. Why is the opening line one that can be interpreted in two ways? What are the two interpretations?
2. Judging from the other particulars in the poem, why is Nobody a "queer fellow"? Explain why you do or do not share that opinion of him.
3. Why did the speaker in the poem once have a yellow rose? Why is it in a trunk now?
4. How should society treat people who act like Nobody? Give reasons for your response.
5. Which of the men—the speaker or Nobody—do you most admire? Why? If you admire neither of them, give reasons for that response and explain just what your response is.

Suggestion for writing

1. Imagine what Nobody would do in a season other than autumn. Write a short paper describing those activities. Make certain that they are consistent with the impression you have of him in the poem.

INDIANS TODAY, THE REAL AND THE UNREAL

Vine Deloria

Indians are like the weather. Everyone knows all about the weather, but none can change it. When storms are predicted, the sun shines. When picnic weather is announced, the rain begins. Likewise, if you count on the unpredictability of Indian people, you will never be sorry.

One of the finest things about being an Indian is that people are always interested in you and your "plight." Other groups have difficulties, predicaments, quandaries, problems, or troubles. Traditionally we Indians have had a "plight."

Our foremost plight is our transparency. People can tell just by looking at us what we want, what should be done to help us, how we feel, and what a "real" Indian is really like. Indian life, as it relates to the real world, is a continuous attempt not to disappoint people who know us. Unfulfilled expectations cause grief and we have already had our share.

Because people can see right through us, it becomes impossible to tell truth from fiction or fact from mythology. Experts paint us as they would like us to be. Often we paint ourselves as we wish we were or as we might have been.

The more we try to be ourselves the more we are forced to defend what we have never been. The American public feels most comfortable with the mythical Indians of stereotype-land who were always THERE. These Indians are fierce, they wear feathers and grunt. Most of us don't fit this idealized figure since we grunt only when overeating, which is seldom.

To be an Indian in modern American society is in a very real sense to be unreal and ahistorical. In this book we will discuss the other side—the unrealities that face *us* as Indian people. It is this unreal feeling that has been welling up inside us and threatens to make this decade the most decisive in history for Indian people. In so many ways, Indian people are re-examining themselves in an effort to redefine a new social structure for their people. Tribes are reordering their priorities to account for the obvious discrepancies between their goals and the goals whites have defined for them.

Indian reactions are sudden and surprising. One day at a conference we were singing "My Country 'Tis of Thee" and we came across the part that goes:

Land where our fathers died
Land of the Pilgrims' pride . . .

Some of us broke out laughing when we realized that our fathers undoubtedly died trying to keep those Pilgrims from stealing our land. In fact, many of our fathers died because the Pilgrims killed them as witches. We didn't feel much kinship with those Pilgrims, regardless of who they did in.

We often hear "give it back to the Indians" when a gadget fails to work. It's a terrible thing for a people to realize that society has set aside all non-working gadgets for their exclusive use.

During my three years as Executive Director of the National Congress of American Indians it was a rare day when some white didn't visit my office and proudly proclaim that he or she was of Indian descent.

Cherokee was the most popular tribe of their choice and many people placed the Cherokees anywhere from Maine to Washington State. Mohawk, Sioux, and Chippewa were next in popularity. Occasionally I would be told about some mythical tribe from lower Pennsylvania, Virginia, or Massachusetts which had spawned the white standing before me.

At times I became quite defensive about being a Sioux when these white people had a pedigree that was so much more respectable than mine. But eventually I came to understand their need to identify as partially Indian and did not resent them. I would confirm their wildest stories about their Indian ancestry and would add a few tales of my own hoping that they would be able to accept themselves someday and leave us alone.

Whites claiming Indian blood generally tend to reinforce mythical beliefs about Indians. All but one person I met who claimed Indian blood claimed it on their grandmother's side. I once did a projection backward and discovered that evidently most tribes were entirely female for the first three hundred years of white occupation. No one, it seemed, wanted to claim a male Indian as a forebear.

It doesn't take much insight into racial attitudes to understand the real meaning of the Indian-grandmother complex that plagues certain whites. A male ancestor has too much of the aura of the savage warrior, the unknown primitive, the instinctive animal, to make him a respectable member of the family tree. But a young Indian princess? Ah, there was royalty for the taking. Somehow the white was linked with a noble house of gentility and culture if his grandmother was an Indian princess who ran away with an intrepid pioneer. And royalty has always been an unconscious but all-consuming goal of the European immigrant.

The early colonists, accustomed to life under benevolent despots, projected their understanding of the European political structure onto the Indian tribe in trying to explain its political and social structure. European royal houses were closed to ex-convicts and indentured servants, so the colonists made all Indian maidens princesses, then proceeded to climb a social ladder of their own creation. Within the next generation, if the trend continues, a large portion of the American population will eventually be related to Powhattan.

While a real Indian grandmother is probably the nicest thing that could happen to a child, why is a remote Indian princess grandmother so necessary for many whites? Is it because they are afraid of being classed as foreigners? Do they need some blood tie with the frontier and its dangers in order to experience what it means to be an American? Or is it an attempt to avoid facing the guilt they bear for the treatment of the Indian?

The phenomenon seems to be universal. Only among the Jewish community, which has a long tribal-religious tradition of its own, does the mysterious Indian grandmother, the primeval princess, fail to dominate the family tree. Otherwise, there's not much to be gained by claiming Indian blood or publicly identifying as an Indian. The white believes that there is a great danger the lazy Indian will eventually corrupt God's hard-working people. He is still suspicious that the Indian way of life is dreadfully wrong. There is, in fact, something *un-American* about Indians for most whites.

I ran across a classic statement of this attitude one day in a history book which was published shortly after the turn of the century. Often have I wondered how many Senators, Congressmen, and clergymen of the day accepted the attitudes of that book as a basic fact of life in America. In no uncertain terms did the book praise God that the Indian had not yet been able to corrupt North America as he had South America:

It was perhaps fortunate for the future of America that the Indians of the North rejected civilization. Had they accepted it the whites and Indians might have intermarried to some extent as they did in Mexico. That would have given us a population made up in a measure of shiftless half-breeds.

I never dared to show this passage to my white friends who had claimed Indian blood, but I often wondered why they were so energetic if they did have some of the bad seed in them.

Those whites who dare not claim Indian blood have an asset of their own. They *understand* Indians.

Understanding Indians is not an esoteric art. All it takes is a trip through Arizona or New Mexico, watching a documentary on TV, having known *one* in the service, or having read a popular book on *them.*

There appears to be some secret osmosis about Indian people by which they can magically and instantaneously communicate complete knowledge about themselves to these interested whites. Rarely is physical contact required. Anyone and everyone who knows an Indian or who is *interested,* immediately and thoroughly understands them.

You can verify this great truth at your next party. Mention Indians and you will find a person who saw some in a gas station in Utah, or who attended the Gallup ceremonial celebration, or whose Uncle Jim hired one to cut logs in Oregon, or whose church had a missionary come to speak last Sunday on the plight of Indians and the mission of the church.

There is no subject on earth so easily understood as that of the American Indian. Each summer, work camps disgorge teenagers on various reservations. Within one month's time the youngsters acquire a knowledge of Indians that would astound a college professor.

Easy knowledge about Indians is a historical tradition. After Columbus "discovered" America he brought back news of a great new world which he assumed to be India and, therefore, filled with Indians. Almost at once European folklore devised a complete explanation of the new land and its inhabitants which featured the Fountain of Youth, the Seven Cities of Gold, and other exotic attractions. The absence of elephants apparently did not tip off the explorers that they weren't in India. By the time they realized their mistake, instant knowledge of Indians was a cherished tradition.

Missionaries, after learning some of the religious myths of tribes they encountered, solemnly declared that the inhabitants of the new continent were the Ten Lost Tribes of Israel. Indians thus received a religious-historical identity far greater than they wanted or deserved. But it was an impossible identity. Their failure to measure up to Old Testament standards doomed them to a fall from grace and they were soon relegated to the status of a picturesque species of wildlife.

Like the deer and the antelope, Indians seemed to play rather than get down to the serious business of piling up treasures upon the earth where thieves break through and steal. Scalping, introduced prior to the French and Indian War by the English,* confirmed the suspicion that Indians were wild animals to be hunted and skinned. Bounties were set and an Indian scalp became more valuable than beaver, otter, marten, and other animal pelts.

* Notice, for example the following proclamation:

Given at the Council Chamber in Boston this third day of November 1755 in the twenty-ninth year of the Reign of our Sovereign Lord George the Second by the Grace of God of Great Britain, France, and Ireland, King Defender of the Faith.

By His Honour's command
J. Willard, Secry.
God Save the King

Whereas the tribe of Penobscot Indians have repeatedly in a perfidious manner acted contrary to their solemn submission unto his Majesty long since made and frequently renewed.

I have, therefore, at the desire of the House of Representatives . . . thought fit to issue this Proclamation and to declare the Penobscot Tribe of Indians to be enemies, rebels and traitors to his Majesty. . . . And I do hereby require his Majesty's subjects of the Province to embrace all opportunities of pursuing, captivating, killing and destroy-all and every of the aforesaid Indians.

And whereas the General Court of this Province have voted that a bounty . . . be granted and allowed to be paid out of the Province Treasury . . . the premiums of bounty following viz:

For every scalp of a male Indian brought in as evidence of their being killed as aforesaid, forty pounds.

For every scalp of such female Indian or male Indian under the age of twelve years that shall be killed and brought in as evidence of their being killed as aforesaid, twenty pounds.

What do you think?

1. What are the difficulties that get in the way of American Indians gaining accurate self-knowledge? Explain in what ways these difficulties differ from those that confront Americans in general.
2. What are the sources of most of the ideas you have about American Indians: how they live, speak, make their living and so on? In general, do you feel that you know them as a people? Why or why not?
3. How and why has scalping become identified more closely with the American Indians than with either non-Indian Americans or the English? What effect might this association have on how the majority of Americans view Indians?
4. Explain how an expression such as "give it back to the Indians" could influence anyone's attitude toward Indians. Or, if you disagree with the author on this point, explain why such an expression has little or no effect on the opinions of others.
5. Notions about Indian blood carrying both desirable and unwanted qualities are described here. What other ideas have you heard about characteristics that blood carries? Argue for or against the validity of one such idea.

Suggestions for writing, and reading, and viewing

1. Write a review (500 to 1000 words) of a Western you've seen recently. Comment in some length on the treatment of Indians. Would Deloria approve or not approve of their depiction? Explain the reasons for your opinion.
2. Recall as thoroughly as possible all of the films, television shows, articles, books, and illustrations you have seen depicting Indians. Then write a paper in which you imagine that you are an American Indian and are reacting to the general picture of yourself. Describe as fully as possible who you are, in a paper of 750 words.
3. The book from which this chapter was taken is *Custer Died for Your Sins,* written by Vine Deloria, Jr., who is a Sioux Indian. Other chapters that are recommended are: Chapter 4, "Anthropologists and Other Friends"; Chapter 8, "The Red and the Black"; and Chapter 10, "Indians and Modern Society." The book is available in paperback.
4. *Circle of the Sun* (National Film Board of Canada, 1960; 30 min., color). A film showing the dilemma faced by today's North American Indian who must sometimes choose between holding onto the traditional customs and relinquishing them in order to ease his transition into the American "mainstream."

PUERTO RICANS

Olga Cabral

Your language ricochets
arpeggios of sun
in lightless tunnels of long subway jails.
Your children's eyes, plums
plucked from purple orchards,
the bloom still on them.
And your plumage—tropical
you go in quick, small flocks,
your narrow bones arrayed
in such thin rainbows!
By day your hours are squeezed
in the winepress of sweatshop factories,
at night you return
to pigeonholes in time-cracked tenements,
to bowers above the sticky balustrades,
to sour serenades of stairs that creak
through calendars of endless poverty,
to the cracked bathtub in the hall—not yours,
to the water faucet stricken with drouth this morning.
Yet once inside, the sun has been swept tidy,
the lamplight wiped and polished, and a guitar
on the wall plays a soft anthem to itself,
and soon some laughter washes the whole day clean.

Fiestas come most frequently to you,
for you insist on bloom,
like a strange plant, marooned,
exploding lost suns from some drab windowsill.
And so it is on Sundays
your little girls emerge
like newborn butterflies,
all in mango or like shy egrets;
and your tiny, fertile women
self-conscious in cinnamon and tamarind,
and your agile men in muscatel,
mauve as sea-fans and as graceful, pressed
precisely, though the price-tag's there
on the lapel, under the pawnshop gardenia,
and none of it's yet paid for.

Who stole your sky?
Who pulled the earth from under your brown tree-toes?
Who banished you from hills of parrot-green
to the cold cities of the cold north
with their slums, waiting
with their sweatshops, waiting
with their jails?
Who lashed you forth with whips of sugar cane
to live on heartbreak street,
the last address of vanished immigrants?
For now it is you, it is your turn:
Spicks!—

Yes—same old whiplash,
same old heartbreak street.

But in the cold nights, shivering
between the sour stone walls
you dream of a white goat tethered to the dawn,
of the sun like a red rooster
crowing from village to village,
of the white goat's milk set out in calabashes—
but you awake in a strange land, weeping,
because it was only a dream,
the white goat went a long time ago
and on the green hillsides the rotted shanty towns
squat in their death-traps above the grinning oleandars;
the windows are rifled sockets,
the rooftops long eaten by rats,
and the tears of the women are dry as the empty pots.
Ai! There is nothing to go back to!
Though the heart is there, home must be—
here.

And so, dear *companeros,* you are here:
to struggle among us, to take root, to dream.
Salud to the brave heart you bring us
that never forgets to buy flowers
with Friday's skinned paychecks;
salud to your sun-island's gift,
the uprooted wealth of your land—your own
lighthearted, heartbroken, deft, dark
musical selves.

What do you think?

1. Colors are important in this poem. Underline each color that is either named or suggested by the poet. What is the poet's object in writing such a colorful poem?
2. The poet uses two Spanish words in the poem. One is in line 70, *companeros,* and the other is in line 75, *salud.* By closely examining the *context,* can you correctly guess the meaning of these words?
3. Describe the overall image of the city, which emerges from the poem. How does it compare with your feelings and observations of the city?
4. How does New York City compare to Puerto Rico, according to this poem? Which locale appeals to you? Why? Why would a Puerto Rican choose to live in New York City in light of the view of life provided in the poem?
5. Throughout the poem, does Miss Cabral refer to typical ideas about Puerto Ricans or does she make fresh and personal observations? Defend your answer by reference to particular lines in the poem.

Suggestions for further reading

1. *The People of Puerto Rico* by Julian M. Steward and others (University of Illinois, Champaign), published in 1956, and *Worker in the Cane* by Sidney W. Mintz (Yale University, New Haven), published in 1960, are two books about life in Puerto Rico that might interest you.
2. Sweatshop factories are referred to in line 12. They were an interesting and tragic part of the industrial history of this country. You can learn more about them and other working patterns of the early part of the twentieth century by checking in the *Dictionary of the Social Sciences* or a similar reference book.

ought to

I I I I have

don't like

I

I

want to I

I

I

I I I I IIIIII I I I I I III probably will III IIIIIIIIIIIII

I I I

I I

do it I I

I I I

I I I

am not I I

I I I

I I I

too am I I

I I I

I I I

buried I I II I

I I II I

I I

think I II

I I

I I II

wonder I

I I II

I I

would I II

I I

I I II

am pretty sure I

I

wish I

I

I

know

have got to

I I I I I I I I I I I I I I I I I I I I I I I I I I I IIIIIII I I I I

shall

cannot
could
was
am

"I Ought to Have" by Michael S. Bell, from *Red Book Collation Son Sun Eye I*, © 1970. Used by permission of author.

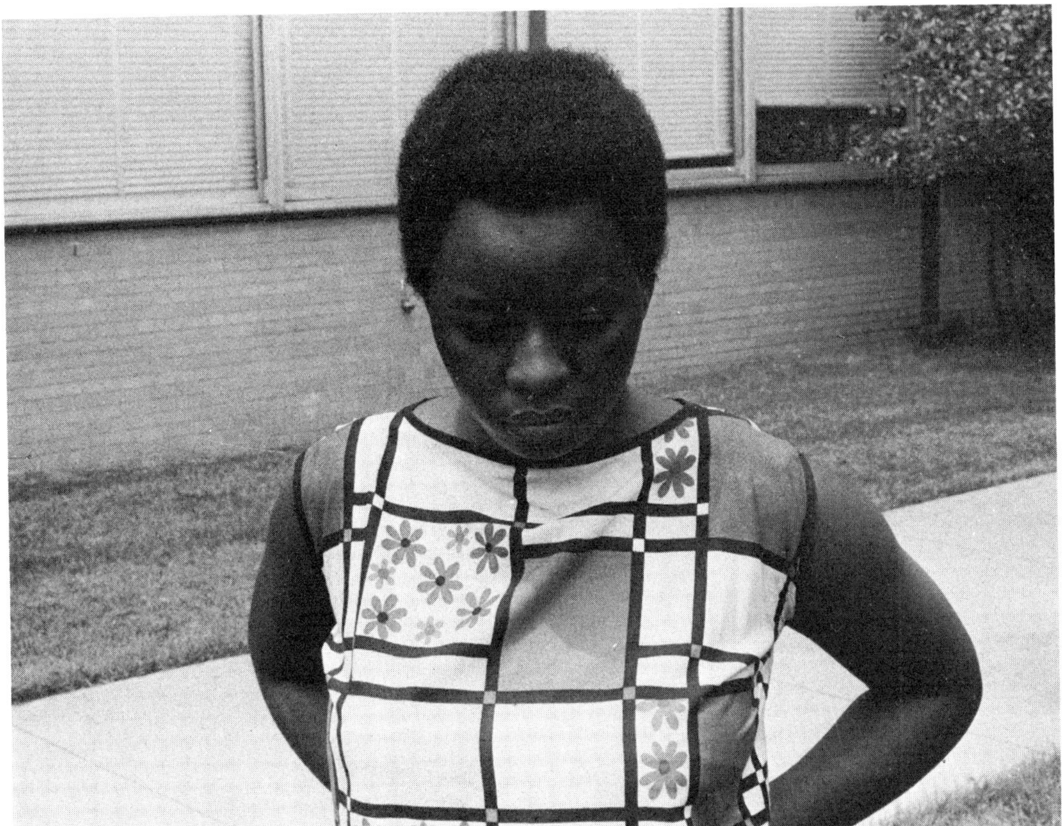

Elihu M. Williams

What do you think?

1. Can you find reasons for the poet using the pronoun *I* so many times in the poem? Name those reasons. How do you feel about the use of the pronoun? Explain in some detail.
2. Are the phrases that accompany the pronoun common ones in your life? In the lives of others? What do you think the poet is getting at on the basis of your answers?
3. How do you feel about the way the poem is set up? Would you prefer a conventional stanza form? Does this setup add or take away from the impact of the poem?
4. Is this a poem or a design? Explain how you distinguish between what is visual and what is written art.

"TO BE THAT SELF WHICH ONE TRULY IS" A THERAPIST'S VIEW OF PERSONAL GOALS

Carl Rogers

THE QUESTIONS: "What is my goal in life?" "What am I striving for?" "What is my purpose?" These are questions which every individual asks himself at one time or another, sometimes calmly and meditatively, sometimes in agonizing uncertainty or despair. They are old, old questions which have been asked and answered in every century of history. Yet they are also questions which every individual must ask and answer for himself, in his own way. They are questions which I, as a counselor, hear expressed in many differing ways as men and women in personal distress try to learn, or understand, or choose, the directions which their lives are taking.

In one sense there is nothing new which can be said about these questions. Indeed the opening phrase in the title I have chosen for this paper is taken from the writings of a man who wrestled with these questions more than a century ago. Simply to express another personal opinion about this whole issue of goals and purposes would seem presumptuous. But as I have worked for many years with troubled and maladjusted individuals I believe that I can discern a pattern, a trend, a commonality, an orderliness, in the tentative answers to these questions which they have found for themselves. And so I would like to share with you my perception of what human beings appear to be striving for, when they are free to choose.

SOME ANSWERS: Before trying to take you into this world of my own experience with my clients, I would like to remind you that the questions I have mentioned are not pseudo-questions, nor have men in the past or at the present time agreed on the answers. When men in the past have asked themselves the purpose of life, some have answered, in the words of the catechism, that "the chief end of man is to glorify God." Others have thought of life's purpose as being the preparation of oneself for immortality. Others have settled on a much more earthy goal—to enjoy and release and satisfy every sensual desire. Still others—and this applies to many today—regard the purpose of life as being to achieve—to gain material possessions, status, knowledge, power. Some have made it their goal to give themselves completely and devotedly to a cause outside of themselves such as Christianity, or Communism. A Hitler has seen his goal as that of becoming the leader of a master race which would exercise power over all. In sharp contrast, many an Oriental has striven to eliminate all personal desires, to exercise the utmost of control over himself. I mention these widely ranging choices to indicate some of the very different aims men have lived for, to suggest that there are indeed many goals possible.

In a recent important study Charles Morris investigated objectively the pathways of life which were preferred by students in six different countries—India, China, Japan, the United States, Canada, and Norway. As one might expect, he found decided differences in goals between these national groups. He also endeavored, through a factor analysis of his data, to determine the underlying dimensions of value which seemed to operate in the thousands of specific individual preferences. Without going into the details of his analysis, we might look at the five dimensions which emerged, and which, combined in various positive and negative ways, appeared to be responsible for the individual choices.

The first such value dimension involves a preference for a responsible, moral, self-restrained *participation in life,* appreciating and conserving what man has attained.

The second places stress upon delight in vigorous action for the overcoming of obstacles. It involves a confident initiation *of change,* either in resolving personal and social problems, or in overcoming obstacles in the natural world.

The third dimension stresses the value of a self-sufficient *inner life* with a rich and heightened self-awareness. Control over persons and things is rejected in favor of a deep and sympathetic insight into self and others.

The fourth underlying dimension values a *receptivity* to persons and to nature. Inspiration is seen as coming from a source outside the self, and the person lives and develops in devoted responsiveness to this source.

The fifth and final dimension stresses *sensuous enjoyment,* self-enjoyment. The simple pleasures of life, an abandonment to the moment, a relaxed openness to life, are valued.

This is a significant study, one of the first to measure objectively the answers given in different cultures to the question, what is the purpose of my life? It has added to our knowledge of the answers given. It has also helped to define some of the basic dimensions in terms of which the choice is made. As Morris says, speaking of these dimensions, "it is as if persons in various cultures have in common five major tones in the musical scales on which they compose different melodies."

ANOTHER VIEW: I find myself, however, vaguely dissatisfied with this study. None of the "Ways to Live" which Morris put before the students as possible choices, and none of the factor dimensions, seems to contain satisfactorily the goal of life which emerges in my experience with my clients. As I watch person after person struggle in his therapy hours to find a way of life for himself, there seems to be a general pattern emerging, which is not quite captured by any of Morris' descriptions.

The best way I can state this aim of life, as I see it coming to light in my relationship with my clients, is to use the words of Søren Kierkegaard—"to be that self which one truly is." I am quite aware that this may sound so simple as to be absurd. To be what one is seems like a statement of obvious fact rather than a goal. What does it mean? What does it imply? I want to devote the remainder of my remarks to those issues. I will simply say at the outset that it seems to mean and imply some strange things. Out of my experience with my clients, and out of my own self-searching, I find myself arriving at views which would have been very foreign to me ten or fifteen years ago. So I trust you will look at these views with critical scepticism, and accept them only in so far as they ring true in your own experience.

AWAY FROM FAÇADES: I observe first that characteristically the client shows a tendency to move away, hesitantly and fearfully, from a self that he is *not.* In other words even though there may be no recognition of what he might be moving toward, he is moving away from something. And of course in so doing he is beginning to define, however negatively, what he *is.*

At first this may be expressed simply as a fear of exposing what he is. Thus one eighteen-year-old boy says, in an early interview: "I know I'm not so hot, and I'm afraid they'll find it out. That's why I do these things. . . . They're going to find out some day that I'm not so hot. I'm just trying to put that day off as long as possible. . . . If you know me as I know myself—. (*Pause*) I'm not going to tell you the person I really think I am. There's only one place I won't cooperate and that's it. . . . It wouldn't help your opinion of me to know what I think of myself."

It will be clear that the very expression of this fear is a part of becoming what he is. Instead of simply *being* a façade, as if it were himself, he is coming closer to being *himself,* namely a frightened person hiding behind a façade because he regards himself as too awful to be seen.

AWAY FROM "OUGHTS": Another tendency of this sort seems evident in the client's moving away from the compelling image of what he "ought to be." Some individuals have absorbed so deeply from their parents the concept "I ought to be good," or "I have to be good," that it is only with the greatest of inward struggle that they find themselves moving away from this goal. Thus one young woman, describing her unsatisfactory relationship with her father, tells first how much she wanted his love. "I think in all this feeling I've had about my father, that *really* I *did* very much want a good relationship with him. . . . I wanted so much to have him care for me, and yet didn't seem to get what I really wanted." She always felt she had to meet all of his demands and expectations and it was "just too much. Because once I meet one there's another and another and another, and I never really meet them. It's sort of an endless demand." She feels she has been like her mother, submissive and compliant, trying continually to meet his demands. "And really *not* wanting to be that kind of person. I find it's not a good way to be, but yet I think I've had a sort of belief that that's the way you *have* to be if you intend to be thought a lot of and loved. And yet who would *want* to love somebody who was that sort of wishy washy person?" The counselor responded, "Who really would love a door mat?" She went on, "At least I wouldn't want to be loved by the kind of person who'd love a door mat!"

Thus, though these words convey nothing of the self she might be moving toward, the weariness and disdain in both her voice and her statement make it clear that she is moving away from a self which *has* to be good, which *has* to be submissive.

Curiously enough a number of individuals find that they have felt compelled to regard themselves as bad, and it is this concept of themselves that they find they are moving away from. One young man shows very clearly such a movement. He says: "I don't know how I got this impression that being ashamed of myself was such an *appropriate* way to feel. . . . Being ashamed of me was the way I just *had* to be. . . . There was a world where being ashamed of myself was the best way to feel. . . . If you are something which is disapproved of very much, then I guess the only way you can have any kind of self-respect is to be ashamed of that part of you which isn't approved of. . . .

"But now I'm adamantly refusing to do things from the old viewpoint. . . . It's as if I'm convinced that someone said, 'The way you will *have* to be is to be *ashamed* of yourself—so *be* that way!' And I accepted it for a long, long time, saying 'OK, that's me!' And now I'm standing up against that somebody, saying, 'I don't care *what* you say. I'm *not* going to feel ashamed of myself!' " Obviously he is abandoning the concept of himself as shameful and bad.

AWAY FROM MEETING EXPECTATIONS: Other clients find themselves moving away from what the culture expects them to be. In our current industrial culture, for example, as Whyte has forcefully pointed out in his recent book, there are enormous pressures to become the characteristics which are expected of the "organization man." Thus one should be fully a member of the group, should sub-

* I cannot close my mind, however, to the possibility that someone might be able to demonstrate that the trends I am about to describe might in some subtle fashion, or to some degree, have been initiated by me. I am describing them as occurring in the client in this safe relationship, because that seems the most likely explanation.

ordinate his individuality to fit into the group needs, should become "the well-rounded man who can handle well-rounded men."

In a newly completed study of student values in this country Jacob summarizes his findings by saying, "The main overall effect of higher education upon student values is to bring about general acceptance of a body of standards and attitudes characteristic of collegebred men and women in the American community. . . . The impact of the college experience is . . . to *socialize* the individual, to refine, polish, or 'shape up' his values so that he can fit comfortably into the ranks of American college alumni."

Over against these pressures for conformity, I find that when clients are free to be any way they wish, they tend to resent and to question the tendency of the organization, the college or the culture to mould them to any given form. One of my clients says with considerable heat: "I've been so long trying to live according to what was meaningful to other people, and what made no sense at *all* to me, really. I somehow felt so much *more* than that, at some level."So he, like others, tends to move away from being what is expected.

AWAY FROM PLEASING OTHERS: I find that many individuals have formed themselves by trying to please others, but again, when they are free, they move away from being this person. So one professional man, looking back at some of the process he has been through, writes, toward the end of therapy: "I finally felt that I simply *had* to begin doing what *I wanted* to do, not what I thought I *should* do, and regardless of what other people feel I *should* do. This is a complete reversal of my whole life. I've always felt I *had* to do things because they were expected of me, or more important, to make people like me. The hell with it! I think from now on I'm going to just be me—rich or poor, good or bad, rational or irrational, logical or illogical, famous or infamous. So thanks for your part in helping me to rediscover Shakespeare's—'To thine own *self* be true.'"

So one may say that in a somewhat negative way, clients define their goal, their purpose, by discovering, in the freedom and safety of an understanding relationship, some of the directions they do *not* wish to move. They prefer not to hide themselves and their feelings from themselves, or even from some significant others. They do not wish to be what they "ought" to be, whether that imperative is set by parents, or by the culture, whether it is defined positively or negatively. They do not wish to mould themselves and their behavior into a form which would be merely pleasing to others. They do not, in other words, choose to be anything which is artificial, anything which is imposed, anything which is defined from without. They realize that they do not value such purposes or goals, even though they may have lived by them all their lives up to this point.

TOWARD TRUST OF SELF: Still another way of describing this pattern which I see in each client is to say that increasingly he trusts and values the process which is himself. Watching my clients, I have come to a much better understanding of creative people. El Greco, for example, must have realized as he looked at some of his early work, that "good artists do not paint like that." But somehow he trusted his own experiencing of life, the process of himself, sufficiently that he could go on expressing his own unique perceptions. It was as though he could say, "Good artists do not paint like this, but *I* paint like this." Or to move to another field, Ernest Hemingway was surely aware that "good writers do not write like this." But fortunately he moved toward being Hemingway, being himself, rather than toward some one else's conception of a good writer. Einstein seems to have been unusually oblivious to the fact that good physicists did not think his kind of thoughts. Rather than drawing back because of his inadequate academic preparation in physics, he simply moved toward being Einstein, toward thinking his own thoughts, toward being as truly and deeply himself as he could. This is not a phenomenon which occurs only in the artist or the genius. Time and again in my clients, I have seen simple people become significant and creative in their own spheres, as they have developed more trust of the processes going on within themselves, and have dared to feel their own feelings, live by values which they discover within, and express themselves in their own unique ways.

What do you think?

1. According to the article, when are people *not* free to choose what they want to be? Describe an important experience you've had in which you were not free.
2. Explain, in your own words, why Rogers thinks it is valuable for a person to move away from what he is *not*. What recent experiences have you had in which you were more receptive to what others thought you were like than what you actually were?
3. What are the implications of the study made by Charles Morris of the relationship between the values favored by a particular culture and the values that individuals within that culture select? Be as specific as possible in your answer.
4. In what ways and to what extent have the values stressed in American culture influenced your personal values? If you also identify with a subculture, in what ways have its values affected your own?
5. What are the impediments that stand in the way of persons learning to trust themselves?
6. Has Rogers described a life goal that is identical or similar to your own? Explain which one it is or, if necessary, provide your own description if it does not appear in the article.
7. Explain how the man in the W. H. Auden poem, "The Unknown Citizen," is like and different from the client in the article who says, "I've been so long trying to live according to what was meaningful to other people. . . ." (p. 38).
8. The article by Deloria, on page 24, mentions barriers to knowing one's self which Rogers does not take into account. What are they?

Suggestions for writing, reading, and viewing

1. Write a short paper (750 words) in which you describe, in considerable detail, how your school attempts to socialize you so that you will reflect in your behavior or thinking a particular value that it esteems. Be specific about the nature of the value; whether it is, for example, social, ethical, political, and so on.
2. Write a moderately long paper (2000 words) in which you argue for or against the notion that there would be no progress or constructive change in American society if every individual conformed strictly to society's expectations.
3. *To Kill a Mockingbird* by Harper Lee is a novel about the consequences of nonconformity on the part of a lawyer in a small Southern town. It is available in paperback, and is recommended to students wishing to do further reading on this subject.
4. *Howard* (National Film Board of Canada, 30 min.) is a film showing an adolescent caught between his own tendency to follow the direction of his friends, who have a broad view of life and its possibilities, and his parents, who have more narrow aspirations for him.

MEDI-HAIR ADVERTISEMENT

If you are one of the haves this message is not directed to you! This message is directed to have nots—who are missing out on many of life's pleasures. The pleasure of looking young and dynamic, no matter what your age may be. The pleasure of getting interested looks from the fair sex. So you're married? Don't you think your wife will enjoy having a younger and better looking you? Get into the swing of things. Come on into the Now world. Don't resign yourself to a prematurely aged appearance.

Do you know you can have a full head of hair in 4 hours precisely matched to your own—that can't come off no matter what you are doing? Hair that will look and feel like your own. Hair that can be styled as you wish, brushed, combed, shampooed. We're not talking about a phony looking toupee, or weave, or transplant. We're talking about MEDI-HAIR, the astonishing medical hair replacement process that is giving newfound joy to thousands of bald and balding men coast to coast.

You don't need to remain bald unless you want to. You can arrange for a free private consultation by telephoning MEDI-HAIR 943-2559, Or mail the coupon below for our free brochure in plain envelope. Act Now!

MEDI-HAIR INTERNATIONAL

700 N. MICHIGAN

CHICAGO, ILL. 60611

Offices also in Beverly Hills, Seattle, Denver, Phoenix, Dallas, Portland, Detroit, New York, Miami and other principal cities in America & Europe.

MEDI-HAIR TEL. 943-2559

700 N. MICHIGAN AVENUE
SUITE 314, CHICAGO, ILL. 60611

GENTLEMEN:

☐ Please send me your Free brochure.

☐ Please contact me to arrange a consultation without cost or obligation.

Name ....

Address................ City........ Zip......

Bus. Phone..........Home Phone.........ST I-31

What do you think?

1. In general, why would most persons be resentful of being referred to as "have nots"? How might a person's self-concept be affected if he were repeatedly called a "have not"?
2. What are life's pleasures, according to the advertisement, that the bald or balding man may be missing? What other pleasures, of value to you, are *not* hinted at here? Explain how having more hair would enhance one's chances of enjoying these pleasures.
3. Is there a direct relationship between looking young *and* looking dynamic, as the ad hints there is?
4. In your opinion, does the "newfound joy" obtained by men who have had their hair replaced derive merely from their having more hair or from the things that happen because they have more hair? Which of these alternatives does the advertisement emphasize? Speculate on why there is this emphasis.
5. Why do the advertisers give the assurance that their free brochure will come in a *plain* envelope and that the consultation will be *private?*
6. Based on the content of this advertisement, how would you generalize about the personal values of many Americans?

Suggestions for writing and drawing

1. In a local newspaper, locate an advertisement that appeals to something other than the reader's vanity and desire for having a good time. Analyze what the exact appeal of the advertisement is and speculate on why it would be successful with a given audience. Attach the advertisement to your short paper (500 words).
2. Rewrite the MEDI-HAIR INTERNATIONAL advertisement so that it appeals to a different audience, such as women, barbers, or actors.
3. Illustrate the advertisement showing what a "have not" looks like and what he is forced to do for fun. Contrast this with a picture of a "have" who is enjoying one of life's pleasures.

2
I'VE GOTTA BE ME
(From the Broadway Musical, "GOLDEN RAINBOW")
Music and Lyrics by
WALTER MARKS
Slowly and firmly
Wheth - er I'm
L.H.
Cmaj7
C6
Dm7
G7
Dm7
right
or wheth-er I'm
wrong
Wheth-er I
find
a
place in
this
live!
not mere - ly sur - vive!
And I won't give up this dream
of
p
G7
Cmaj7
C6
(Tacet)
F6
Em7
world
or nev - er be - long,
I've Got - ta Be
Me!
I've Got - ta Be
life
that keeps me a - live!
I've Got - ta Be
Me!
I've Got - ta Be
© Copyright 1967 by DAMILA MUSIC, INC., 40 West 55th Street, New York, N. Y.
International Copyright Secured
Made in U. S. A.
All Rights Reserved

3
F6 Em7 F6 Em7 Am7 Fmaj7 Dm7(sus) G7 (Tacet)
Me! What else can I be but what I am? I want to
Me! The dream that I
L.H.
F6 Em7 Dm7 Dm7(sus) Cmaj7 C6 (Tacet) Bm7(sus)
see makes me what I am! That far a-way prize,
E7 Am(sus) Am Dm G7 Cmaj7
A world of suc-cess, It's wait-ing for me if I heed the call.
C6 (Tacet) Fmaj7 F6 (Tacet) Em7 Am7 (Tacet)
I won't set-tle down, or set-tle for less, As long as there's
I've Gotta Be Me - 3

4
Am7 (sus) D9 Dm7 (sus) G7 (Tacet) Cmaj7
half a chance that I can have it all! I'll go it a - lone.
C6 Dm7 G7 Dm7 G7
That's how it must be. I can't be right for some-bod-y else if I'm not right for
L.H.
Cmaj7 C6 (Tacet) F6 Em7 F6 Em7
me! I've got-ta be free! I've got-ta be free! Dar - ing to
ritard
F6 Em7 F6 Dm7(sus) Cmaj7 Dm7 C6
try to do it or die! I've Got-ta Be Me!
ritard
a tempo
I've Gotta Be Me - 3

I'VE GOTTA BE ME

Lyrics by Walter Marks

Whether I'm right or whether I'm wrong
Whether I find a place in this world or never belong,
I've Gotta Be Me!
I've Gotta Be Me!
What else can I be but what I am?

I want to live! not merely survive!
And I won't give up this dream of life that keeps me alive!
I've Gotta Be Me!
I've Gotta Be Me!
The dream that I see makes me what I am!

That faraway prize, a world of success,
It's waiting for me if I heed the call.
I won't settle down, or settle for less,
As long as there's half a chance that I can have it all!

I'll go it alone. That's how it must be.
I can't be right for somebody else if I'm not right for me!
I've gotta be free!
I've gotta be free!
Daring to try to do it or die!
I've Gotta Be Me!

What do you think?

1. Does the song title make sense? Doesn't everyone have to be himself? Explain.
2. Does the writer show a low regard for truth or morality when he says that he's got to be himself even though he may be wrong? Do you approve of this attitude? Does your behavior reflect the same or a different attitude?
3. What different kinds of answers can you give to the question raised in the first verse: "What else can I be but what I am?" What reasons are there for persons being something other than genuine? Is that kind of behavior honest? Explain.
4. The songwriter suggests there is a difference between "living" and "surviving." What does he mean? Do you agree?
5. Interpret the line, "The dream that I see makes me what I am."
6. On the basis of the various sentiments expressed here, describe the speaker in terms of his character and personality. Is he admirable? Would you choose him for a friend? Why or why not?

Suggestions for listening and writing

1. There are several recordings of this song; however, the one by Della Reese (ABC Record: S-636 *I gotta be me . . . this trip out*) is especially forceful. After listening to it, discuss what her rendition adds to or takes away from the lyrics. If possible, compare Miss Reese's recording with those of other singers.
2. Check in a record catalog for song titles which indicate that a song is concerned with self-identity or discovery. For example, "Go Away—Find Yourself" recorded by Jerry Butler. Listen to a couple of the songs and report in writing or orally to the class on the variety of reasons given for the person finding himself *and* on the different methods recommended for self-discovery.
3. Expand the project in suggestion 2 by writing a short paper (500 words) in which you select two song lyrics and compare their views of Americans' desire for self-knowledge, its prevalence, its nature, and the reasons for it.
4. Write a very short (300 words) paper in which you evaluate the methods recommended for self-discovery in any one of the songs that you listen to outside of class or even the method suggested in "I've Gotta Be Me."

But there was something missing and I knew what it was: Trina. I couldn't get her out of my mind. I couldn't walk through familiar streets without thinking, There's where we used to go, *or* There's were we used to eat.

from Down These Mean Streets by Piri Thomas, 1967. Reprinted by permission of Alfred A. Knopf, Inc.

PART 2

"I COULDN'T GET HER OUT OF MY MIND . . ."

For better or worse, the prospect of being loved is a prominent preoccupation in our society. The advertising theme of innumerable items evolves from Boy-Meeting-Girl situations. Lyrics of popular songs frequently are about the beginnings of romance. Girls are urged to be feminine; they are informally brought up (and sometimes even formally taught) to be feminine and boys are urged to be masculine, not because these are worthwhile ends in themselves, but because, as a consequence, they will be more attractive persons to the opposite sex.

The selections in this section cover a broad range of material. We begin with characters from Miss Peach's comic strip who use the very serious jargon of love and romance to fit their own self-centeredness. We end the section with song lyrics that express a vital linkage between selfhood and the experience of being loved. Both selections dramatize commonly encountered human behavior and concepts.

Love is thought to move to marriage in our society and the readings move similarly. A poem examines some popular fantasies about marriage; an essay describes the various styles of marriage which women who are unusually talented enter into; another essay humorously explodes the myth of the husband and wife being married "happily ever after."

The questions raised here about the nature of love and marriage and the conflicting viewpoints expressed about the amount of room either state permits for individual development hopefully will assist the reader in reaching his own conclusions about the value of both.

MISS PEACH

Mell Lazarus

Mell Lazarus. Courtesy of Publishers-Hall Syndicate

What do you think?

"Miss Peach" I

1. Francine explains why she can commit herself to Arthur. Is it a reasonable explanation or not? Explain.
2. How do you imagine Arthur feels in the last panel? Should he go steady with Francine or not? Give the reasons for your answer.

"Miss Peach" II

1. Arthur asks Francine if she *merely* likes him. What does the wording of that question imply about the relative importance of liking and loving? Does that implication reflect your own evaluation of the worth of those feelings?
2. What does Francine accomplish by using the phrasing she does in answer to Arthur's question? Do you think he will be satisfied with her response? Why or why not?

Suggestion for drawing

1. Draw another panel for comic strip II. Indicate by the words in the bubble exactly how Arthur reacted to Francine's answer. Be prepared to defend your panel by having reasons in mind as to why he reacted your way.

SNAG

Victor H. Cruz

1
i thought of you
early morning
my eyes still not open
your eyes leaning against the wall
& the beautymark behind your knee

(but i'm making this up; am i)

the way you threw your arms
into my coat
& yelled it's too big
but did not matter

anyway
it's early morning

2
who are they over there
singing in a corner
beer cans in hands
passing Luchow's
not looking in to see their boss
or to smell the food

early Sunday mornings
i do things like this
or i think of something better.

What do you think?

1. How is the title related to the central thought of the poem? Provide as many different defensible interpretations as possible.
2. How can you distinguish fantasy from reality in the poem? For example, is the speaker remembering a girl who actually existed? Be prepared to defend your response.
3. What part does fantasy play in most relationships between young men and women that you're familiar with? What, in your opinion, is the *proper* role of fantasy in a man-woman relationship?
4. Explain the relationship between Parts 1 and 2 of the poem.
5. In your own words, what is the central thought of the poem?

Suggestions for listening and writing

1. "I Have Dreamed," a song from the musical, *The King and I,* depicts a situation in which a person has *only* his fantasies about a love-relationship with another. If this song is available, listen to it and examine the lyrics. Write a short paper (500 words) in which you set forth the advantages or disadvantages of this kind of thorough indulgence in fantasy. If the song is not available, possibly there is another song with similar sentiments that is popular. If so, use those lyrics in the way suggested above.

A TREE. A ROCK. A CLOUD

Carson McCullers

"A Tree. A Rock. A Cloud" by Carson McCullers. First published in *Harper's Bazaar*, November, 1942.

It was raining that morning, and still very dark. When the boy reached the streetcar café he had almost finished his route and he went in for a cup of coffee. The place was an all-night café owned by a bitter and stingy man called Leo. After the raw, empty street the café seemed friendly and bright: along the counter there were a couple of soldiers, three spinners from the cotton mill, and in a corner a man who sat hunched over with his nose and half his face down in a beer mug. The boy wore a helmet such as aviators wear. When he went into the café he unbuckled the chin strap and raised the right flap up over his pink little ear; often as he drank his coffee someone would speak to him in a friendly way. But this morning Leo did not look into his face and none of the men were talking. He paid and was leaving the café when a voice called out to him:

"Son! Hey, son!"

He turned back and the man in the corner was crooking his finger and nodding to him. He had brought his face out of the beer mug and he seemed suddenly very happy. The man was long and pale, with a big nose and faded orange hair.

"Hey, son!"

The boy went toward him. He was an undersized boy of about twelve, with one shoulder drawn higher than the other because of the weight of the paper sack. His face was shallow, freckled, and his eyes were round child eyes.

"Yeah, mister?"

The man laid one hand on the paper boy's shoulder, then grasped the boy's chin and turned his face slowly from one side to the other. The boy shrank back uneasily.

"Say! What's the big idea?"

The boy's voice was shrill; inside the café it was suddenly very quiet.

The man said slowly: "I love you."

All along the counter the men laughed. The boy, who had scowled and sidled away, did not know what to do. He looked over the counter at Leo, and Leo watched him with a weary, brittle jeer. The boy tried to laugh also. But the man was serious and sad.

"I did not mean to tease you, son," he said. "Sit down and have a beer with me. There is something I have to explain."

Cautiously, out of the corner of his eye, the paper boy questioned the men along the counter to see what he should do. But they had gone back to their beer or their breakfast and did not notice him. Leo put a cup of coffee on the counter and a little jug of cream.

"He is a minor," Leo said.

The paper boy slid himself up onto the stool. His ear beneath the upturned flap of the helmet was very small and red. The man was nodding at him soberly. "It is important," he said. Then he reached in his hip pocket and brought out something which he held up in the palm of his hand for the boy to see.

"Look very carefully," he said.

The boy stared, but there was nothing to look at very carefully. The man held in his big grimy palm a photograph. It was the face of a woman, but blurred, so that only the hat and the dress she was wearing stood out clearly.

"See?" the man asked.

The boy nodded and the man placed another picture in his palm. The woman was standing on a beach in a bathing suit. The suit made her stomach very big, and that was the main thing you noticed.

"Got a good look?" He leaned over closer and finally asked: "You ever seen her before?"

The boy sat motionless, staring slantwise at the man. "Not so I know of."

"Very well." The man blew on the photographs and put them back into his pocket. "That was my wife."

"Dead?" the boy asked.

Slowly, the man shook his head. He pursed his lips as though about to whistle and answered in a longdrawn way: "Nuuu— —" he said, "I will explain."

The beer on the counter before the man was in a large brown mug. He did not pick it up to drink. Instead he bent down and, putting his face over the rim, he rested there for a moment. Then with both hands he tilted the mug and sipped.

"Some night you'll go to sleep with your big nose in a mug and drown," said Leo. "Prominent transient drowns in beer. That would be a cute death."

The paper boy tried to signal to Leo. While the man was not looking he screwed up his face and worked his mouth to question soundlessly: "Drunk?" But Leo only raised his eyebrows and turned away to put some pink strips of bacon on the grill. The man pushed the mug away from him, straightened himself, and folded his loose crooked hands on the counter. His face was sad as he looked at the paper boy. He did not blink, but from time to time the lids closed down with delicate gravity over his pale green eyes. It was nearing dawn and the boy shifted the weight of the paper sack.

"I am talking about love," the man said. "With me it is a science."

The boy half slid down from the stool. But the man raised his forefinger, and there was something about him that held the boy and would not let him go away.

"Twelve years ago I married the woman in the photograph. She was my wife for one year, nine months, three days, and two nights. I loved her. Yes . . ." He tightened his blurred, rambling voice and said again: "I loved her. I thought also that she loved me. I was a railroad engineer. She had all home comforts and luxuries. It never crept into my brain that she was not satisfied. But do you know what happened?"

"Mgneeow!" said Leo.

The man did not take his eyes from the boy's face. "She left me. I came in one night and the house was empty and she was gone. She left me."

"With a fellow?" the boy asked.

Gently the man placed his palm down on the counter. "Why naturally, son. A woman does not run off like that alone."

The café was quiet, the soft rain black and endless in the street outside. Leo pressed down the frying bacon with the prongs of his long fork: "So you have been chasing the floozy for eleven years. You frazzled old rascal!"

For the first time the man glanced at Leo. "Please don't be vulgar. Besides, I was not speaking to you." He turned back to the boy and said in a trusting and secretive undertone: "Let's not pay any attention to him. O.K.?"

The paper boy nodded doubtfully.

"It was like this," the man continued. "I am a person who feels many things. All my life one thing after another has impressed me. Moonlight. The leg of a pretty girl. One thing after another. But the point is that when I had enjoyed anything there was a peculiar sensation as though it was laying around loose in me. Nothing seemed to finish itself up or fit in with the other things. Women? I had my portion of them. The same. Afterward laying around loose in me. I was a man who had never loved."

Very slowly he closed his eyelids, and the gesture was like a curtain drawn at the end of a scene in a play. When he spoke again his voice was excited and the words came fast—the lobes of his large, loose ears seemed to tremble.

"Then I met this woman. I was fifty-one years old and she always said she was thirty. I met her at a filling station and we were married within three days. And do you know what it was like? I just can't tell you. All I had ever felt was gathered together around this woman. Nothing lay around loose in me any more but was finished up by her."

The man stopped suddenly and stroked his long nose. His voice sank down to a steady and reproachful undertone: "I'm not explaining this right. What happened was this. There were these beautiful feelings and loose little pleasures inside me. And this woman was something like an assembly line for my soul. I run these little pieces of myself through her and I come out complete. Now do you follow me?"

"What was her name?" the boy asked.

"Oh," he said. "I called her Dodo. But that is immaterial."

"Did you try to make her come back?"

The man did not seem to hear. "Under the circumstances you can imagine how I felt when she left me."

Leo took the bacon from the grill and folded two strips of it between a bun. He had a gray face, with slitted eyes, and a pinched nose saddled by faint blue shadows. One of the mill workers signaled for more coffee and Leo poured it. He did not give refills on coffee free. The spinner ate breakfast there every morning, but the better Leo knew his customers the stingier he treated them. He nibbled his own bun as though he grudged it to himself.

"And you never got hold of her again?"

The boy did not know what to think of the man, and his child's face was uncertain with mingled curiosity and doubt. He was new on the paper route; it was still strange to him to be out in the town in the black, queer early morning.

"Yes," the man said. "I took a number of steps to get her back. I went around trying to locate her. I went to Tulsa where she had folks. And to Mobile. I went to every town she had ever mentioned to me, and I hunted down every man she had formerly been connected with. Tulsa, Atlanta, Chicago, Cheehaw, Memphis . . . For the better part of two years I chased around the country trying to lay hold of her."

"But the pair of them had vanished from the face of the earth!" said Leo.

"Don't listen to him," the man said confidentially. "And also just forget those two years. They are not important. What matters is that around the third year a curious thing begun to happen to me."

"What?" the boy asked.

The man leaned down and tilted his mug to take a sip of beer. But as he hovered over the mug his nostrils fluttered slightly; he sniffed the staleness of the beer and did not drink. "Love is a curious thing to begin with. At first I thought only of getting her back. It was a kind of mania. But then as time went on I tried to remember her. But do you know what happened?"

"No," the boy said.

"When I laid myself down on a bed and tried to think about her my mind became a blank. I couldn't see her. I would take out her pictures and look. No good. Nothing doing. A blank. Can you imagine it?"

"Say, Mack!" Leo called down the counter. "Can you imagine this bozo's mind a blank!"

Slowly, as though fanning away flies, the man waved his hand. His green eyes were concentrated and fixed on the shallow little face of the paper boy.

"But a sudden piece of glass on a sidewalk. Or a nickel tune in a music box. A shadow on a wall at night. And I would remember. It might happen in a street and I would cry or bang my head against a lamppost. You follow me?"

"A piece of glass . . ." the boy said.

"Anything. I would walk around and I had no power of how and when to remember her. You think you can put up a kind of shield. But remembering don't come to a man face forward—it corners around sideways. I was at the mercy of everything I saw and heard. Suddenly instead of me combing the countryside to find her she begun to chase me around in my very soul. *She* chasing *me,* mind you! And in my soul!"

The boy asked finally: "What part of the country were you in then?"

"Ooh," the man groaned. "I was a sick mortal. It was like smallpox. I confess, son, that I boozed. I fornicated. I committed any sin that suddenly appealed to me. I am loath to confess it but I will do so. When I recall that period it is all curdled in my mind, it was so terrible."

The man leaned his head down and tapped his forehead on the counter. For a few seconds he stayed bowed over in this position, the back of his stringy neck covered with orange furze, his hands with their long warped fingers held palm to palm in an attitude of prayer. Then the man straightened himself; he was smiling and suddenly his face was bright and tremulous and old.

"It was in the fifth year that it happened," he said. "And with it I started my science."

Leo's mouth jerked with a pale, quick grin. "Well, none of we boys are getting any younger," he said. Then with sudden anger he balled up a dishcloth he was holding and threw it down hard on the floor. "You draggle-tailed old Romeo!"

"What happened?" the boy asked.

The old man's voice was high and clear: "Peace," he answered.

"Huh?"

"It is hard to explain scientifically, son," he said. "I guess the logical explanation is that she and I had fled around from each other for so long that finally we just got tangled up together and lay down and quit. Peace. A queer and beautiful blankness. It was spring in Portland and the rain came every afternoon. All evening I just stayed there on my bed in the dark. And that is how the science come to me."

The windows in the streetcar were pale blue with light. The two soldiers paid for their beers and opened the door—one of the soldiers combed his hair and wiped off his muddy puttees before they went outside. The three mill workers bent silently over their breakfasts. Leo's clock was ticking on the wall.

"It is this. And listen carefully. I meditated on love and reasoned it out. I realized what is wrong with us. Men fall in love for the first time. And what do they fall in love with?"

The boy's soft mouth was partly open and he did not answer.

"A woman," the old man said. "Without science, with nothing to go by, they undertake the most dangerous and sacred experience in God's earth. They fall in love with a woman. Is that correct, son?"

"Yeah," the boy said faintly.

"They start at the wrong end of love. They begin at the climax. Can you wonder it is so miserable? Do you know how men should love?"

The old man reached over and grasped the boy by the collar of his leather jacket. He gave him a gentle little shake and his green eyes gazed down unblinking and grave.

"Son, do you know how love should be begun?"

The boy sat small and listening and still. Slowly he shook his head. The old man leaned closer and whispered:

"A tree. A rock. A cloud."

It was still raining outside in the street: a mild, gray, endless rain. The mill whistle blew for the six-o'clock shift and the three spinners paid and went away. There was no one in the café but Leo, the old man, and the little paper boy.

"The weather was like this in Portland," he said. "At the time my science was begun. I meditated and I started very cautious. I would pick up something from the street and take it home with me. I bought a goldfish and I concentrated on the goldfish and I loved it. I graduated from one thing to another. Day by day I was getting this technique. On the road from Portland to San Diego——"

"Aw shut up!" screamed Leo suddenly. "Shut up! Shut up!"

The old man still held the collar of the boy's jacket; he was trembling and his face was earnest and bright and wild. "For six years now I have gone around by myself and built up my science. And now I am a master, son. I can love anything. No longer do I have to think about it even. I see a street full of people and a beautiful light comes in me. I watch a bird in the sky. Or I meet a traveler on the road. Everything, son. And anybody. All strangers and all loved! Do you realize what a science like mine can mean?"

The boy held himself stiffly, his hands curled tight around the counter edge. Finally he asked: "Did you ever really find that lady?"

"What? What say, son?"

"I mean," the boy asked timidly, "have you fallen in love with a woman again?"

The old man loosened his grasp on the boy's collar. He turned away and for the first time his green eyes had a vague and scattered look. He lifted the mug from the counter, drank down the yellow beer. His head was shaking slowly from side to side. Then finally he answered: "No, son. You see, that is the last step in my science. I go cautious. And I am not quite ready yet."

"Well!" said Leo. "Well well well!"

The old man stood in the open doorway. "Remember," he said. Framed there in the gray damp light of the early morning, he looked shrunken and seedy and frail. But his smile was bright. "Remember I love you," he said with a last nod. And the door closed quietly behind him.

The boy did not speak for a long time. He pulled down the bangs on his forehead and slid his grimy little forefinger around the rim of his empty cup. Then without looking at Leo he finally asked:

"Was he drunk?"

"No," said Leo shortly.

The boy raised his clear voice higher. "Then was he a dope fiend?"

"No."

The boy looked up at Leo, and his flat little face was desperate, his voice urgent and shrill. "Was he crazy? Do you think he was a lunatic?" The paper boy's voice dropped suddenly with doubt. "Leo? Or not?"

But Leo would not answer him. Leo had run a night café for fourteen years, and he held himself to be a critic of craziness. There were the town characters and also the transients who roamed in from the night. He knew the manias of all of them. But he did not want to satisfy the questions of the waiting child. He tightened his pale face and was silent.

So the boy pulled down the right flap of his helmet and as he turned to leave he made the only comment that seemed safe to him, the only remark that could not be laughed down and despised:

"He sure has done a lot of traveling."

What do you think?

1. When the stranger touched the young boy, he "shrank back uneasily" (Page 55); when the stranger told the boy he loved him, the men at the counter laughed. Comment on the appropriateness of those responses. Comment on the reasonableness of the boy's suspicion that the transient is either drunk or crazy.
2. What is the significance of the stranger inviting the boy—who is a minor—to have a beer with him?
3. Clearly, Leo would not listen to the stranger's story. What reasons can you provide for the boy listening? Why do you think the stranger tells his story? Why does he grasp the boy's jacket collar? Why is he trembling?
4. Some of the boy's questions may seem inappropriate. Do you think his questions would be more in line with the things the transient is relating if he were older? If age makes a difference in understanding or appreciating, why doesn't the transient insist on telling his story to Leo?
5. The transient considers love a science. Do you have the impression that he has sincerely developed a "science" or is this a ruse to escape future relations with women? What clues does the story offer which help you to answer this question?
6. The author touches on circumstances that encourage persons to seek love and those that they fear once they are "in love." What are those circumstances? Would the same items appear on your personal list of characteristics found in persons *before* and *while* being "in love"?
7. Considering the ideas about love advanced in this story, how would you summarize the act of loving. How does it compare with your own notion?

Suggestions for writing and viewing

1. The stranger married Dodo after knowing her only three days. Write a paper (1000 words) on any aspect of a short courtship which interests you. For example, you might discuss the notion that a person can "fall in love" at first sight.
2. *The Semantics of the Popular Song* (National Educational Television, 30 min.). This film contrasts the attitude toward love developed by the lyrics of popular songs and the attitude projected by the blues. It poses the question of whether popular songs make attainment of emotional maturity more difficult. The film is recommended to provide visual alternatives to the notion of love advanced in "A Tree. A Rock. A Cloud."

ASK ANN LANDERS

Her guy and her best friend

Dear Ann Landers: Until six weeks ago I was going with a very interesting guy. A buddy of his came to town and asked me to get him a date. So I fixed him up with my best friend. The four of us went out together. After that evening my very interesting guy never called me again. He has been seeing my "friend" almost every night.

I tried to act as if I didn't care, but I cared plenty. Not because I lost him to her, but because she thought so little of our friendship that she accepted a date with him when she knew he was mine. Finally I got fed up pretending. I lost my cool and told her exactly how I felt. She was dumbfounded—acted as if she had no idea I was hurt.

Am I justified in my feelings that she betrayed me? Please comment. KANSAS CITY KITTY

Dear Kitty: The guy you refer to as "yours" obviously was not. You didn't lose him. You never had him. A woman rarely loses a man to someone else. He first loses his interest in HER—then someone else comes along.

Bury the hatchet and pass the peace pipe.

Reprinted by permission of Ann Landers, Publishers-Hall Syndicate, Chicago Sun-Times, Daily News Building, Chicago, Illinois 60611.

What do you think?

1. Is the Kansas City Kitty's problem a common one? Have you ever been involved in such a situation? Did you resolve it satisfactorily? Explain how.
2. What's your opinion of Kitty's behavior? Was she wise to act as if she didn't care? To lose her cool? To write to Ann Landers? Give reasons for each response.
3. What is implied by Kitty's saying, ". . . but I cared plenty . . . because she thought so little of our friendship that she accepted a date with him when she knew he was mine." Is she rationalizing? Do you think Kitty's friend was honestly dumbfounded or was she pretending? Should Kitty maintain her friendship with this girl? Give reasons for your opinion.
4. Is Ann Landers correct in saying that Kitty never really had the fellow? How can you judge whether someone belongs to you?

Suggestions for writing and research

1. Write a very short letter (200-300 words) to Ann Landers in which you assume the role of Kitty's girlfriend. Make clear whether you knew that Kitty liked the fellow in question.
   (a) The second step in this writing project would be for one of your fellow students to write Ann Lander's response to your letter. Caution the person that he must be prepared to defend his response on the basis of the nature of the advice offered in answer to Kitty.
2. Read the advice column that is carried in the local newspaper for at least two weeks. Write a short (300 words) evaluative report in which you explain why you do or do not respect the kinds of advice that the writer gives. Clip two or three columns that you consider typical and submit them as evidence along with your report.

IS LOVE AN ART?

Erich Fromm

Is love an art? Then it requires *knowledge* and *effort.* Or is love a pleasant sensation, which to experience is a matter of chance, something one "falls into" if one is lucky? This little book is based on the former premise, while undoubtedly the majority of people today believe in the latter.

Not that people think that love is not important. They are starved for it; they watch endless numbers of films about happy and unhappy love stories, they listen to hundreds of trashy songs about love—yet hardly anyone thinks that there is anything that needs to be learned about love.

This peculiar attitude is based on several premises which either singly or combined tend to uphold it. Most people see the problem of love primarily as that of *being loved,* rather than that of *loving,* of one's capacity to love. Hence the problem to them is how to be loved, how to be lovable. In pursuit of this aim they follow several paths. One, which is especially used by men, is to be successful, to be as powerful and rich as the social margin of one's position permits. Another, used especially by women, is to make oneself attractive, by cultivating one's body, dress, etc. Other ways of making oneself attractive, used both by men and women, are to develop pleasant manners, interesting conversation, to be helpful, modest, inoffensive. Many of the ways to make oneself lovable are the same as those used to make oneself successful, "to win friends and influence people." As a matter of fact, what most people in our culture mean by being lovable is essentially a mixture between being popular and having sex appeal.

A second premise behind the attitude that there is nothing to be learned about love is the assumption that the problem of love is the problem of an *object,* not the problem of a *faculty.* People think that to *love* is simple, but that to find the right object to love—or to be loved by—is difficult. This attitude has several reasons rooted in the development of modern society. One reason is the great change which occurred in the twentieth century with respect to the choice of a "love object." In the Victorian age, as in many traditional cultures, love was mostly not a spontaneous personal experience which then might lead to marriage. On the contrary, marriage was contracted by convention—either by the respective families, or by a marriage broker, or without the help of such intermediaries; it was concluded on the basis of social considerations, and love was supposed to develop once the marriage had been concluded. In the last few generations the concept of romantic love has become almost universal in the Western world. In the United States, while considerations of a conventional nature are not entirely absent, to a vast extent people are in search of "romantic love," of the personal experience of love which then should lead to marriage. This new concept of freedom in love must have greatly enhanced the importance of the *object* as against the importance of the *function.*

Closely related to this factor is another feature characteristic of contemporary culture. Our whole culture is based on the appetite for buying, on the idea of a mutually favorable exchange. Modern man's happiness consists in the thrill of looking at the shop windows, and in buying all that he can afford to buy, either for cash or on installments. He (or she) looks at people in a similar way. For the man an attractive girl—and for the woman an attractive man—are the prizes they are after. "Attractive" usually means a nice package of qualities which are popular and sought after on the personality market. What specifically makes a person attractive depends on the fashion of the time, physically as well as mentally. During the twenties, a drinking and smoking girl, tough and sexy, was attractive; today the fashion demands more domesticity and coyness. At the end of the nineteenth and the beginning of this century, a man had to be aggressive and ambitious—today he has to be social and tolerant—in order to be an attractive "package." At any rate, the sense of falling in love develops usually only with regard to such human commodities as are within reach of one's own possibilities for exchange. I am out for a bargain; the object should be desirable from the standpoint of its social value, and at the same time should want me, considering my overt and hidden assets and potentialities. Two persons thus fall in love when they feel they have found the best object available on the market, considering the limitations of their own exchange values. Often, as in buying real estate, the hidden potentialities which can be developed play a considerable role in this bargain. In a culture in which the marketing orientation prevails, and in which material success is the outstanding value, there is little reason to be surprised that human love relations follow the same pattern of exchange which governs the commodity and the labor market.

The third error leading to the assumption that there is nothing to be learned about love lies in the confusion between the initial experience of *"falling"* in love, and the permanent stage of *being* in love, or as we might better say, of "standing" in love. If two people who have been strangers, as all of us are, suddenly let the wall between them break down, and feel close, feel one, this moment of oneness is one of the most exhilarating, most exciting experiences in life. It is all the more wonderful, and miraculous for persons who have been shut off, isolated, without love. This miracle of sudden intimacy is often facilitated if it is combined with, or initiated by, sexual attraction and consummation. However, this type of love is by its very nature not lasting. The two persons become well acquainted, their intimacy loses more and more its miraculous character, until their antagonism, their disappointments, their mutual boredom kill whatever is left of the initial excitement. Yet, in the beginning they do not know all this: in fact, they take the intensity of the infatuation, this being "crazy" about each other, for proof of the intensity of their love, while it may only prove the degree of their preceding loneliness.

This attitude—that nothing is easier than to love—has continued to be the prevalent idea about love in spite of the overwhelming evidence to the contrary. There is hardly any activity, any enterprise, which is started with such tremendous hopes and expectations, and yet, which fails so regularly, as love. If this were the case with any other activity, people would be eager to know the reasons for the failure, and to learn how one could do better—or they would give up the activity. Since the latter is impossible in the case of love, there seems to be only one adequate way to overcome the failure of love—to examine the reasons for this failure, and to proceed to study the meaning of love.

The first step to take is to become aware that *love is an art,* just as living is an art; if we want to learn how to love we must proceed in the same way we have to proceed if we want to learn any other art, say music, painting, carpentry, or the art of medicine or engineering.

What are the necessary steps in learning any art?

The process of learning an art can be divided conveniently into two parts: one, the mastery of the theory; the other, the mastery of the practice. If I want to learn the art of medicine, I must first know the facts about the human body, and about various diseases. When I have all this theoretical knowledge, I am by no means competent in the art of medicine. I shall become a master in this art only after a great deal of practice, until eventually the results of my theoretical knowledge and the results of my practice are blended into one—my intuition, the essence of the mastery of any art. But, aside from learning the theory and practice, there is a third factor necessary to becoming a master in any art—the mastery of the art must be a matter of ultimate concern; there must be nothing else in the world more important than the art. This holds true for music, for medicine, for carpentry—and for love. And, maybe, here lies the answer to the question of why people in our culture try so rarely to learn this art, in spite of their obvious failures: in spite of the deep-seated craving for love, almost everything else is considered to be more important than love: success, prestige, money, power—almost all our energy is used for the learning of how to achieve these aims, and almost none to learn the art of loving.

Could it be that only those things are considered worthy of being learned with which one can earn money or prestige, and that love, which "only" profits the soul, but is profitless in the modern sense, is a luxury we have no right to spend much energy on?"

What do you think?

1. Do you agree that most people today are more concerned with the problem of *being loved* than the problem of *being able to love?* Are you using the same proofs for your position as Fromm uses for his argument? Explain.
2. Fromm says that people today ". . . listen to hundreds of trashy songs about love." Would you consider the song on page 103 an example of such? Why or why not? Can you name other examples among songs which are currently popular which fit the author's description?
3. What qualities are most highly valued in a person of the opposite sex among members of the group you most associate with? Good looks? Money? A new car? Or other things?
   What reasons can you give for why these particular things are most highly valued?
4. The divorce rate is high in this country; one sociologist reports that there are 1000 divorces a day. Do you think this rate would drop if we arranged marriages on the basis of factors such as social position, religious background, and mutual economic standing? Why or why not?
5. Do you agree that "Our culture is based on the appetite for buying . . ."? Can you think of groups within our culture for whom this is *not* true? Are they in the mainstream or on the margins of society? Explain your answer.
6. Is your own idea of what happens when two people "fall in love" different from Fromm's? Do you agree with the opinion that feelings of antagonism and mutual boredom necessarily grow which smother the initial feelings of excitement? Explain your response.
7. How do you imagine Erich Fromm would respond to the idea of ownership of someone which is expressed in the letter to Ann Landers, p. 62: ". . . she accepted a date with him when she knew he was mine."

Suggestions for writing

1. Write a short paper in which you describe "The Lovable Man" (or "Woman"). Provide a clear picture of how he (or she) looks, dresses, talks, and thinks. Also indicate what his relationship is to such institutions as the church, school, government, and his family.
2. Question 2 in the first group can be turned into a writing assignment. You can select a song that is currently popular and write a paper in which you show that it either is or is not a "trashy" love song. One way to go about this is to begin by quoting the pertinent lyrics and then comment on their significance insofar as they reflect a particular view of what love is, how it comes about, and what a person can expect from love.

I BREAK EASILY

Barbara Howard

I break easily—
he knows that, yet he does not;
we still communicate through telephone booths,
with each other's picture stuck in our hands
like arbitrary gifts of Fate . . .

laconic notes scribbled between appointments
are hidden in the crevices of our
meeting places . . .
holding hands &/or making love in the park
behind a rock, near a tree, above a spring yet
below a bubbling Hell—we still whisper—but not for
the right reasons—

staring momentarily at each other
as the elevator closes;
we must meet downstairs
where the hall is subdued by
a nonfunctional door,
a place which the maintenance man
ignores—
& we must meet there do some
ignoring
because everyone knows . . .

clandestine arrangements are not
terrible, they are painful—
I am aware of this pain, &
so is he, yet he is not;
we are two branches discouraged from
becoming one tree or spending any other
time together—
he knows all this, yet he does not;
& I know all this, yet I cannot stop . . .

What do you think?

1. Often in poetry, we find ideas expressed in such a fashion that two or more meanings can be gathered from them. This feature is called deliberate ambiguity. Some of the examples of such ambiguity in this poem follow. Provide at least two different interpretations for each.
   (a) "I break easily" (line 1).
   (b) "He knows that, yet he does not" (line 2).
   (c) "He knows all this yet he does not" (line 30).
2. Deliberate ambiguity is used in writing other than poetry. Sometimes you find it in advertising and in political speeches or statements. Bring examples that you find in newspaper or magazine articles to class, and be prepared to explain the multiple meanings.
3. Provide as many reasons as you can why the lovers in the poem must meet secretly. Why do you think the poetess didn't provide an explanation?
4. Do you think there is a special kind of excitement about a "secret" affair? What are the special problems in such affairs? Explain both answers in detail.
5. In general, what is the apparent attitude of American society toward "secret" affairs? Explain what difference such factors as the age and the marital status of the persons involved makes. Is your attitude a different one or similar to that of society in general? Why?

Suggestions for writing

1. A number of films and popular songs have been based on "secret" affairs. Write a short paper (500 words) in which you describe one film or song of this kind, in such fashion that someone who is unfamiliar with it will get a clear understanding of why the affair must not be generally known. Give your own explanation for the popularity of the film or song.

MISS PEACH

Mell Lazarus

MISS PEACH
By Mell Lazarus
ARTHUR, YOU REALLY LOVE THE FLOWERS AND TREES AND BROOKS, DON'T YOU?
YES.
-BUT THIS UNREQUITED LOVE DEPRESSES ME...
MELL LAZARUS 8-25

Mell Lazarus. Courtesy of Publishers-Hall Syndicate

What do you think?

1. Unlike the stranger in "A Tree. A Rock. A Cloud." Arthur doesn't seem to love these objects because they are steps in a process to something greater. He seems to love them as an end in themselves. Do you think this is healthy or not?
2. Arthur is depressed by unrequited love. Is this the usual reaction? Would Fromm describe Arthur as a person who has the correct idea about loving versus being loved?

HAPPILY EVER AFTER (THEY THINK)

Ernest Havemann

We are about to look in on Ruth Doe Harris (Mrs. George K.). Address: 132 Abbington Road, in a suburb fifteen miles from the city limits. Age: thirty. Religion: Protestant. Husband's occupation: junior executive, American Chemical Company.

No. 132 Abbington Road is the kind of address to which every young girl aspires. The house is freshly painted white frame, split level, four bedrooms, set on a half acre of immaculate lawn. The lights shine cheerfully behind green awnings. In the back yard, roses are blooming; nicotiana perfumes the quiet air; robins are bobbing across the grass.

It is early evening of a Friday in late June, and a new moon is rising in a cloudless and still bright sky. It is a perfect evening, the kind celebrated in song. June, moon. Sky above, love.

Inside the house Ruth Doe Harris has just finished feeding Pamela, age five, and Roger, age four. She is a handsome young woman, blonde and blue-eyed, trim and shapely in tapered slacks and an open-throated white blouse. She wears sandals; her toenails are bright red. She has the first golden beginnings of a summer suntan. She is the kind of young matron who could, with her two good-looking children, pose for an ad.

She takes the children to bed; she reads to them. Being an old-fashioned sort of mother who likes to bring up her children on the same fare she herself enjoyed as a child, she reads *Cinderella.* The unhappy stepdaughter goes to the ball; the glass slipper is lost; the Prince comes searching. At the end Ruth Harris reads the magic words which conclude all fairy tales: "They got married and lived happily ever after."

The children are tucked in. Ruth Harris goes downstairs. She checks the casserole atop her spotless electric range, then goes to the living room. No sign as yet of George K.; he is late. She turns on the radio and picks up the afternoon newspaper. While she reads, the tunes that come from the loudspeaker are "Some Enchanted Evening," "Why Do I Love You?", "I'll Always Be in Love with You." In the newspaper, a beauty column advises her how to make her hair irresistible to men. *Dear Abby* is telling a teen-ager how to recognize true love when it comes along.

She finishes the paper and turns on the television set. An old movie is showing. She watches a boy who is hopelessly in love with a girl and a girl who is hopelessly in love with the boy go through a series of unfortunate misunderstandings, but she is not unduly worried because she knows that in movies of this type the hero and heroine always get together at the end; they marry and live happily ever after.

In a little while she turns off the movie. She is beginning to get annoyed. George K. is now nearly an hour late. She is sorry that she did not have pork chops instead of a casserole for dinner, so that she could accuse him of ruining the meal. She makes herself a martini and broods. There is always the chance that George K. may have been in an accident. He may have been killed.

Eventually footsteps approach up the front walk. She rushes to the door, not knowing whether she is relieved or angry. She says nothing until he has kissed her. Then—possibly because it was a routine, unexciting, cousinly kiss—she blurts almost without meaning to: "Where have you been? You're an hour late."

He shrugs. "I had to work."

She starts to say, "You could have called me." But before the words have formed she sees that he is lying. George is a poor liar; she can tell every time. "You stopped for some drinks with the boys," she says.

He smiles guiltily.

"You could at least have let me know," she says. "How many did you have?"

"Not too many."

Her blue eyes narrow slightly as she makes a survey. He seems all right, but she does not want to take any chances. "Well," she says dubiously, "we'd better eat. Everything's ready. It's been ready for an hour."

"Wait a minute," says George K. "It was hot in the city. I had to stand halfway home on the bus. Let's have a drink and take it easy."

Although not at all sure of her facts, she says, "You've had enough already."

"Don't be a prig."

"Don't be a drunk."

"Darling," he says patiently, "I had a terrible day at the office. Old Smothers is getting worse all the time. We were standing at the bar trying to figure how to murder him quietly. None of us can stand him a week longer."

"I had a hard day, too," Ruth Harris says. "Pamela fell and skinned her knee. Roger got into a fight with that new boy down the street. The dishwasher broke down and the repairman says he can't come until Monday."

"So we both had a hard day. Let's sit down and relax."

He has removed his jacket and loosened his tie and is in the kitchen mixing a drink.

"At least I didn't run down to the saloon and get home an hour late," Ruth Harris says.

He does not reply. They go into the living room and there is a long silence, because they both know that anything they say is likely to lead to trouble. Ruth turns on the radio. Someone sings "My Darling," and then "So in Love." She picks up a magazine and starts reading a novelette telling how love came to a small-town librarian in the form of a glamorous stranger. George picks up a novel he has been reading: a glowing account of an artist's life and loves. The music stops momentarily and the announcer talks about a soap guaranteed to give women the kind of skin men love to touch.

It is now eleven o'clock Saturday morning. George K. and Ruth Doe Harris are attending a wedding at the Second Presbyterian Church at the edge of the city. It is an inconvenient hour for a wedding, but couples who get married in June cannot be choosers. The church is booked for weddings all day, an hour apart, every hour from 10 A.M. through 8 P.M. Ruth's sister Jane Doe, the bride, and John Smith, the groom, who did not set the date of their wedding until a month ago, were lucky to find an hour open at all.

The flowers that banked the altar for the ten-o'clock ceremony have been removed, the new flowers for Jane Doe and John Smith put in place. The wedding party, including Ruth Doe Harris as matron of honor, perfectly stunning in a yellow chiffon dress, has arrived by rented Cadillac. The church is filling up with friends, relatives, and neighbors, all wearing the bittersweet, romantic, indulgent smiles deemed appropriate for weddings.

The bride walks down the aisle, holding tight to her father's arm, and the customary sigh of admiration and regret sweeps the church. All brides are beautiful in their wedding gowns, and Jane Doe is more beautiful than most. Every heart in the church beats faster. Mrs. Doe weeps. Husbands and wives sitting side by side in the pews instinctively reach for each other's hands. A hidden voice sings "Oh, Promise Me" and "I Love You Truly." Jane Doe's cheeks are flushed; her eyes are swimming; this is the moment she has been waiting for all her life. She can barely repeat the marriage vows, so shaken is she by excitement and fulfillment.

In the anteroom of the church afterward, the bride and groom shake hands with the departing guests. Everyone is smiling now, even Mrs. Doe. "Congratulations," the guests murmur. "All happiness." "You're a very lucky young man." "You were a beautiful bride." "May you both live happily ever after." And inevitably someone says, "May all your troubles be little ones."

The reception is at a restaurant ten miles away, not the closest restaurant by any means, nor even the best, but the only one that had a private room available for luncheon. All the others in the neighborhood had been booked for months. The food is not particularly good; the punch has a strange taste, but nobody minds. Everybody is busy making nostalgic conversation, dancing with the bride, and taking pictures. It seems that every guest has brought a camera, for nothing holds so much fascination for amateur photographers as a wedding.

When the bride finally departs, tossing her bouquet away as she goes, there is a scramble among the bridesmaids. They half believe the old adage that whoever catches the bouquet will be the next to marry, and of course every one of them can hardly wait for that day to come. The girl who captures the bouquet feels a sense of triumph even now.

George K. and Ruth Doe Harris return home. Ruth kicks her slippers off as she enters the door; she has not worn high heels for so many consecutive hours in many months; her feet hurt and her calves ache. They kiss the children and pay off the babysitter. Ruth gets out of the yellow chiffon dress, hangs it up with a sigh, and changes into slacks. George changes into an old pair of levis, a dark blue sports shirt, and loafers. They are both still thinking about the wedding.

"Well," says George K., "another good man gone wrong."

It is one of those jokes that men invariably make after a wedding, and to Ruth it is not very funny. She resents it. She herself is thinking how beautiful her sister Jane looked, and how handsome the bridegroom in his rented morning suit. She slams the closet door shut on the yellow dress and goes downstairs to start preparing the children's supper. Her eyes are unaccountably filled with tears.

George K., not noticing, goes out to mow the lawn. If he hurries, he can finish the whole thing by the time Ruth calls him to dinner. He goes about his work cheerfully, whistling "There Is Nothing Like a Dame."

It is night time. Ruth and George Harris celebrated the wedding in the family by opening a bottle of wine at the dinner table. They watched television awhile; then, growing sentimental, they turned it off and talked about their own wedding day, their honeymoon, the birth of their two children. They are in bed now; they have made love; they are about to drift off to sleep.

Ruth Harris feels drowsily contented; she is tired but happy; she is also a little sad. "George?" she asks.

From the other twin bed he answers, "Yes?"

"Are you ever sorry you married me?"

"Of course not."

She smiles. "I'll bet you are."

"Absolutely never," he insists.

"Wasn't she beautiful?"

"Who?"

"Jane."

"Oh. Sure, she was beautiful."

"George?"

"Yes?"

"Do you suppose those two kids have any idea what marriage is really like?"

"Did you?"

"No," Ruth admits. "Did you?"

"Of course not," George says. "Well, they'll find out soon enough, won't they?"

They go to sleep. Across the nation, the radio stations are still broadcasting their songs: "Embraceable You," "I Can't Believe That You're in Love with Me," "My Man I Love Him So," "That Old Black Magic Called Love." Boy is still meeting girl on the television screens and in wide-screen technicolor at the movie houses. The Sunday papers are out with new columns of advice to the lovelorn. Somewhere a lady novelist sits up late, describing the utterly devastating profile of her hero.

Jane Doe and John Smith are miles away now, on the first night of their honeymoon. Although they are thinking only of each other and feel isolated from the world, they have plenty of company: there are thousands and thousands of other young couples who are in the same delightful situation or baffling predicament. Something like 170,000 couples get married every June, most of them on weekends. On any Saturday night in June, the nation's hotels, motels, and resorts are absolutely bursting with honeymooners.

All the newlyweds were brought up on the fairy tales; all of them saw the movies, read the novels, and sang the songs. They all expect to live happily ever after.

Will they? Of course not. The fairy tales are a fraud. Nobody—man or woman, married or unmarried, rich or poor, tall or short, fat or lean—lives happily all the time.

Will that old black magic continue to send icy fingers up and down their spines? Of course not. The love songs are a delusion. Very few people feel those icy fingers even before marriage, much less after. (Although many people try very hard to pretend that they feel them, because they have been persuaded that they should.)

Will they quarrel, bicker, and occasionally wish that fate had never thrown them together? Yes, alas, they will. Such is human nature.

Despite all this, can they be happy though married? Of course they can. Despite all the grousing by disillusioned husbands and wives, despite the high divorce rate, there is a vast amount of happiness, comfort, and even ecstasy in American marriage—and there would be a lot more if people did not enter upon it with such unreasonable hopes, expectations, and demands.

Fact Number One is simply this: marriage is not easy. It never was, as far back as one can find in recorded history. It is probably more difficult in the United States of today than it ever was before. It is a job requiring lengthy training and diligent effort, and all too many young people lack the preparation and are loath to do the work.

What do you think?

1. What segments in our culture does the author hold partly responsible for the perpetuation of myths about the nature of love and marriage? Are there other primary sources?
2. Are Mr. and Mrs. George K. Harris a typical couple? Explain why or why not in detail. Do they illustrate the kind of love Erich Fromm commends in his essay, "Is Love an Art?" (Page 64.)
3. The author uses the wedding of Ruth Harris' sister to illustrate a number of opinions about the general attitude of American society toward marriage. Explain the significance of the following observations.
   (a) That the guests at the wedding are wearing smiles which are "bitter-sweet, romantic and indulgent."
   (b) That the bride has been "waiting all her life" for her wedding.
   (c) That the guests make unoriginal statements, such as "You're a very lucky young man," "You were a beautiful bride," and "May all your troubles be small ones."
4. Would you consider George and Ruth *happy?* Explain your answer. What is your response to the author's question, ". . . can they [couples] be happy though married?" (page 74.) What does the very question suggest?

Suggestions for writing and reading

1. The author mentions three once-popular songs: "Some Enchanted Evening;" "Why Do I Love You;" and "I'll Always Be in Love With You." Check the lyrics of these songs either by looking at the sheet music or by listening to recordings of them. Then write a short paper (500 words) describing the concept of love which any one of the songs advances.
2. Using the resources in the library, find out what you can about *why* the month of June is the favorite one for marriages in America. Write a short paper (500 words) based on your findings.
3. Write a letter of advice to Jane Doe and her husband giving them several hints as to how to keep their marriage reasonably satisfactory. Use sections from "Happily Ever After" if they will help to strengthen your suggestions.
4. In American society, unlike many Eastern and African ones, there are only a limited number of ceremonies that permit groups of friends and relatives to come together and celebrate specific achievements. List as many of those ceremonies as you can. Comment on the value of these kinds of ceremonies for the central figures and the other participants.
5. The following book is recommended for those who are interested in reading more about some of the differences between American marriages and marriages that are characteristic of other societies: *Love Match and Arranged Marriage* by Robert O. Blood (1967). This book compares marriage arrangements and styles in Tokyo, Japan and Detroit, Michigan.

Suggestion for viewing

1. The short film, *Happy Anniversary* (Contemporary Films, 12 min; black and white), is about the problems incurred when a husband gets caught in a traffic jam and is late for his anniversary celebration. It is recommended for stimulation of discussion and writing experiences.

I GOT A GAL

Marion Montgomery

Marion Montgomery, "I Got a Gal" from *Southern Writing in the Sixties* (1966) by Louisiana State University Press. Reprinted By permission of Louisiana State University Press, Baton Rouge.

It was nearly eight o'clock and the August sun was already hot behind the chinaberry tree when he got water in the A-model and called Sara to come on and get in. She didn't answer. He stood in the shade leaning on the spare tire waiting a minute. Then he went over to where he could look in the window. He couldn't see in the dim room at first.

"It's time we was going," he said. A fly cleaned its hind legs on the window sill, pointing its rear at him.

"I know it."

"Well, you'd better hurry up," he said. He could make out the back of her head a little. Sitting in front of the mirror brushing that long wavy hair again.

"You can just wait, Jim Patterson," she said, "because I'm not a-going till I get myself ready."

The fly he was watching crawled out of the edge of shade to where another one was dozing on the bleached pine window sill, and then both went whirling out into the sunlight. A year ago he would have already been in town by this time, but that was before they had to have the car. That was when they drove Tilly and his daddy's buggy the ten miles. But that wasn't for long after they got married.

He walked over and threw the empty bucket down beside the well curbing and wiped his hands on an old rag. First of all, he had slept late. That was what Sara said they could do once they got a car. They wouldn't have to get such an early start with the automobile. So he slept late, almost to six-fifteen. The car would be the ruination of him yet. If he slept till six-fifteen on Saturday, no telling what time it would be Sunday. And then Monday . . .

At six-thirty, after he finally roused Sara, he had gone out to see about the car. He tossed a rolled-up burlap bag in the back seat and picked up the water bucket. The radiator leaked and you had to put in water every five miles—or after half an hour when it was just resting under the chinaberry tree. But when he got the radiator filled he noticed that the left rear tire was flat. He had had to fix a flat on the way home last Saturday, and now there was one even before they got started. Old Man Lebius had let the car sit up under his shed till the tires near rotted off before he sold it to Sam Benson. And then he, Jim, had let Sara and that crooked mule dealer sell it to him for a hundred and twenty-five dollars. But Sara had to have a car. Arguments hadn't been worth a toot in a whistle factory to Sara. He finally gave in and bought it.

He finally bought that five-dollar jar of cream too, and that ought to have been enough. Sara had seen it in the Sunday funny papers one week, and had hounded him for the next two till he let her send off for it. She kept the clipping stuck in the edge of the bureau mirror where she could see it the first thing in the morning and the last thing before she blew out the lamp at night just in case she might forget to mention it. He argued about that cream. She was only seventeen. When she got her first baby they would get bigger.

"I seen too many yearlings come in," he said. "You don't need no New York cream. All you need is a youngun to nuss."

"It ain't New York, it's Paris." She pointed out the name too, *La Contour for Mademoiselle.* "That's French. Sudy Lou's husband said it was. He's been to France. He ought to know."

"Sudy Lou's husband be damned," he said. "It says New York right on the paper here. That's where you send the money, ain't it?"

That's where he sent the money. After she cried and pouted and burned the biscuits and undercooked the blackeyed peas. She left the clipping stuck in the mirror frame with its French words and New York address and what looked to Jim like a big radio tower in the background and a lot of black-headed women pushing balloons ahead of them. The cream came all right, a piddling little old jar of white stuff about the size of a Vick's salve. And Sara kept burning the biscuits. She like to have worn out the tape measure the first two weeks too, and kept talking about how the cream was working. But he couldn't see a bit of difference in the world. Still couldn't.

He got the patching on the innertube that was already so patched it looked like somebody had shot it with number nine bird shot. He got the boot worked back into place. But the water had leaked out of the radiator and he had to fill it again. When Tilly stuck her head over the lot gate and brayed at him, he picked up a clod of dirt and threw it hard as he could. It shattered against the barn and sprayed dirt all over the mule.

Then he stomped into the house. Sara was still at the mirror. Used to he'd have had his breakfast over with and done, and she hadn't even got the coffee made. So by the time they got the coffee made and the biscuits done, there wasn't anything to do but fill the radiator again before they left. Sara said he ought to have waited anyhow.

So there it was nearly eight o'clock, and they hadn't started yet. He hung the rag he'd been wiping his hands with back on the nail at the well curb.

"Sara," he yelled again. "Sara, if you're going with me you'd better git on out here. I have to fill this damn croakersack of a radiator again, I'm going to walk."

The front screen door banged and Sara came down the steps. No wonder she was late. Dressed up in her Sunday dress, big green and red flowers on it, and that hat and everything. It looked like ever since he got the automobile she spent most of her time either getting ready to go to town on Saturday or talking about getting ready. She didn't even fix his breakfast till she got her hair all primped up and put some of the cream on. No blessed wonder it took him so long to get to the field.

"I'm coming," Sara said. She climbed up in the front seat and Jim set the water bucket in the back. He was about to get in when Tilly brayed at him again. He reached down and got another clod of dirt and threw it over the car at the mule. A scattering of it managed to get on Sara's dress and she began brushing it off like it was something worse than dirt.

He slammed the door and stepped on the starter. He turned the key in the switch two or three times and tried again. There was a puny groan once from the motor, and then it didn't do any good to step on the starter anymore. Jim sat there a minute, clutching the wheel in both hands.

"What's the matter now?" asked Sara.

"The matter is that I ought never let you talk me into getting this damn heap of junk, that's what the matter is." He got out and slammed the door behind him. Tilly was back at the lot gate with her head over watching when Jim got the bridle off the peg. But Tilly wanted to play. She kicked up her heels and ran around and around the lot. He finally hemmed her up in a corner and got a rope around her neck, but she wouldn't take the bit. Stubborn as Sara sometimes. He twisted her nose sharply and slipped the piece of steel between her teeth. Then he yanked her ears through the halter and led her into the barn. All that time Sara just sat there in the car watching, clasping her hands and unclasping them. When Jim came out of the barn with Tilly, she had on her plow harness. He scraped his shoes on a clump of bermuda grass.

He didn't say a word to Sara. When he got Tilly around in front of the A-model, he hitched the traces around the bumper. Then he got on the running board so he could guide the car with one hand and hold the plow lines with the other.

"All right now, git up!"

Tilly just stood there, looking back over her shoulder at Jim and then at the automobile. "Git up, goddamn it!" She moved forward till she took up the slack. Then she looked back at him again.

"I wish you wouldn't cuss so, Jim," Sara said softly, looking down at her hands. "Mama says it don't sound right. I never heard Sudy Lou's husband cuss a-tall, and he was in the Army."

Jim went around in front of Tilly and grabbed her halter with both hands. She strained a little and the car began moving.

"Two mistakes an old fool like me ought never make," he said between his teeth at Tilly. "One is marry a little old gal that's too young and full of mama and going. Other is to buy a fool automobile."

Tilly pulled half-heartedly at the unfamiliar burden. He slapped her on the side with the plow lines and hollered at her again. He could see Sara sitting up there holding on to the door for dear life though the car was only going at a creep. The second time he slapped Tilly she got the devil in her tail and started hard as she could go. They got to the little rise and over it before he could get her stopped. The mule and the car were well on their way to the bottom of the hill with the A-model gaining when Jim managed to get in and step on the brakes. Tilly jerked up tight in her harness and just stood there panting and trembling.

"I ought never to have sold my buggy to that mule stealer."

Sara was white and scared, but she was quiet for a change. Jim left her holding the brake on with both feet while he got out and scotched a rock under the front wheel. Then he unhitched Tilly and led her to the barn. When he got back to the car, he moved the rock, gave the car a little shove, and jumped in. He pushed the clutch in, wrestled the gears into second from neutral, and let the wheels turn the motor. The first time it didn't catch. He leaned forward. They were nearly at the bottom of the hill when he tried again, and this time the motor caught and sputtered and started.

When they got out to the highway and things seemed to be going all right, Sara loosened up. "Maybe we ought to get another one," she said.

Jim was still hunched over the wheel gritting his teeth when the black Chevrolet came whizzing up alongside, slowed down, and the driver started honking his horn at them. He didn't even look. Sudy Lou's husband. He'd done the same thing when he had that little old Ford and Jim and Sara rode to town in the buggy. The black car shot on ahead so they could see its jewelled mud flaps and exhaust. All that show and all that Sunday talk at Sara's mama's house was what got her started harping on trading the buggy in the first place. Nothing would do but Jim must see about getting an automobile. It took two weeks for the fancy cream. She wore him down in a month about the car. She like to have drove him crazy till he couldn't stand it any more and spoke to Sam Benson. Sam wanted Tilly, but Jim wouldn't trade her. They finally traded for the A-model, and Jim shelled out a hundred and twenty-five dollars for it, twenty-five of it credit for the buggy. But that hadn't satisfied Sara for long.

"If we was to just get us a little better one, Jim," she said, "we wouldn't have all this trouble like this. You wouldn't have to fill the radiator and fix the tires and all. It would be a lot better."

"The next trade I make," Jim said, "is going to be for my buggy. It's already ten o'clock. If we'd been driving Tilly, we'd already be there and out of this sun. Next trade is going to be for my buggy again."

Sara pouted then for awhile, but Jim didn't care. He had made up his mind, no matter if she did pout and wheedle.

They were three and a half miles from home when the car choked, ran another few yards gasping. It sounded like the gas tank was empty. He managed to get the car off the road on the shoulder before it stopped rolling. Then he got out. He cut off a piece of pop-gun elder beside the road and stuck it down in the tank. It came out damp. He smelled it. It was gas. He raised the hood and poked around at the spark plugs. He couldn't find anything wrong. Only thing it could be, he decided, was the fuel line choked up.

"Maybe if we'd just get us a better one," Sara said, "we wouldn't keep having this trouble." She said it like it was a new idea she'd just thought of. The sun was really coming down on Jim's neck now. He got in and stepped on the starter again.

"Maybe we ought to stop and see Sam Benson on the way in," Sara said. "Sudy Lou's husband says . . ."

Jim reached in the back seat and got the rolled-up burlap bag. He unrolled it slowly, watching Sara coldly as her red pout changed to white. She put her hand over her mouth when he pulled the .38 Special out of the sack. Then he walked around to the raised hood and fired four shots into the motor, pausing a second after each. Sara sat there with her lip trembling, watching wide-eyed and silent. He clicked the cylinder out in his palm and blew the smoke from the barrel, looking at Sara through the windshield. Then he wrapped the gun up in the burlap and stuck it under his arm. He held a steady pace toward town, not looking back and not seeing Sara burst into tears. When he was nearly out of sight, she pulled off her shoes and headed for home.

Jim stopped off at Walt Jenkins' place before he got to town. He found Walt out at the barn and sold him what was left of the car for ten dollars. Then he tramped on to town, the burlap bag under his arm. When he got to the Happy House Restaurant he went in and drank two beers. By that time he was feeling a little better and on the way out he bought two pints of blackberry wine. What was left of the ten dollars he stuffed in a hip pocket. He stopped off in the men's room and drank a quarter of one of the pints and wrapped the bottles in the burlap bag with the gun.

Down the street he bought a ticket to the jungle movie and watched a black-headed woman push her balloons all over the screen. He wondered if she used French cream. He asked the lady next to him and she got up and moved. Then he started talking to a fellow in front of him and the people got to shushing him. When the black-headed woman's fellow commenced swinging on long vines, he began to feel sick. He got up and went to the men's room and washed his face. That made him feel a little better and he drank another quarter.

But he didn't go back and watch the rest of the picture show. He walked around the courthouse square looking for Sudy Lou's husband and the black Chevrolet. He couldn't find them. After awhile he thought about the mule trader and got mad again. He tried to stop a fellow and tell him about it, but the man laughed and said he had to go. Jim stood looking after him a long minute. Then he struck out for Sam Benson's buy-and-trade mule barn. Sam hadn't sold the buggy when he got there, and that sure was good. He traded for it, giving Sam five dollars down. Then he worked at the buggy top till he got it collapsed and tied. Sam loaned him a mule till Sunday, and it was dusk when he got her hitched to the buggy and started home.

Every time a car passed him on the big road, he stood up and waved his hat and shouted. Then he would take another pull at the blackberry wine. When the buggy swung in the side yard, the moon was up and he was singing.

Ducks in the pond and geese in the ocean
Hi ho diddle um day

He stopped under the chinaberry tree and put the borrowed mule in the barn lot. Tilly wanted to play again, but he hemmed her up in a stall and got the bit in her mouth.

Devil's in a woman if she takes the notion
Hi ho diddle um day

He brought her out into the moonlight and hitched her to the buggy. Around and around the house then, singing and shouting at the moon and the car lights down on the highway every once in awhile. By the bottom of the second pint he could hardly get the old girl unharnessed. He patted her on the neck, telling her what a good mule she was. So happy he could cry. He stood there with his arm around Tilly's neck crying for a long time. He drained the empty bottle once more and threw it out across the cotton field, watching it flash in the moonlight. Then he started toward the house to find the French cream, singing again.

I got a gal on Sourwood Mountain
Hi ho diddle um day
She won't come and I won't come git her
Hi ho diddle um day.

Sara pretended she was asleep as long as he would let her.

What do you think?

1. What tricks does Sara use to get her way with Jim? Itemize them in two categories: harmless and costly ones.
2. Is Sudy-Lou's husband perfect? Answer this question first from Sara's viewpoint and then from Jim's viewpoint. Speculate on Sudy-Lou's own opinion of him.
3. What is the significance of Sudy-Lou's husband being referred to as her husband rather than by name?
4. In what ways does the closeness—both physical and emotional—of Sara to her mama add to Jim's problems? Does this closeness alleviate or increase Sara's own problems?
5. When Jim pulled the gun from the burlap bag, who or what did you think he was going to shoot? What earlier clues in the story helped you anticipate his target? What is the point of this action?
6. What is the first clue you picked up that Jim was drunk? Are his drunken activities harmful? Defend your answer.
7. Would Jim probably have sold the car and bought back the buggy if he had been sober? Make your comment broad enough to clarify whether Jim is weak, flexible, whether he has been transformed into a puppet by his love for Sara, or something other than these choices.
8. Another way of describing Jim is by focusing on Sara. How would you describe her, in relation to him: Dominating? Selfish? Stubborn? Or something other than these choices?
9. Is this a good or a bad marriage? Give reasons for your opinion. Which of the two persons seems best suited for marriage? Explain your answer.
10. Apparently Jim is considerably older than Sara. He blames her youth for some of their troubles. He says it was a mistake for him to "marry a little old gal that's too young and full of mama and going." How does your own experience and observations correspond with this statement?
11. In a few sentences express the main idea of this story. For example, is it chiefly about how other peoples' opinions can affect a marriage? Or is it about the problems of a marriage in which the persons are of significantly different ages? Whatever your response, be prepared to defend your answer.

Suggestions for writing, listening, and viewing

1. Attempting to acquire and keep material things and a status that others have is called "Keeping Up With the Joneses." It is a life-style that is often talked about in magazine and newspaper articles. Do some research in the library or among your friends and relatives on the subject. Write a paper (1000 words) in which you discuss the feelings that motivate men and women who try to "keep up" in this way.
2. Speculate on what happens after Jim goes into the house. Then write a short paper (500 words) that describes the activities and dialogue between Sara and Jim during the thirty-minute period that begins when the story ends.
3. "Our Ages or Our Hearts" is a song about a love affair between a man who is 34 years old and a woman who is 21. Listen carefully to the words so that you can discuss the problems that they encounter *because* of the age difference. Comment on whether you consider the lyrics realistic or not. An excellent recording is on Atlantic Records, SD 8230, by Miss Roberta Flack. The LP record is entitled, *First Take.*
4. *Have I Told You Lately that I Love You?* (University of Southern California, 1958, 17 min.). This film presents, in symbolic fashion, a typical day in the life of an upper middle class American family. It suggests that their reliance on machines has seriously affected their relations with each other.

Maurice Sackett/D.P.I.

MARRIAGE

Gregory Corso

Should I get married? Should I be good?
Astound the girl next door with my velvet suit and faustus hood?
Don't take her to movies but to cemeteries
tell all about werewolf bathtubs and forked clarinets
then desire her and kiss her and all the preliminaries
and she going just so far and I understanding why
not getting angry saying You must feel! It's beautiful to feel!
Instead take her in my arms lean against an old crooked tombstone
and woo her the entire night the constellations in the sky—
When she introduces me to her parents
back straightened, hair finally combed, strangled by a tie,
should I sit knees together on their 3rd degree sofa
and not ask Where's the bathroom?
How else to feel other than I am,
often thinking Flash Gordon soap—
O how terrible it must be for a young man
seated before a family and the family thinking
We never saw him before! He wants our Mary Lou!
After tea and homemade cookies they ask What do you do for a living?

Should I tell them? Would they like me then?
Say All right get married, we're losing a daughter
But we're gaining a son—
And should I then ask Where's the bathroom?

O God, and the wedding! All her family and her friends
and only a handful of mine all scroungy and bearded
just wait to get at the drinks and food—
And the priest! he looking at me as if I masturbated
asking me Do you take this woman for your lawful wedded wife?
And I trembling what to say say Pie Glue!

I kiss the bride all those corny men slapping me on the back
She's all yours, boy! Ha-ha-ha!
And in their eyes you could see some obscene honeymoon going on—
Then all that absurd rice and clanky cans and shoes
Niagara Falls! Hordes of us! Husbands! Wives! Flowers! Chocolates!
All streaming into cozy hotels
All going to do the same thing tonight
The indifferent clerk he knowing what was going to happen
The lobby zombies they knowing what
The whistling elevator man he knowing
The winking bellboy knowing
Everybody knowing! I'd be almost inclined not to do anything!
Stay up all night! Stare that hotel clerk in the eye!
Screaming: I deny honeymoon! I deny honeymoon!
running rampant into those almost climactic suites
yelling Radio belly! Cat shovel!
O I'd live in Niagara forever! in a dark cave beneath the Falls
I'd sit there the Mad Honeymooner
devising ways to break marriages, a scourge of bigamy
a saint of divorce—

But I should get married I should be good
How nice it'd be to come home to her
and sit by the fireplace and she in the kitchen
aproned young and lovely wanting my baby
and so happy about me she burns the roast beef
and comes crying to me and I get up from my big papa chair
saying Christmas teeth! Radiant brains! Apple deaf!
God what a husband I'd make! Yes, I should get married!
So much to do! like sneaking into Mr Jones' house late at night
and cover his golf clubs with 1920 Norwegian books
Like hanging a picture of Rimbaud[1] on the lawnmower
like pasting Tannu Tuva postage stamps all over the picket fence
like when Mrs Kindhead comes to collect for the Community Chest
grab her and tell her There are unfavorable omens in the sky!
And when the mayor comes to get my vote tell him
When are you going to stop people killing whales!
And when the milkman comes leave him a note in the bottle
Penguin dust, bring me penguin dust, I want penguin dust—

Yet if I should get married and it's Connecticut and snow
and she gives birth to a child and I am sleepless, worn,

up for nights, head bowed against a quiet window, the past behind me,
finding myself in the most common of situations a trembling man
knowledged with responsibility not twig-smear nor Roman coin soup—
O what would that be like!
Surely I'd give it for a nipple a rubber Tacitus[2]
For a rattle a bag of broken Bach records
Tack Della Francesca[3] all over its crib
Sew the Greek alphabet on its bib
And build for its playpen a roofless Parthenon[4]

No, I doubt I'd be that kind of father
not rural not snow no quiet window
but hot smelly tight New York City
seven flights up, roaches and rats in the walls
a fat Reichian wife screeching over potatoes Get a job!
And five nose running brats in love with Batman
And the neigbors all toothless and dry haired
like those hag masses of the 18th century
all wanting to come in and watch TV
The landlord wants his rent
Grocery store Blue Cross Gas & Electric Knights of Columbus
Impossible to lie back and dream Telephone snow, ghost parking—
No! I should not get married I should never get married!
But—imagine If I were married to a beautiful sophisticated woman
tall and pale wearing an elegant black dress and long black gloves
holding a cigarette holder in one hand and a highball in the other
and we lived high up in a penthouse with a huge window
from which we could see all of New York and even farther on clearer days
No, can't imagine myself married to that pleasant prison dream—

O but what about love? I forget love
not that I am incapable of love
it's just that I see love as odd as wearing shoes—
I never wanted to marry a girl who was like my mother
And Ingrid Bergman was always impossible
And there's maybe a girl now but she's already married
And I don't like men and—
but there's got to be somebody!
Because what if I'm 60 years old and not married,
all alone in a furnished room with pee stains on my underwear
and everybody else is married! All the universe married but me!

Ah, yet well I know that were a woman possible as I am possible
then marriage would be possible—
Like SHE[5] in her lonely alien gaud waiting her Egyptian lover
so I wait—bereft of 2,000 years and the bath of life.

[1] Rimbaud: a Belgian poet whose work expresses a strong desire for the spiritual world.
[2] Tacitus: a Roman historian.
[3] Della Francesca: an Italian painter of the 15th century.
[4] Parthenon: a 5th century temple in Athens, Greece.
[5] SHE: an African sorceress whom death apparently can't touch.

What do you think?

1. In the first section of the poem, why does the speaker equate getting married with "being good"? Why would it be appropriate to take the girl next door to the cemetery? What is the American myth about "the girl next door" and courtship?
2. Why would the speaker hesitate to ask where the bathroom is, in that first section? How can you ascertain whether he is serious about the activities he'd like to participate in in that section?
3. What elements in the speaker's vision of the honeymoon make it a desirable experience? An undesirable one?
4. In the second vision of marriage, what does the phrase, "a trembling man knowledged with responsibility" (lines 77-78) mean? Why would you agree or disagree that being a father can have this effect?
5. Why does Corso call the fourth vision of marriage a "pleasant prison dream"?
6. Each conventional act described in the poem is followed by a description of an unconventional one. What point is Corso making by use of this pattern?
7. Which of the following does the speaker in the poem seem most interested in throughout the poem: The object of love? The process of loving? Or alternative kinds of marriage with no consideration for loving? In light of your answer which of the other writers you've read in this section is Corso most like?
8. In your own words, what is the theme of the poem? In what ways does it reflect or conflict with your own feelings about marriage?

Suggestions for writing and viewing

1. Select that version of married life described in the poem which appeals most to you. Write a short paper (500 words) in which you explain its appeal.
2. Write a paper (750 words) in which you describe the perfect marriage. In some detail explain how the husband or wife feels about himself and the marriage.
3. At certain points in the poem, Corso uses nonsense phrases: "radio belly," "apple deaf," and so on. Write a paper (750 words) in which you create your own nonsense phrases and describe the formal or serious setting in which you would like to use them. Explain how you think observers would be affected by your words and what feelings you think you would experience in saying them.
4. *A Day in the Country* (37 min.; black and white; Contemporary Films) is recommended as a stimulant to discussion or for a writing experience. It is about a young Parisian girl who falls in love with a man she meets at a picnic; she marries someone else and years later sees the man of her dreams and senses the happiness she might have known with him.

LAUGHING BOY

Oliver LaFarge

I

Time passing and corn growing cannot be seen; one can notice only that the moon has become so much older, the corn so much higher. With a new life almost more regular than the old, yet far more thrilling, with a rich supply of silver and choice turquoise, with horses to trade and a cornfield to care for, and all the world made over new, time for Laughing Boy went like a swift, quiet river under cottonwood trees. For him, life—which had never been a problem—was solved and perfected, with none of Slim Girl's complication of feeling that such happiness was too good to last. Had he sat down at T'o Tlakai to compose a song of perfection, he could not have imagined anything approaching this.

It had always been a pleasure to him to work in the corn, to help make the green shafts shoot up, to watch them dance, and contrast their deep, full green with the harsh, faded desert. Among his people corn was a living thing; to make a field beautiful was not so far from making a fine bracelet, and far more useful. He drew the precious water into his field thriftily. At its corners he planted the four sacred plants.

Slim Girl did not understand it at first; she had rather wanted to bar it as entailing unnecessary labour, but decided not to say anything. He saw that she thought it dull, drudging work. He did not try to explain it to her directly, but told her the story of Natinesthani and the origin of corn, and taught her the songs about the tall plant growing. When the stalks were past waist-high, he took her to the field at evening,

Paolo Koch/Rapho Guillumette

while sunset brought the drab clay bluffs to life with red, and a soft breeze made the leaves swing and whisper. He made her see the whole field in contrast, and the individual hills, the slender plants and their promise, talking to her of Corn Maiden and Pollen Boy, and of how First Man and First Woman were made from corn. Her eyes were opened to it then, as much through understanding how he felt as through what she objectively beheld. After that she worked with him a little, to please him, although she never cared for the backbreaking toil in itself.

His silver sold well. His craftsmanship was fine, his invention lively, and his taste in turquoise most exacting. It was strong, pure stuff, real Northern Navajo work, untouched by European influence. Other Indians would buy it in the store, and its barbaric* quality caught the tourist's eye. Slim Girl got in touch with the Harvey agent, finding him a ready buyer at good prices. She liked to think, then, of the many places along the railroad in which strangers were paying for her husband's work.

She had learned not to care much for general opinion of herself, and was surprised to find that this tangible evidence of her mythical husband's existence, this visible means of support, made a pleasant difference in the trader's attitude towards her, and eventually in the looks she received from men throughout the town. There was a surprised feeling that she must have been telling the truth about herself, and a grateful decrease in attempts to scrape unwelcome acquaintance with her. As for George Hartshorn, her American, he developed an increased jealousy that she knew how to use.

To complete her idyll, she wanted to weave, and she found it harder than she had expected. She had been taken to school young, before she had become skilled, and now it was almost all forgotten. Laughing Boy even had to teach her the names of her tools. She wondered, as he watched her struggling with the stubborn warp, if he were laughing at her inside himself, if she seemed ridiculous to him. Many times she would have given up had it not been for her natural determination of character, and for knowing how anomalous and incomplete to him was the house in which the woman could not make a blanket. She dearly longed to reconstruct that scene, but after just a little her back would ache, her forearms grow heavy, and in the backs of her hands would be sharp pains, while the threads were like demons to outwit her. The patient, monotonous spinning was pure torture, and she knew little or nothing of dyes.

Of course, her first blanket was an ambitious one, elaborately designed. The conception was simplified in the making, and the finished product was a quarter of the originally intended size. When she cut the sorry object from the loom, and looked at it, all crooked, irregular, and full of holes, she could have cried. She hid it from him. Many of her later attempts, not fit to go under a saddle or be sold, she destroyed, but this was the first thing she had made. It was a sad failure, but she could see what it was meant to be, and she kept it.

She wove perfectly plain strips that might serve to be sat on, and even many of these were hopeless. At times, despite her husband's encouragement, in his absence she would curse fluently in English and yank at the strings. Few things could make her lose control of herself thus; she wondered at herself for continuing. It was an offering to her beloved and, unconsciously, an expiation for a guilt she had not admitted.

II

On a day when the corn was nearly ripe, she went to work in the field. Tiring, she sat down to rest where she could watch two stalks, with their silk just showing against

* Characterized by simplicity and purity of artistic design.

the sky. Low on the horizon the beginnings of a storm darkened the blue. She called Laughing Boy.

'Show me how they draw the corn in the sandpictures.'

'I do not think I should show you that. You are a woman, and you have never seen the true gods in the Night Chant.'

'Perhaps you are right.'

He was making a decision.

'I shall show you.' He drew in the sand. 'We do it like this. Here is blue, here yellow. Here are the tassels, the silk.'

'Why do you show me?'

'You are not like ordinary people, you have a strength of your own. I do not think any harm will come to you.'

She looked from the conventionalization to the growing stalks; she divided the threatening sky into a design. Her first, elaborate blanket had been a built-up, borrowed idea, her later ones were uninteresting accidents. Now she saw her work complete, loving it and the task of making it. Now she really had something to tell her loom.

She was impatiently patient with the dyeing and spinning, needlessly afraid that she would lose her inspiration. When she was ready, she worked so steadily that Laughing Boy warned her of the fate of women who wove too much, and forced her to let a day go by. Her muscles were much tougher now, and her fingers had grown clever and hard among the strands.

She managed for him to be away with his horses during the last two days, when she finished it. He had not yet returned when, a little despondently, she locked in the selvage, unrolled it on the frame, and sat back on her heels to smoke and look. She did not see what she had conceived. She did not see a living design, balanced and simple, with mated colours. She saw thin, messy workmanship, irregular lines, blunders, coarsenesses. At one place she had forgotten to lock the blue into the green weft, sunlight showed through. The counting of stitches was uneven. The blanket was not even a rectangle.

She went quickly away from the house, walking hurriedly and smoking fiercely.

'I am not a Navajo; it is not given to me to do these things. Mother was happy when she wove, she was beautiful then. I cannot make anything, and he is gifted. He will despise me in the end. Being able to make something beautiful is important to him. He will feel his house empty without the sound of weaving. They said I was gifted, that man who came that time. "My child, just stick to the things of your people and you will do something. You have it." "Mr. Waters is a very famous artist, you must pay attention to what he says, my dear. He expressed himself much pleased with your pictures. I am sure the whole class is proud of Lillian to-day." Those crayons were easy. Perhaps he would like that. But I want to weave. There is nothing the matter with me. No use. *God damn it to hell! God damn me! Chindi, mai, shash, Jee-Cri!* Well, let's go and look at it. There's his pony in front of the house. Come on.'

He had taken down the blanket and was pegging it out carefully. All he said was,

'Where are your wool cards?'

She brought them, two implements like very sharp curry-combs, used to prepare the wool for spinning. She sat down to watch him, thinking, 'Perhaps I shall get very drunk. That might help.'

He carded the face of the blanket energetically, so roughly that it seemed a gratuitous insult even to her poor work. The very coarseness of her spinning served his purpose, as the sharp teeth scraped and tore across the design. She wondered if he were trying to efface it. He stood up.

'Now come here and look.' He put his arm over her shoulder. 'You have thought well. The picture is beautiful.'

The scraping had torn loose a long wool nap, almost a fur, fluffy and fine, that covered all the errors of the weaving. The sharp edges were lost, but the lovely combination she had dreamed of was there, soft and blurred, as though one saw it through tears. She could see how good her conception had been, how true and sure. She had made a beautiful thing. She looked and looked.

He loosened the pegs and turned up the untouched side. As he turned it, he jerked at the corners, throwing the uncertain weave out of shape. It looked like a child's work.

'I am not telling you a lot of things. I am just letting you see something. I think you understand it.'

'I understand. You will be able to put my next blanket under your saddle, and be proud of it. Thank you.'

III

After that there were long, flawless days when they were at home together, he at his forge, she at her loom, time passing with the thump of the batten, the ring of the hammer or rasp of the file. There were chatter and laughter, songs, and long, rich silences. Work then was all love and inspiration.

She had known a good many different kinds of pleasure, but this was a new richness, something that did not exhaust itself, but grew, a sharing of achievement, designs, colours; fingers, hands, and brain creating, overcoming. There was the talk and hummed songs. There was a great deal to be silent about. It came to her as she was weaving the coloured threads to her intent, Why was this not enough?

This is it. This is the thing I have always wanted. There is nothing better; why endanger it. Why not let that man go now? Why not just do this?

The batten thumping down on the weft, the hammer ringing on white metal.

As long as I keep on my way, there is danger. I could never go back to what used to be now. This is what is worth while. A hogan in the Northern desert would be beautiful now.

Sure fingers interlocking dark blue and black, driving the toothed stick down over the juncture.

I cannot stop halfway now. I am making a new trail of beauty. When I get through, it will be wonderful. Nothing will ever have been like our life.

Lifting the treadle to let a line of crimson follow the shuttle through the design.

We shall command money, money will command everything. I have herded sheep, their dust in their lungs, hot, a little girl howling at the sheep. We shall be above that. *Aigisi hogahn hojoni.* A little girl watching old Light Man drive by to his summer camp in a buckboard behind two spanking pintos.

A tiny touch of white brings the red meander to life, and deepens the thunderous background.

Navajo women are growing old when Americans are just getting really strong. I am not going to turn into a fat old squaw. My dear, my dear, will you be gay when you are old? Your silver is beautiful. Is anything in the world worth the risk of separating your forge and my loom?

The blue shuttle goes under six warp strands, the black, coming under two, meets it. A close weave looks like a true diagonal.

Are you afraid now, Came With War? I can handle these men. I make my own trail, and I do not stop halfway. I shall make something perfect, that nobody else has made. If I stop now, I might as well stop work on this blanket, after all it cost me to learn to make it. I shall pay myself back for everything that has been.

A single weft strand has no thickness at all, and a blanket is long. It needs patience to finish it, and to make it beautiful, one must not be afraid of the colours.

Laughing Boy, having done his thinking and made up his mind, did not mull over his decision, any more than when he had started a bracelet; he worried whether it ought to have been a necklace. If he did think of other forms, it was only in reflecting that after this was done he would make more, and always more.

You make your dies out of iron files, you get some small piece of iron from a trader for your anvil. In a hard wooden board you cut depressions for hammering out bosses and conchos and hemispheres for beads. When you have bought or made your tools, and have your skill, you go ahead. You make many things, rings, bracelets, bow-guards, necklaces, pendants, belts, bridles, buttons, hatbands. No two are alike, but they are all of the silver, or of silver and turquoise.

Having what he had, he went ahead with living. There were many days, all different, some of high emotion, some of mere happiness, but they were all made of the same stuff; there was one element beautified in all of them. So he worked, content.

When he had made something that had truly satisfied him, he would give it to her, saying, 'That is for you. There is no use selling that to Americans, they do not understand.'

It always pleased her, but she would appraise the jewelry carefully, checking it against their mutual profits, his sales and horse trades, her blankets, and what she brought from the town. If it could be paid for, she put it away, otherwise she required that it be earned. Her primitive banking won his astonished admiration. For her, it was a happy symbol that their fortune, however earned, should be stored in things of beauty.

And every day, at the end, the sun went down and the harsh horizons dimmed. Then there was the magic drink ready for him, and after that a banquet. They spoke dreamily in the firelight, side by side, and knew a great intimacy. They were not two individuals, but two parts who together made a whole, and there was no cleavage between them.

What do you think?

1. At one point in the story, Slim Girl expresses her concern that the happiness she feels is so good that it is bound to be lost. Why would she or anyone else harbor this feeling? In your opinion do people generally have faith that happiness or unhappiness will be long-lived? How do you explain this?
2. One reason Slim Girl learns to weave is to please her husband. Considering how difficult it is for her, what motivates her to continue trying? Is she trying to make *unnatural* changes in herself in order to please Laughing Boy? Explain your answer.
3. Characterize the kinds of things that make life meaningful for Laughing Boy. How do they differ from the things that Slim Girl values? Whose preferences are most similar to the possessions and activities that make your life meaningful? Explain in some detail.
4. What kinds of experiences contribute most to the intimacy that Laughing Boy and Slim Girl feel with one another? Based on your observations of other couples, is their work or play or leisure together the experience that brings them closest together? How do you explain this phenomenon?
   (a) Laughing Boy says on page 89, "I am not telling you a lot of things. I am just letting you see something." What kinds of things does this remark tell you about his relationship to Slim Girl?
5. Several ideas are offered in the story for how a person's thinking and behavior are influenced by his being either Indian or white. Explain why you agree or disagree with this kind of thinking.

Suggestions for writing

1. Laughing Boy mentions stories about the origin of corn. What non-Indian tales do you know that explain the origin of certain things in nature or of the world itself? Write a short paper in which you relate this tale.
2. Create your own story of how something was created. Make your story sufficiently logical that it will not be dismissed as being thoroughly ridiculous.

ASK ANN LANDERS

The other side of the marriage gap

Dear Ann Landers: Now that you've put the in-laws in their place by printing Eight Ways To Break Up A Son's Or Daughter's Marriage, will you please give equal time to the other side?

I have prepared a simple list of rules which might help preserve the sanity and health of parents with married children.

(1) Settle your own arguments. Don't drag us into your family fights and ask us to take sides.

(2) Buy what you can afford. When you made the decision to marry, you announced to the world that you were old enough to stand on your own two feet. Prove it.

(3) Don't assume we are willing to sit with your children or have them dumped on us at your convenience. When we want them for the day or the night, we'll let you know. We raised ours. Please raise yours.

(4) Don't assume that because you married Marcia or John that we enjoy the company of his or her parents. On certain occasions, both in-laws should be present, but don't foist them on us.

(5) Don't take it for granted that you can borrow our car, our boat, our lawn mower, our silverware and table linen for your parties, etc. Ask first. And be courteous enough to return our property in the same condition in which you received it—for example, gas in the tank of the car, tablecloth clean and ironed, etc.

Respectfully yours MOTHER AND DAD

Dear M and D: Your suggestions are excellent, and I'm sure they'll be the topic of many dinner table discussions—by both generations! Thanks for writing.

Reprinted by permission of Ann Landers, Publishers-Hall Syndicate, Chicago Sun-Times, Daily News Building, Chicago, Illinois 60611.

What do you think?

1. Do you agree with all five points in the letter? If so, what is it about them that you consider reasonable or appropriate? Do you agree with only some of them? Which ones and why?
2. Using your own words, how would you describe the type of relationship that "Mother and Dad" prefer between in-laws? What is their attitude toward the subject of their letter? Be specific.
3. What effect do certain words and phrases have on you? Words such as "drag", "dumped", "foist", and "take it for granted", for example?
4. Sometimes we hear about extended families living together in our society. Is this preferable to the nuclear kind of family that "Mother and Dad" seem to prefer? What advantages and disadvantages can you think of in each arrangement?

Couple at Foot of Stairs by George Segal. Collection of the Museum Boymans van Beuningen, Rotterdam, Netherlands, Courtesy of Sidney Janis Gallery, New York.

PROBLEMS OF COEXISTENCE: GIFTED WOMEN AND THE MEN THEY MARRY

Joan Dash

"Problems of Coexistence: Gifted Women and The Men They Marry," by Joan Dash. From *Mademoiselle Magazine,* March 1968. Used by permission of author.

"Woman's principal work in life is hardly left to her own choice; nor can she drop the domestic charges devolving on her . . . for the exercise of the most splendid talents ever bestowed. And yet she must not shrink from the extra responsibility implied by . . . such talents. She must not hide her gift in a napkin." Thus the novelist Elizabeth Gaskell, in the cozy imagery of the 19th century, considered the vexing question of talented women and marriage; nor is the issue much altered since then, except in its urgency. More gifted women are trained today for a greater variety of careers than ever before, yet we continue to ponder what, precisely, is required for a marriage to succeed when one partner is a gifted woman, desirous of making the most of her talents, yet pathetically eager to keep her marital happiness.

Varying viewpoints can be derived from the sea of statistics that surrounds us on every side, or the rushing waters of modern psychology that we, true children of the Age of Freud, lap up unceasingly. But statistics are often deceptive and psychological casebooks are best left to experts; only the past—biography, history, letters—offers sure ground. By standing firmly rooted in today and looking backward, we achieve perspective. We have, moreover, the singular advantage of looking at people who do not know they are being watched; we survey the marriages of the past when the game is over.

To judge the marriages of a number of gifted women is to see them broadly, in caricature as it were. Our pictures will be exaggerated, unscientific, perhaps ludicrously so, as well as inconclusive—but they will be nonetheless revealing. We will be tempted to see, with our cartoonist's eye, three categories—and to caption them as supplementary, complementary, and collaborative marriages (our captions referring to the husbands in each case).

It was the economist Sidney Webb who described himself quite amiably as "one of those supplementary males often found among the lower crustacea." This was not an accurate description in his particular case, yet Webb, the rotund little man with the Cockney accent who ended his days as Baron Passfield, was frequently outdistanced—in the world's eye at least—by his beautiful and talented wife. Although married women have often refused promotion rather than surpass their husbands in rank or in salary, the man who can lightheartedly call himself a supplementary male remains a rarity; the wife who can hear him so label himself without a shudder for his masculinity is rarer still. But the marriage of Sidney and Beatrice Webb was a notable success—so much so that they came to exude an almost aggressive aura of conjugal contentment that vastly amused their fellow-Socialist G. B. Shaw: "Beatrice every now and then when she felt she needed a refresher . . . would rise from her chair, throw away her pen and hurl herself on her husband in a shower of caresses which lasted until the passion for work resumed its sway; then they wrote and read authorities for their footnotes until it was time for another refresher."

The Webbs had one marked advantage over many a similar couple; they married when Beatrice was already distinguished, and Sidney had every reason to suspect he might one day play second fiddle to his wife's virtuoso first. Marriages are younger nowadays, wives often in college, their talents untried, their goals uncertain. It is a platitude of marriage counseling that the successful marriage is likely to be one contracted in maturity, and this is even truer for the extraordinary woman. She must have time—time at least to learn that she is extraordinary, time to learn what she requires of a marriage and of a husband. She may conclude—has sometimes concluded in the past—that she needs a husband who is willing to make over his life to fit hers, for this is what the supplementary husband actually does.

Eugen Boissevain was such a man. Edna St. Vincent Millay was 31 when she married him—a tiny, redheaded woman, electrically magnetic, moody, often shy; confident of her already renowned creative powers, yet changeable as the ocean she loved. "At times she was so afflicted by self-consciousness and dislike for the external world that she could hardly utter a word," so Vincent Sheean describes her.

Eugen Jan Boissevain was not her first love, but unlike the others he was neither poet nor esthete. Rather precisely the opposite—at 43 a huge man and strikingly handsome, massive and virile, he imparted an air of absolute competence. He had made a fortune in business—hardly the sort one would suggest for the role of supplementary male. Yet from the very first this was the part he chose for himself, the part Miss Millay allowed him to play.

A peaceful, serene, harmonious marriage it was not, but Miss Millay was clearly never created for peace and harmony. She was, to her readers in the 1920's, the dazzling creature who burned her candle at both ends, a magnificent lyricist whose works—*Renascence, The Harp Weaver, The Buck in the Snow,* for example—exuded a pagan delight in the joys of physical love. In Boissevain, she found an absolute and lifelong devotion. He guarded her against the world and its multiple terrors, remodeled his own life to fit her needs, left the business world far behind him for the isolation of their farm in upstate New York where, for the 26 years of their life together, the poet could be assured of the solitude she required.

For months on end she saw no human being there except her husband, who nursed her, cooked for her, and walked five miles through winter snows to reach post office and telephones. As a poet, Miss Millay matured and perfected her gifts; as a woman she held fast to her one security, Eugen. At a public dinner she once implored the committee, "I can't sit with strangers only. . . . Please, I must have Eugen sitting beside me. I don't know what will happen if he isn't there."

The marriage of a woman as rare as Miss Millay is surely an extreme case, and yet far from unique. The immortal Colette, who married twice for love and twice disastrously, was married a third time when she was past 50 to a man 15 years younger. Her union with Maurice Goudeket lasted 20 years—serene, productive years for Colette, during which Goudeket devoted himself solely to the task of seeing that his wife received ". . . the greatest consideration possible, and her person those honors of which I judged that none could be too great for her."

Among stage people and singers, this sort of marriage is common. Many a stage or screen star of today is married to a man who has become her manager, devoting his life to the furtherance of her career, occasionally leaving a promising professional interest of his own to do so.

And the women who should probably have married a "supplementary male," but didn't, fill the pages of biography. Edith Wharton—a lady of strong character as well as driving talent—married at 20, and first discovered her career as a novelist when in her 30's. Of Teddy Wharton, a shadowy, well-bred, and nervous gentleman, little is remembered except that he was "a Teddy bear gone sour," "more equerry than husband," having neither interests of his own nor enough interest in his wife's work to fill his life. Katherine Mansfield, lovely, mercurial, tormented as much by her search for an unknown fulfillment as she was by the consumption that killed her, might have found her fulfillment, as well as a greater maturity of her talents, had she avoided marriage with the splendidly handsome John Middleton Murry. For Murry had his own overwhelming quest to pursue—"he had never claimed to be a husband. Would Katherine have been his partner if he had?" one biographer remarks. Murry was not free to devote his life to answering Katherine's cry for help. Theirs was a tormented marriage, and hers a remarkable talent that never reached its fullest flower.

Margaret Higgins was yet another who fell in love at 20—a pretty redheaded nurse, who could not have suspected her need for a supplementary male since she was unaware that she was remarkable at all. The man she married, William Sanger, was an impetuous romantic, longing to give up his career in architecture to paint. His friends were the exciting Socialist figures of New York at the turn of the century.

A suburban interlude followed their marriage in 1903; three babies, a house of their own, domestic serenity with William, returning from a day of work, more than willing to do the dinner dishes so Margaret could read, write, or study. It was only when the babies had passed their infancy that Margaret felt the first pangs of a growing discontent with suburbia—she expressed a fear of becoming "kitchen-minded." The great world to which Sanger had introduced her was clamoring at her door. When their new house was destroyed by fire, Margaret took it as a singular portent; she insisted that they move to Manhattan.

Here, both Sangers plunged into Socialist activities, and Margaret returned for a while to nursing. Her motives seem to have been purely practical ones—no conscious desire for a glorious career, but rather a need to plan against what she called her husband's extravagance. Systematic, efficient, determined, she feared that her husband was repeating her father's sad life of dreams and improvidence. But in reality it was less a need for money than the siren song of freedom that called her back to work and, later, into the crusade for birth control—into headlines and prison, to India and Japan, to friendships with Havelock Ellis and H. G. Wells. Sanger tugged backward. His amiability seemed to evaporate; he objected strenuously to his wife's working and, even more, to the rumblings of discontent with domestic life. Although Margaret never blamed him, his growing touchiness—jealousy even—felt like bonds of iron.

While nursing on New York's Lower East Side, Margaret was confronted with mothers dying of self-induced abortion while their infants roamed the garbage-littered streets. She had found her crusade. In 1913, the Sangers sailed for Europe, William to paint, Margaret to search for birth-control information. When she had found it, William was still content with his painting. They agreed that she would return with the children while he remained in Europe for a while.

But it proved a permanent separation—after 12 years of marriage—only formalized into divorce many years later. Mrs. Sanger, impelled essentially by a selfless need to serve humanity, flew headlong into her crusade; she writes to a friend, "Where is the man to give me what the [birth-control] movement gives in joy and interest and freedom?" Sanger, from Europe, wrote to plead that "no work is so great that two should miss the sweetness of life." Margaret never doubted his loyalty or his love; but what she required of a husband, if she was to have one at all, was an almost complete sacrifice of self.

Sometimes the sacrifice to marriage must be made by the woman, especially when the man she marries is not emotionally equipped to submerge his life in hers, or is not, on the other hand, involved in a prosperous career, out of which he can reach from time to time to furnish the requisite support for a difficult and complex female character. Then it is the woman who may decide to hide her gift in a napkin, because she would rather be a reasonably happy wife than an unhappy genius. In Charlotte Brontë and the story of her brief but pathetically happy marriage, we glimpse this choice. One can only speculate on Charlotte's ultimate development as wife and writer, because of her early death. All the same, one is apt to find the speculation irresistible, partly because Charlotte herself is irresistible—few novelists have proved so tempting to biographers; partly also because of her husband's curious attitude toward her career, an attitude that can only be described as ambivalent.

"I cannot for the life of me see those interesting germs of goodness in him you described; his narrowness of mind always strikes me chiefly." So Charlotte first pictures her future husband in a letter to a friend. Arthur Bell Nicholls came in 1845 to Haworth parsonage, to serve as curate for eccentric old Patrick Brontë. Brontë's daughter Charlotte was amused rather than impressed, but then curates in general were only fodder for her sharp wit. It was her portrait of Nicholls as a "decent, decorous, conscientious" curate in the novel *Shirley,* no doubt combined with the sudden, exciting revelation of Charlotte as the nationally successful novelist Currer Bell, which seem to have first opened Nicholls's eyes to her attractions as a woman.

Once smitten, the decorous and conscientious gentleman began to sulk and brood until Dr. Brontë called him "an unmanly driveler." His first proposal was refused by Charlotte. She was 36 years old and at the height of her fame; she had buried two beloved sisters, battled penury and loneliness and failure, and long since resigned herself to spinsterhood. If Nicholls was intrigued by Charlotte's fame and talent, she seems to have been attracted at first only by the bitter pain with which he took her refusal. The petulant objections of her father—who wanted a rich, spectacular match for her, if any—were not the strongest obstacles in the way of the marriage. Stronger still was Charlotte's awareness that "he is not intellectual. There are many places into which he could not follow me intellectually." But he loved her. Charlotte had been offered marriage before, but never before had she been offered love. It was too great a prize to refuse.

Charlotte's fears of having chosen second-best began to evaporate with the honeymoon. At last she knew what it was to be wanted, to have every moment accounted for. Arthur flourished, put on weight, commanded his wife, even, in the tenderest way, bullied her. And she thrived, discovering in her husband ". . . an affectionate . . . a high-principled man; and if, with all this, I should yield to regrets that fine talents, congenial tastes and thoughts are not added . . . I should be presumptuous."

Yet we find Arthur declaring that a clergyman's

wife has little time for writing. He was jealous of Currer Bell; he was extremely possessive of Charlotte Brontë. All the same, a new novel was begun and discussed with Arthur. Pregnancy, and a dangerous flare-up of tuberculosis intervened; Charlotte took to her bed. Nine months after the wedding, in her last moments of life, she cried out to her husband, "Oh, I am not going to die, am I, He will not separate us, we have been so happy?"

Charlotte's innumerable biographers disagree on her future as a writer—but few foresee anything but a happy marriage had she lived. Her novels furnish absolute proof that to her the beloved wife and mother was the most enviable of beings. After her death, Arthur maintained that Charlotte would have continued to write with his fullest support. But there are many reasons to believe that his declarations belied his innermost needs, for Arthur kept her letters and manuscripts hidden, refused to baptize a parish infant with her name—showed every sign of clutching Currer Bell to his bosom, rather than share her with an admiring world. Moreover, one cannot but feel that the demands of motherhood, combined with the happiness of familial affections fulfilled, would have left Charlotte with no overpowering need to write.

One suspects, indeed knows, that many gifted women today have been faced with a similar choice—and for reasons like Charlotte's, or for other reasons growing out of the complex interplay of society's pressures on the modern woman, choose to let their creative talents lie fallow while they retire to the suburbs and the production of large families. For some it doubtless is the right choice; and there is no way of judging, just how wrong the others are.

For many remarkable women, the answer lies in the selection of a husband who will willingly support a working wife—"support" here having a specialized meaning. The question is less one of financial backing than a matter of emotional support. Female genius is in no way exempt from the handicaps of male genius. It is difficult to live with; it is likely to be encased in a delicate, even an inflammable structure, neurotic, uneven, in daily need of props. A husband who works in a similar field, who offers a sturdiness of temperament, an unflagging patience, as well as clear-sighted professional advice, has a marked advantage for such a woman. Virginia Stephen had the good fortune to marry an editor whose opinion she could respect, and whose disciplined, even character offered invaluable ballast to her own fluctuating temper. And what sort of mate is handier for a high-strung writer than a capable editor? One can only compare it to the good fortune of the mother who raises eight difficult children under the eye of a pediatrician husband. In such a marriage, the husband acts as emotional and professional complement to his wife. He doesn't disappear behind the scenes as does the supplementary male—and yet, as in the case of Virginia Stephen and Leonard Woolf, the husband's greatest single accomplishment is indubitably his wife.

When they met, Virginia Stephen at 30 had not yet published her first novel, but her latent qualities must have been evident. Clearly, the shy young woman with the elongated face, tremendous eyes, and "fierceness" of manner could never submerge herself in her husband's life. Moreover, she had suffered a nervous breakdown some years before. Leonard Woolf must have been well aware of the overwhelming task he was about to undertake.

Into Virginia's hitherto circumscribed life, whose central props had been art, literature, and the conversation of the learned, Woolf brought the great world. Editor, economist, and tireless worker for the British Labor Party, he opened her eyes to the grubby and unending struggles of the working classes. But more than this, Leonard Woolf possessed in abundance those very qualities Virginia believed to be most painfully lacking in herself. He was eminently rational and disciplined. Mastering his own nervous shyness, he served as ballast to Virginia's soaring flights and torturing descents of emotion. Her admiration for him—amounting at times to a kind of awe—only increased with the years.

Each of Virginia's novels—*The Voyage Out, To The Lighthouse,* among them—was fearfully submitted to Leonard before another eye had seen it. His critical approval was an absolute necessity to her, for even success failed to strengthen her self-esteem. And when, in her early 50's at the start of World War II, Virginia chose death by drowning rather than run the risk of another nervous breakdown, her last lines were addressed to Leonard: "I owe all my happiness in life to you. I cannot go on and spoil your life."

Other women, who chose, as Virginia did, out of the careful judgment of their mature years, found similar success in unions with complementary men. George Eliot was 34 at the time of her liaison with George Lewes, "the ugliest man in London," and an editor and publisher with whom she lived happily for more than two decades. Her happiness is all the more remarkable since the divorce laws of 19th-century England prevented Lewes from marrying; yet, even as London wallowed in the smog of Victorian morality, it revered George Eliot, visited her, honored her despite her irregular household. She trusted Lewes's critical judgment implicitly. He was critic, counselor, and prop against torturing self-doubts about her writing.

And Elizabeth Barrett Browning—for all that her husband is counted today a far greater poet than she ever was—must be properly considered as having made a "complementary" marriage. For in their own time, she was the genius—a heroine of Victorian romance, imprisoned by parental tyranny as well as by invalidism. He was the sturdy, sure-footed, all-but-unknown who released her from her prison by sheer force of character. Elizabeth was 38 at the time of their elopement; Browning was 32, and penniless. It was Elizabeth's income that made their marriage possible, and Browning's personal strength, as well as the reassuring power of his love for one who persisted in believing herself unlovable and unworthy, which brought her to health, to motherhood, and to the creation of her few enduring works.

Seemingly the most truly "modern" of our three prototypes is the collaborative marriage, presupposing as it does equality of talent and temperament, as well as increasing equality of professional opportunity. In yet another way, collaborative unions are especially modern, for they occur most often in those fields—science, business, medicine, education—where women are comparatively recent entrants. Science, in particular, encourages teamwork; literature, once almost the only field wide open to female talent, is lonely work.

Women of vital talent in science are numerous today; but female geniuses in science are still rare, possibly because science and womanhood are basically at odds. To speak of female genius in science is to think immediately of Marie Curie, twice a Nobel Laureate, and the only scientist ever so distinguished, regardless of sex.

Many a young woman today, embarking on a career in physics or chemistry, dreams of becoming another Marie Curie; but the dreams of a high-minded girl are different from those of a matron and mother, no matter how high-minded. The Curies retained to the end of their days, despite marriage and parenthood, a youthful disregard for the world—for fame, for recognition, for possessions, for the simplest requirements of personal comfort and ease. They seem, in their personal lives, almost a pair of medieval ascetics, with science their religion—which they served through a total forgetfulness of self. It is impossible to read Marie's account of her husband's life, or their daughter's account of Marie's, without being moved to tears, not for their triumphs or their sorrows, but for the inaccessible heights of their unselfishness. If Marie Curie wanted a pretty dress, a vacation cruise, or an opera box, such longings were buried in a single-minded search for scientific truth.

Theirs was a marriage marked by tenderness and mutual admiration. Pierre, as a young man, had written that "women of genius are rare, and the average woman is a positive hindrance to a serious-minded scientist." He was 35 when he found a woman, seven years younger and as dedicated as he, with whom he worked for two years, enduring cold, fatigue, and sickness, to isolate radium salts in "... that miserable shed . . . [where] we passed the best and happiest years of our life."

It was for that two years' work that the Curies were jointly awarded the Nobel Prize. After her husband's accidental death at the age of 47, Marie worked alone to isolate the element radium, for which she received the second Nobel award.

While Pierre did not possess the physical vitality typical of the experimental physicist, his wife did. Pierre's qualities were deeper and perhaps rarer ones. Marie speaks of "his detachment from all vanity and from those petty faults one sees in oneself and . . . that one judges indulgently but not without aspiring to a more perfect ideal." Nevertheless, despite the reverence with which she describes his character and his intellectual attainments, Mme. Curie was herself a woman of stubborn and indomitable purpose. Had she never married Curie, she would undoubtedly have pursued her profession with the same unwavering direction she showed when, left a widow, she took up the threads of his career as well as her own. Just as her physical being required neither comfort nor ease, so did her emotional being require no reassurance, no coddling—only enough serenity so that work might go on.

While theirs was a rewarding life together, Marie Curie is always recalled as a grave, sad figure, a woman who wore the plainest of dark dresses and rarely laughed. Perhaps ascetics are always somber, and especially ascetic Poles. More likely the answer is that the Curies were not searching for happiness any more than they were working for money—they could have been rich many times over had they chosen to patent the process for isolating radium salts; instead they gave radium freely to the uses of medical science, and left the search for happiness to those who required it. What the Curies wanted instead—hard work, high thinking, and solitude—they had, along with its austere rewards.

On a lesser plane, one recalls the collaborative marriages of the Gilbreths—time-and-motion-study engineers immortalized in *Cheaper by the Dozen;* the botanist Wanda Farr and her husband; Victor and Mary Putnam Jacobi, doctors and fellow pioneers in the early years of modern pediatrics. Indeed, the history of women in medicine is studded with female doctors who married fellow students and spent their lives in active collaboration with their mates. Sarah Adamson, Lydia Folger Fowler, Rachel Brooks Gleason come to mind. Because science is a continually demanding life, such women tend to lose themselves in their work, to choose their husbands without looking up from the microscope as it were. No other woman has yet attained the scientific distinction of Marie Curie, but many have found similar satisfaction in working with a husband of the same bent, the same training, and a more-or-less equal talent.

Of marriage more than of any other human endeavor, *"Plus ça change, plus c'est la même chose."* Whether we turn to biography or to modern psychology for enlightenment, we are likely to decide that extremely youthful marriage presents peculiar dangers. The man who marries an extraordinary woman deserves, at the very least, to know in advance just what he is getting into. And the talented woman, for her own heart's comfort as well as her work, deserves to be old enough, at least, to know what she is asking of the man she chooses—just how much support she requires if she is to fulfill her talents. It is indeed, as Charlotte Brontë once wrote, a perilous and wonderful thing to be a wife. And with the higher stakes for which the gifted woman plays, come greater wonder and greater peril.

What do you think?

1. The author indicates that gifted women may have goals in mind in getting married which differ from those of other women. Describe the gifted women's goals. Do they differ from the goals that men seem to have in mind when they get married? Explain your answer.
2. Why do you agree or disagree with the author when she writes that marriages made later in life are more likely to be happy ones?
3. Explain, as fully as possible, what adjustments a husband and wife must make because of the wife's talents. How do your ideas differ from Mrs. Dash's? Speculate on the reasons for your differences of opinion.
4. Sprinkled throughout the essay are remarks which suggest that the writer holds certain "scientific" ways of analyzing matters. Why do you share or disagree with her sentiments about experts versus laymen in such fields as psychology? Why does she say that psychological casebooks are best left to so-called experts?
5. In the first paragraph, why does the author say that the gifted woman is "pathetically eager" to keep her marital happiness? Would a term such as "understandably" or "predictably" be more acceptable? Why or why not? Does the remainder of the article support her opening statement? Explain.

Suggestions for reading

1. Read the article in *Ebony* Magazine, "First Black Woman on Capitol Hill" (February, 1969), which is about Shirley Chisholm, Congresswoman from New York State. In light of Mrs. Dash's article, is Shirley Chisholm's marriage a successful one? Is it successful in your own terms?
2. Do some research in the reference book, *Reader's Guide to Periodical Literature* on the subject of gifted women. Do the magazine articles express similar ideas and attitudes about them? About their marriages? Is there largely agreement or disagreement with the ideas of Mrs. Dash?

"You're Nobody 'Till Somebody Loves You" words and music by Russ Morgan, Larry Stock, and James Cavanaugh. Copyright 1944 by Southern Music Publishing Co., Inc. Used by permission.

3
D7+ G B7 E7(-9) E7 Dmi E7 B7 E7
Slowly
YOU'RE NO-BOD-Y 'TIL SOME-BOD-Y LOVES YOU, You're
mp-mf
Ami D7 G6 Bmi7 G6 Bmi G6 D7+
no - bod - y till some - bod - y cares; You
Bmi7 C#dim. Ami7
may be king, you may pos - sess the world and its gold, But
A9+ A9 Ami7 D7 Ami7 D7 D7+
gold won't bring you hap - pi - ness when you're grow - ing old; The
You're Nobody 'Til etc. - 3

4
G
B7
E7(-9)
E7
Dmi
E7
B7
E7
world still is the same, you'll nev-er change it, As
Ami
E7
Ami
E7
Ami
C
sure as the stars shine a-bove; YOU'RE NO-BOD-Y 'TIL
C♯dim.
G
D+
B♭mi7(♭5)
E7
Ami
E7
Ami
A7
D7
Optional
SOME-BOD-Y LOVES YOU, So find your-self some-bod-y to
r.h.
1. G
E♭maj.7
F9
D♭
E♭7
D7
D7+
2. G
Cmi7
G6
love. YOU'RE love.
f
mf
mf
l.h.
pp
You're Nobody 'Til etc.,-3

YOU'RE NOBODY 'TIL SOMEBODY LOVES YOU
Words by Russ Morgan, Larry Stock, and James Cavanaugh

Some look for glory,
It's still the old story
Of love versus glory,
And when all is said and done,—

You're nobody 'til somebody loves you,—
You're nobody till somebody cares;
You may be king, you may possess the world
  and its gold,
But gold won't bring you happiness when you're
  growing old;

The world still is the same,
You'll never change it,
As sure as the stars shine above;

You're nobody 'til somebody loves you,
So find yourself somebody to love.

What do you think?

1. Which of these statements or implications made in the song do you agree of disagree with? Be prepared to explain why:
   (a) That love and glory are in conflict.
   (b) That money won't bring happiness when you're growing old.
   (c) That you'll never change the world.
2. Can you imagine what possible beneficial or harmful effects these lyrics might have on a listener? Explain.
3. Explain how a person can find somebody to love. Do agencies that claim to match persons by computerized information interfere with or assist this search?
4. Interpret the various meanings of the statement, "You're nobody 'til somebody loves you." Do you agree with all or some of those interpretations? Explain. Are there writings in the section on Self-Identity which conflict with or reinforce that idea? What are they?
5. How does the key idea of this song compare with Eric Fromm's statement, "Most people see the problem of love primarily as that of *being loved,* rather than that of *loving*" (p. 64)? Explain.

Suggestions for writing

1. Write a paper (500 words) in which you describe the things that you think happen to most of the people you know when they are in love. Explain, in your paper, whether they seem to become more sure of *who* they are. Provide any reasons for this change that seem reasonable to you.
2. Write a paper (500 words) in which you discuss 3 to 5 ways in which people "look for glory." Include in your discussion some commentary on whether you approve of the methods, and why; whether society, as a whole, approves, and why; and whether the methods used promise success in attaining that glory.
3. Find a song which is popular today that discusses what happened to someone when he loved someone else. In a paper (1000 words) discuss whether you find those lyrics believable. It will be necessary to quote all or parts of the lyrics you're discussing.

But wasn't it great to work for a living? I calculated how long it would take to make my first million shining shoes. Too long. I would be something like 997 years old.

from Down These Mean Streets by Piri Thomas, 1967. Reprinted by permission of Alfred A. Knopf, Inc.

PART 3

"BUT WASN'T IT GREAT TO WORK FOR A LIVING?"

Many Americans take for granted the matter of being employed. There are various reasons for this. In some cases they've always had a job with reasonable security. In other cases, they've always felt assured that a job would be available, regardless of the economic state of the country.

As a result, typical concerns about employment include such questions as salary, fringe benefits, and opportunities for advancement. Many of us view a job in terms of what it can do for our social as well as economic status. Few of us, unless we are in a crisis situation, have considered the consequences of underemployment and unemployment. The sections in this part urge the reader to do just that.

Also, in our society, one of the measures of a man—and this may soon be equally true of women—is his job. One social thinker puts it this way:

"It is perhaps not too much to say that only in very exceptional cases can an adult man be genuinely self-respecting and enjoy a respected status in the eyes of others if he does not 'earn a living' in an approved occupational role. . . . more than any other single factor, it [occupational status] determines the status of the family in the social structure, directly because of the symbolic significance of the office or occupation as a symbol of prestige, indirectly because as the principal source of family income it determines the standard of living of the family."[1]

Thus, it is important for us to examine various aspects of employment: among them, both the aspects that are likely to immediately touch the lives of students and those that (though more remote) nevertheless flavor students' lives. Among the questions that arise for the student himself are these: Are the parochial and the romantic jobs thoroughgoingly so? Just how vital it is to one's well being to have a "good" job? How can one's job affect who he is?

Accordingly, the materials in this section deal with some of the ramifications of employment, underemployment, and lack of employment. In "Profession: Housewife," a suburban wife reacts violently to the boredom stemming partly from being *merely* a housewife. Another short story, "The Happiest Man on Earth," describes an extremely depressed economic situation that stems from a breadwinner's not having a job. Two articles—one each from a newspaper and magazine—describe the world of the sports star.

In short, there is wide variety in the kinds of people, settings, and situations that the reader will encounter in this section. However, despite the variety, something consistently comes through: what a person does to earn his living can affect who he is, in his own eyes, as well as his standing in the larger society.

[1] "Age and Sex in the Social Structure of the United States," Talcott Parsons, *Personality in Nature, Society, and Culture*, ed. Clyde Kluckhohn and Henry Murray (Alfred A. Knopf, 1954), 367-368.

MISS PEACH

Mell Lazarus

Mell Lazarus. Courtesy of Publishers-Hall Syndicate

What do you think?

1. Is Mr. Grimmis correct in implying that *yesterday* a person didn't have to have very high aspirations? What period of time is he referring to: twenty years, fifty years, or one hundred years ago? Can you support your impression with evidence?
2. What kind of work would you consider a "good job"? What are the characteristics that make it "good"?
3. Arthur's classmate seems to think that someone will "make" him *Boss of the World.* Do you think this is how people gain powerful positions? If so, why is it this way? If not, how do people get those positions?
4. Arthur says that he wants to be *Boss* also. Is it possible to have two Bosses? Why? Why not?

Suggestions for writing and drawing

1. Some critics of higher education contend that large numbers of students only go to college to get a "union card"—a degree that will admit them into a certain profession. Is this goal satisfactory or not? Are there other goals which you think are worse or better than that one?
   Write a short paper (not over 250 words) in which you set forth the *best* reasons for a student going to college. Be certain to give reasons why you think more highly of these than of some others.
2. Write a brief paper (250 words) in which you describe, in some detail, your own reasons for being in college.
3. Draw a cartoon with 4 to 5 panels in which you show who the *Boss of the World* is and just what kind of aspirations he has. In other words, show whether even he is bothered by desires to be something more or merely something other than what he is.
4. "Stay in School—Don't Be No Fool" was once a popular slogan. Make up several slogans that indicate your opinion about persons who stay in school and those who leave.

THE TRUTH

Ted Joans

IF YOU SHOULD SEE A MAN
walking down a crowded
street
      talking
            ALOUD
TO HIMSELF
            DON'T RUN
                        IN THE
OPPOSITE DIRECTION
                      BUT RUN
TOWARD HIM
              for he is a
                        POET
You have NOTHING to
                      FEAR
FROM THE
           POET
                 BUT THE
           T R U T H

What do you think?

1. What does "truth" mean in this poem?
2. Do you agree that poets tell the truth? (Consider 4 to 6 poets you've read in this book before answering the question.) Do they tell the truth more often than persons in other areas of communication, such as journalists or teachers? Why or why not?
3. From your own observations, what do you think the economic and social status of most poets is in our society? Can you provide any reasons for this?
4. Are there striking examples of poets telling the truth that you've either heard of or read about? If so, bring either the poem to class for discussion or the news item reporting the truth that the poet revealed.
5. Why does the writer of this poem caution you not to run away? Is running the usual response persons have to others who are talking to themselves? Can you provide an explanation for this?
6. There is no punctuation in this poem. Explain how the absence of punctuation affects your understanding of the poem.

Suggestions for writing and reading

1. Look up the etymology of the word "poet." Using the information you find in the dictionary, write a short paper (200-250 words) on one of the following topics:
   (a) Why almost anyone can be considered a poet.
   (b) Whether you prefer the original or the present meaning of the word and the reasons for your preference.
2. Write a paper (1000 words) in which you discuss your own response to poetry writing as a career. Speculate in your paper on how your family and friends would react to your becoming a poet.
3. Write your own poem of no more than fifty words. Do not use any punctuation; instead, stagger the lines and use capitals in such fashion that the reader has certain lines stressed for him and will not confuse the beginning of one thought with the end of another. Select as subject for your poem a description or commentary on someone in a job such as a street cleaner, a school bus driver, or an astronaut.
4. Check in the reference book, *Reader's Guide to Periodical Literature,* for an article on the financial plight of the artist. Do the observations and conclusions in the article reflect your response to question 3 above?

PROFESSION: HOUSEWIFE

Sally Benson

Although the window by the breakfast nook was open, it was very warm. The yellow-and-white gingham curtains hung still and the blue oilcloth showed beads of moisture. Even the painted table top felt damp and sticky, and Joe Grannis was conscious of the discomfort of the hard bench on which he sat. He heard Dorothy tear open the letter and, leaning back as far as he could, he shook out his paper and held it before his face.

In a few minutes she slapped the letter down on the table so hard that the coffee in her cup spilled over into the saucer. "I might have known," she said. "They can't come. At least, she *says* they can't come."

Although it was what he had expected, Joe Grannis lowered his paper and managed to look surprised. "That's funny," he answered. "Maybe some other time."

"Some other time," his wife repeated. "Don't be dumb. The point is they don't want to come, now or any other time."

"I wouldn't say that," he said. "There's no reason why they shouldn't want to come."

Dorothy Grannis lifted her saucer and poured the coffee that had spilled back into the cup. Her face, normally a solid pink, had turned a bright cerise and her hair lay against her forehead with the metallic fixity of a doll's wig. "I'm sorry I asked them in the first place," she told him.

Joe Grannis made a mistake. "Well, you can't say I didn't warn you," he said. "You can't expect to make friends with people who were friends of Louise's. Those things never work out. People feel funny, sort of."

She pushed the sleeves of her chintz house coat further up on her arms with a hard, deliberate gesture and rested her elbows on the table. "Why?" she asked. "From the way you used to talk, I got the impression they were friends of yours. I got the impression that they didn't think so much of *Louise,* that you were the fair-haired boy with them. I got the impression that they couldn't wait until the divorce and everything was over so they could come here again."

She looked around the bright, shiny kitchen and laughed. "My God!" she went on. "If they saw this place now it might be too much for them. They might drop dead. Digging this place out was like excavating. It might be too much for them to see it clean for a change."

Joe Grannis took his watch from his pocket and looked at it. He edged from behind the table and stood up. "Time to go," he said.

"I suppose so," she told him. "You never know the answers to anything. Well, what are we going to do tonight? Sit here and listen to the radio?"

"Now, don't be sarcastic," he answered. "You've got friends of your own. Why don't you call Ruth and Van up and ask them out?"

"And have them wondering why nobody else ever drops in?" she asked indignantly. "That was all right at first. They didn't think anything of it the first few times. But the last time she acted plenty funny about it. Wanting to know if I didn't get lonesome here all day and everything. I'd rather rot."

He looked at her and his face grew set. "Suit yourself," he said. "And since you're speaking of impressions, I got some myself. I got the impression that all you needed to make you happy was a home of your own and to be able to quit work. God knows you sang that tune long enough. Three years, wasn't it? Well, you got what you wanted. You've spent money like a drunken sailor on this place and if you can't make friends for yourself, I can't help you."

"Well, really!" she exclaimed, her voice politely formal. "Really!"

She remained seated at the table until she heard the front door slam behind him, and then she got up and with brisk, efficient movements carried the breakfast dishes to the sink. The sink was of glaring yellow porcelain and the faucets were shiny and new. The hot water on her hands made her feel warmer and she pulled down the zipper of her house coat. Her grasp on the dishes was rough, but she arranged them almost gently in the wire rack to drain.

Pretty soon now the girls would come straggling into the office where she used to work, cool and neat in their new summer dresses. Because the day was warm, the atmosphere about the place would relax and Mannie, the office boy, would be sent to the drugstore for double cokes. There would be gossip and cigarettes in the washroom and speculation as to whether Mr. Ackerman would leave early for a round of golf.

She opened the drawer of the kitchen cabinet and took out a towel, yellow, with blue featherstitching, and dried the dishes hurriedly. Glancing at the clock and seeing that it was not yet nine, she tried to slow her movements. She wiped the breakfast table with a damp cloth and put away the oilcloth doilies.

The dining room was cool and bare. In the centre of the shiny mahogany table was placed an etched silver bowl around which huddled four thin silver candlesticks. Going to the sideboard, she opened the drawers one by one, looking with satisfaction at the rows of silver-plated knives, forks, and spoons lying on their squares of felt. In each drawer was a lump of camphor to prevent tarnishing.

The stairs led out of the dining room and she walked up them to the upstairs hall. Four doors opened out into the hall, but only two of them stood ajar—the door to the bathroom and the one to their bedroom. She liked to keep the extra bedrooms shut off until she felt she could do them over decently. There was little disorder in their own room. Joe's striped silk pajamas lay folded on his bed and her pale-green satin nightgown lay on a chair by the window. She hung these in the closet and then spread the beds, fitting their lavender taffeta covers smoothly.

As she finished, the front-door bell rang briefly, and looking out the window, she saw a man standing there, a leather briefcase under his arm. She loosened her hair slightly about her face and pulled the zipper up on her house coat.

The man who stood at the door was very young and very thin. His light-gray suit was shabby and the coat hung limply from his shoulders. He wore no hat and his fine, light hair was too long and fell untidily over his forehead. He had been looking down when she opened the door, his whole figure drooping, but hearing the sound of the latch, he straightened up to face her, jerking his head up alertly, smiling pleasantly.

"Good morning, Madam," he said.

She stood looking at him for so long without speaking that he shifted his feet in embarrassment, the smile growing fixed on his face.

"Yes?" she asked finally. "Yes?"

He took the briefcase from under his arm, and after struggling with the catch, opened it and drew forth a book, which he held toward her. Its bright, flowered cover looked worn and dirty, as though it had been often handled. She made no motion to take it from him, but he stood bravely facing her, the book in his hand.

"I'm not interested in buying any books," she told him. "Nor anything else."

The young man laughed brightly. "This book, Madam," he said, "is not for sale. It is a gift to you from the company I represent."

"Yes, I know," she answered. "A gift if I subscribe to what?"

The young man lowered his arm, slightly abashed.

"Well?" she asked, raising her eyebrows and putting her head to one side. "Am I right?"

The young man gave another slight laugh. "I can see that you've learned, Madam, that we don't get anything in this world for nothing. A lot of people haven't learned that, and I guess you must be cleverer than average." For a minute he combed his mind to gather up the first rules of salesmanship, which lay scattered there. Then he went on with more assurance. "No, this book is not exactly free, and yet it is free in the sense that you will not actually be paying for this book. What you will be paying for is a three-year subscription to *Good Homes Magazine*. And you will be paying the exact price you would pay if you went to your local dealer. But by taking a subscription now from me, you also will receive this book of five hundred tested recipes, how to set your table for any occasion, and other helpful household hints. So, you see, in a manner of speaking, this book *is* absolutely free. And what is more, Madam, you are permitted to take it now, look it over, and return it to me if you decide you do not care to take a subscription to *Good Homes*."

He smiled triumphantly at her. "Could anything be fairer than that?"

Mrs. Grannis had heard his speech coldly, but now suddenly she opened the door wider and extended her hand for the book. "How long can I keep it before I decide?" she asked.

"For five days, Madam," he told her. Then he dropped his professional manner, and his voice changed. "To tell you the truth, we are supposed to leave them five days. And that's all right for guys that have a car and can come back for them. But I got to figure differently. It's like this—I go to one of these suburbs and spend a day there. I leave a book, if that's what the lady of the house wants, and then I stop by later in the day and pick it up. You see, we're responsible for the books we hand out, and if you don't take a subscription you can't keep the book. The company couldn't afford it. Why, these books cost three dollars to buy."

She stepped back and laid the book on the hall table. "I see," she said. "Well, I'll let you know."

There was something in her gesture that caused the young man to clear his throat anxiously before he spoke again. "May I ask what time will be most convenient for you?"

"Oh, any time," she answered. "I'll be in, all right."

His face cleared. "Well, let's see," he said. "It isn't ten yet and I'll come back about three. That'll give me plenty of time to cover this neighborhood, come back and write out your subscription, and grab a train back to New York. Now, don't think I am too confident, Madam, but I can safely say it will be worth your while to retain the book plus receiving *Good Homes* for three entire years."

He refastened the catch of his briefcase and tucked it under his arm. There was a dark spot where the moisture from his hand had stained the leather. He felt very thirsty and wondered if he dared ask for a drink of water. But the lady acted strange. To be sure, she had taken the book, but you never could tell how people were going to act if you asked for a favor. She might think he was trying to get fresh.

So with the sun beating on his head, he stepped back from the door, smiling. "Good day, Madam," he said. "I will be back later."

Halfway down the path, he turned and called to her. "You're the first lady that's taken a book today. It must be good luck or something."

Mrs. Grannis closed the door and walked into the living room. The glare of the sun hurt her eyes and she lowered the shades. Even then, because of the newness of the light, shiny maple furniture, the room had a sort of glint. She lay down on the couch and closed her eyes, trying to decide whether or not to put on her things and run in to see the girls at the office. She could tell them about the house, she thought, and might even ask them out to see it sometime, although she had almost decided to drop them gradually. Still, you had to see somebody, and with Joe's friends acting the way they did, there didn't seem to be much to look forward to in that direction. The dimness of the room soothed her and she fell asleep.

It was after twelve when she woke up, and her head felt stuffy. She made herself a glass of iced tea, heavily sugared, and toasted a cheese sandwich on the electric grill. Then she dressed leisurely and started for the centre of the village. It was almost three when she arrived back home, her hair freshly washed and waved, her face flushed from sitting under the drier. Remembering the young man, she glanced up and down the street, but he was not in sight. Upstairs, she took off her street things and slipped once more into her house coat. Then, carefully turning back the taffeta spread from her bed, she lay down and lit a cigarette. She heard the bell ring in the kitchen and, propping herself up on one elbow, she peered cautiously out the window. On the steps below stood the young man, who had come for his book. His clothes were even limper than they had been in the morning and he leaned against the side of the door ready to spring into alert attention at the sound of footsteps. She let the curtain drop and lay back on the bed, smoking and staring at the ceiling. The bell rang again, and then, after a few minutes, more urgently.

For a long while she lay there listening to the bell and then she got up and walked silently down the stairs. She picked up the book from the hall table and carried it back to her room. In a few minutes she heard steps once more on the outside walk and the bell began, persistently now. She sat up on the edge of the bed and, taking the book, deliberately and slowly ripped the pages out. When they all lay scattered on the bed beside her, she began tearing them across. With some difficulty she bent the cover. Then, gathering the pieces together, she went to the window and opened it.

The young man looked up at her and the expression on his face changed. He began to smile. "Wake you up?" he asked pleasantly.

She fumbled with the screen and slowly let the torn pages of the book fall to the grass below.

For a minute the young man stared at them, dazed. Without a word he stooped to picked them up, but realizing the hopelessness of his task, he straightened and stood staring up at the window. For a dreadful moment they looked at one another. Then he turned and walked away.

She fastened the screen, lit a cigarette, and lay down again on the bed, smoking and staring at the ceiling.

What do you think?

1. What do the following actions of the characters indicate?
   (a) Joe Grannis' leaning as far as he could on the breakfast-nook bench.
   (b) Dorothy Grannis' loosening her hair before answering the front door. And her lying on the bed smoking and staring at the ceiling.
   (c) The salesman attempting to pick up the pieces of the torn book.
2. Why does the magazine salesman call Mrs. Grannis' behavior "strange"? Do you agree?
3. Were you surprised when Mrs. Grannis tore up the salesman's book? Why did she do it? Were there earlier hints in the story that lead you to expect her to do this or something similar? What were they? What does the salesman represent to her?
4. Can you offer any explanations why she and the salesman share a "dreadful moment" when they look at one another?
5. How does the author of the story feel about Mrs. Grannis? Does she approve of her or not? How can you tell?
6. Does the fact that Mrs. Grannis lives in suburbia have anything to do with her attitude? Are there other factors influencing her attitude?

Suggestions for reading, writing, and listening

1. Assume that either Mr. or Mrs. Grannis is at fault, or that both are to blame, for the monotonous character of their marriage. Write a short paper (500 words) in which you analyze the problem of both or either of them. What would you recommend for them?
2. Write a letter to a column for the lovelorn, such as the Ann Landers column on page 62, in which you pretend to be Mr. Grannis. Explain the problem of you and your wife. Pose the questions that the columnist *most* needs to answer for you.
3. There are several recordings of the song, "Dreams of the Everyday Housewife." Would you say that the day-to-day routine of the woman in the song is comparable to Mrs. Grannis' routine? What does the woman in the song do to break the monotony?
4. H. L. Mencken's essay, "The Feminine Mind," and Elizabeth Hardwick's essay, "The Subjection of Women," treat the role of women in American society quite differently than this short story does. They are available for reading in many school anthologies. If you're interested in more extensive treatment of the subject of the roles women play, read *The Second Sex* by Simone de Beauvoir; *The Feminine Mystique* by Betty Friedan; or *The Black Woman,* edited by Toni Cade. These books are in paperback.

"I'd hate to see this firm go into bankruptcy—would you accept a loan from our union?"

What do you think?

1. The businessmen seem surprised by the offer of the maintenance woman. How many explanations can you find for their surprise?
2. Some of the humor of this cartoon is based on the reversal of *usual* roles. If this were the usual confrontation between executives and maintenance staff, what kind of conversation would be going on? Write your own 2- or 3-line caption.
3. Is the humor here entirely fantastic or is it possible that a union of janitors might have enough money to "bail out" a more prestigious group? Explain your answer.
4. Historically, people who do "dirty work" have been viewed by others as being at the bottom of the ladder of desirable jobs. Is this still the case? Explain why this is true or what has caused a change in attitude. (Indicate the specific jobs you have in mind.)

Suggestion for writing

1. The essay, "Work and the Self," on page 173, discusses job stratification and how it works. After studying it and comparing its ideas to the situation in this cartoon, do you think that people who do "dirty work" are at the bottom of the scale of desirable jobs? Write a short paper (500 words) explaining your opinion and the reasons for it.

TRUANT

Claude McKay

The warbling of a mother's melody had just ended, and the audience was in a sentimental state and ready for the scene that the curtain, slowly drawn, disclosed. A mother in calico print jigged on her knee a little baby, crooning the while some Gaelic folk-words. A colleen sat on a red-covered box, mending a chemise; sitting at her feet, a younger sister with a picture book. Three boys in shirt sleeves and patched pantaloons playing with a red-and-green train on a lacquer-black railroad. A happy family. An antique sitting room, torn wallpaper, two comic chairs, and the Holy Virgin on the mantelpiece. A happy family. Father, fat and round like a chianti bottle, skips into the picture and up leaps boys and girls and mother with baby. The Merry Mulligans!

The orchestra starts at the pointing baton. Squeaky-burlesque family singing. Dancing. Stunting. A performing wonder, that little baby. Charming family of seven. American-famous. The Merry Mulligans, beloved of all lovers of clean vaudeville.

Elihu M. Williams

With them the show finished. Barclay Oram and his wife Rhoda descended from Nigger Heaven, walked up to 50th Street, and caught the local subway train for Harlem. He took the slower train, hoping there would be seats and the passengers not jammed together as always.

Perhaps others had hoped for the same thing. The cars were packed. Rhoda broke up a piece of chewing gum and chewed. She had a large mouth, and she chewed the gum as if she were eating food, opening her mouth so wide that people could see the roof. When they were first married, Barclay had detested her way of chewing gum and told her so. But she replied that it was absurd to let a little thing like chewing gum irritate him.

"Oh, you brown baby!" she had cried, taking his face in her hands and kissing him with the perfumed flavor of her favorite chewing gum on her breath. . . .

"The show was pretty nice, eh?" said Rhoda.

"I am fed up with them; a cabaret in Harlem is better," replied Barclay.

"I don't think so. Anything downtown for a change is preferable to the cheap old colored shows. I'm dead sick of them."

She chewed the gum vigorously, dropping a few pointless phrases that were half-swallowed up in the roar of the train through the enormous gut of the city and the strange staccato talk of voices half-lifted above and half-caught in the roar. Barclay gazed moodily at the many straphangers who were jammed together. None seemed standing on his feet. All seemed like fat bags and lean boxes piled up indiscriminately in a warehouse. Penned up like cattle, the standing closely pressing the seated passengers, kneading them with their knees and blotting out their sight, so that those who had been fortunate to find seats were as uncomfortable as those who had not.

"I thought we'd have a little air in this local box," he said.

"It'll be better at 72nd Street," she said. "Some of them will get out."

"And others will push in. New York City is swarming with people like a beehive."

"Getting thicker and thicker every day," she agreed.

At 135th Street they left the train. Rhoda, as usual, put her hand through her husband's arm as they walked home. The saloons, restaurants, candy stores of the Avenue were crowded. The Chop Suey Palace was doing a good after-theater business.

"Might have some chop suey," suggested Barclay.

"Not tonight," she said. "Betsy's with the Howlands, and they might want to go to bed."

"Ah, yes!" He had forgotten about Betsy, their four-year-old child. Always he forgot about her. Never could he quite realize that he was the father of a family. A railroad waiter, although he was thirty-six, he always felt himself just a boy—a servant boy. His betters whom he served treated him always as a boy—often as a nice dog. And when he grew irritated and snapped, they turned on him as upon a bad dog. It was better for him, then, that, although he was a husband and father, he should feel like an irresponsible boy. Even when sometimes he grew sad, sullen, and disquieted, these were the moods of a boy. Rhoda bossed him a little and never took his moods seriously. . . .

They went straight home. Barclay lighted up the three-room apartment. Rhoda went across the hall to the Howlands' for Betsy. She brought the child in, sleeping on her breast, and bent down that Barclay might kiss her. Then she put her to bed in her little cot beside the dresser.

They had a little supper, cold chicken and beer. . . . They went to bed in the front room that they had made their bedroom. Another room was let to a railroad porter, and the dining room served for eating and sitting room.

Rhoda undressed, rubbed her face and her limbs with cold cream, slipped on a long white gown with pink ribbon around the neck, and lay down against the wall. Barclay laid himself down beside her in his underclothes. During the first six months of their union he had slept regularly in pyjamas. Then he ignored them and began sleeping in his underclothes, returning to the habit of his village boyhood. Rhoda protested at first. Afterwards she accepted it quietly. . . .

Sleep, sweet sleep. . . .

The next morning Rhoda shook Barclay at five o'clock. "O God!" He stretched himself, turned over, and rested his head on her breast.

"Time to get up," she said.

"Yes," he sighed. "God! I feel tired." He stretched his arms, touched, fondled her face, and fell into a slight doze.

Ten minutes more. Rhoda gave him a dig in the back with her knee and cried, "You just must get up, Barclay."

"All right." He turned out of bed. Six o'clock in the Pennsylvania Station for duty, that was life itself. A dutiful black boy among proud and sure white men, so that he could himself be a man in Harlem with purchasing power for wife, child, flat, movie, food, liquor. . . .

He went to the bathroom and washed. Dressed, he entered the dining room, opened a cabinet, and poured out a glass of whisky. That peppered him up and opened his eyes wide. It was not necessary for Rhoda to make coffee. He would breakfast with the other waiters in the dining car. Mechanically he kissed her good-by. She heard him close the door, and she moved over into the middle of the bed, comfortably alone, for an early morning nap.

It was a disastrous trip for Barclay. On the dining car he was the first waiter and in charge of the pantry. As pantryman he received five dollars a month more than the other waiters. It was his job to get the stores (with the steward and chef) from the commissary. He was responsible for the stuff kept in the pantry. There were some waiters and cooks addicted to petty stealing. Butter, cream, cheese, sugar, fruit. They stole for their women in New York. They stole for their women-on-the-side in the stopover cities. Always Barclay had to mount guard quietly. Between him and the raw-voiced, black-bull chef there was an understanding to watch out for the nimble-fingered among the crew. For if they were short in the checking up of the stores, the steward held them responsible. And the commissary held the steward responsible.

This trip Barclay had one of his moody-boy spells. He would not watch the pantry. Let the boys swipe the stuff. He had no pleasure waiting on the passengers. It was often a pleasure, something of an anticipated adventure, each day to meet new passengers, remark the temperature of their looks, and sometimes make casual conversation with a transient acquaintance. But today it was all wrong from the moment he observed them, impatient, crowding the corridor, and the rushing of the dining room as soon as the doors were opened. They filled him with loathing, made him sick of service. SERVICE. A beautiful word fallen upon bad days. No place for true human service in these automatic-serving days.

Mechanically Barclay picked up the dimes and quarters that were left for service. For Rhoda and Betsy. It pleasured him when Rhoda wore pretty clothes. And Betsy loved him more each time he remembered to bring home colored bonbons. What was he going to do with the child? He wondered if he would be able to give her a good education like her mother's. And what would she do? Perhaps marry a railroad waiter like her mother and raise up children to carry on the great tradition of black servitude.

Philadelphia, Harrisburg, Altoona, Pittsburgh. No dice, no coon-can, this trip. His workmates coaxed. Nothing could lift him out of himself. He was a moody boy this trip. The afternoon of the fourth day from New York brought the dining car to Washington. Washington reminded Barclay of a grave. He had sharp, hammering memories of his university days there. For there he had fallen in love. . . .

He went up to 7th Street, loitering through the Negro district, stopping curiously before a house, leaning against a stoop, sniffing here and there like a stray hound. He went into a barrel-house and drank a glass of whisky. The place was sour-smelling, full of black men, dim and smoky, close, but friendly warm.

The hour of his train's departure, approached. Barclay continued drinking. He felt pleased with himself in doing something irregular. Oh, he had been regular for such a long time! A good waiter, an honest pantryman. Never once had he sneaked a packet of sugar nor a pound of butter for his flat. Rhoda would have flung it in the street. He had never given to the colored girls who worked in the yards and visited the dining cars with their teasing smiles. Oh, it was hard to be responsible, hard to be regular.

What would the steward say about his being left in Washington? Maybe he would be drunk himself, for he was a regular souser. Barclay recalled the day when he got helplessly stewed on the Washington run, and the waiters managed the dining car, handed out checks, made change among themselves, and gave the best service they ever did as a crew. At Philadelphia an inspector hopped on the train and took charge of the service. The dining car was crowded. The steward half-roused himself out of his stupor and came lurching through the jam of passengers in the corridor into the diner, to dispute the stewardship with the inspector.

"I'm in charge of this diner," he said in a nerve-biting, imey-wimey voice. "Give a man a chance; treat me like a gen'leman."

Tears trickled down his cheeks. He staggered and swayed in the corridor, blocking the entrance and exit of the guests. Like a challenged mastiff, the inspector eyed him, at the same time glancing quickly from the waiters to the amazed guests. Then he gripped the steward by the scruff of the collar and, with the help of the Pullman conductor, locked him up in a drawing room until the train reached New York.

The crew did not like the steward and hoped they would be rid of him at last. But he was back with them the next trip. The inspector was known as a hard guy, quick to report a waiter if a flask of gin were discovered in his locker. But it was different with the steward. Both men were peers, the inspector being a promoted steward.

"Well, I'm off duty, anyhow," murmured Barclay. He smiled and ordered another drink. The train must have passed Baltimore by then, on its way to New York. What waiter was waiting on the first two tables? "I should worry." He had the warm, luxurious feelings of a truant. He drank himself drunk.

"Something for a change. I've been regular too long. Too awfully regular," he mused.

He rocked heavily out of the barrel-house to a little fried-chicken restaurant. He ate. His stomach appeased, his thoughts turned to a speakeasy. May as well finish the thing in style—be grandly irregular, he thought. He found a speakeasy. Bold-eyed chocolate girls, brown girls, yellow girls. Blues. Pianola blues, gramophone blues. Easy-queasy, daddy-mammy, honey-baby, brown-gal, black-boy, hot-dog blues. . . .

The next day he reported himself at the restaurant-car department in Washington, and was sent home to New York. There at the commissary the superintendent looked him over and said: "Well, you're a case. You wanted a little time off, eh? Well, take ten days."

That was his punishment—ten idle days. He left the commissary walking on air. For three years he had worked on the railroad without taking a holiday. Why? He did not himself know. He had often yearned for a few entirely free days. But he had never had the courage to take them, not for fear of forfeiting the nominal wages, but the tips—his real wages. Nor had he wanted to lose his former dining car. He had liked his work-pals there. A good crew teaming splendidly along together, respectful to and respected by the steward, who was a decent-minded man. Moreover, there was the flat with Rhoda and Betsy. Every day was precious, every tip necessary. . . . Ten days gratuitously thrust upon him with malicious intent. No wages-and-food, no tips. Let him cool his heels and tighten his belt. Yet he was happy, happy like a truant suspended from school.

Freedom! Ten days. What would he do with them? There would be parties. Rhoda loved parties. She had friends in New York who knew her when she was a school-teacher. Whist. Dancing. Movies.

He nosed around the tenderloin district. When he first came to New York he had lived in 40th Street.

He met a pal he had once worked with as elevator boy in a department store. They drank two glasses of beer each and walked up to San Juan Hill.

When Barclay got home, Rhoda, in an orange evening dress, was just leaving for a party. They embraced.

"I phoned up the commissary yesterday and they said you were left in Washington. Bad boy!" She laughed. "Guess I'll fix you something to eat."

"Don't bother. I'm not hungry," said Barclay.

"All right. I'm going on to Mame Dixon's for whist and a little dancing afterwards. You might dress up and come on down and have a little fun."

"Not tonight, honey. We'll have plenty of time to go around together. They gave me ten days."

"Ten days!" she cried. "The rent is due on Friday and the insurance on—on—Ten days! But why did you get left, Barclay?"

"I don't know. Felt rotten the whole trip—tired, blue. Been too punctual all along. Just had to break the habit. Feel a little irresponsible."

"But you might get in bad with the company. How could you, when there's Betsy and me to think of and our social position?"

She broke up a stick of chewing gum and vigorously chewed. "Well, anyway, come on along to Mame's if you feel like it." She rolled the gum with her tongue. "But if you don't, you can bring Betsy over from the Howlands'."

Chewing, chewing, she went out.

"Kill-joy," murmured Barclay. Riding on the subway from San Juan Hill to Harlem, he had been guessing chucklingly at what she would say. Perhaps: "All right, honey-stick, why slave every day? Let's play around together for ten days."

Chewing, chewing. Always chewing. Yet that mouth was the enchanting thing about her. . . . Her mouth. It made me marry her. Her skin was brown and beautiful. Like cat's fur, soft to the fingers. But it was not her fruit-ripe skin. It was her mouth that made me.

Ordinary her face would have been, if it were not for the full, large mouth that was mounted on the ample plane of her features like an exquisite piece of bas-relief.

He went across the hall to the Howlands' and brought back Betsy.

"Candy, daddy, candy!" The happy brown thing clapped her hands and pulled at his pantaloons. He set her on his knee and gave her a little paper packet. He danced her up and down: "Betsy, wupsy, mupsy, pretsy, eatsy plentsy candy."

She wriggled off his knee with the packet and dropped the candies one by one into a small glass jar, gurgling over the colors and popping one into her mouth at intervals. . . . She returned again to Barclay's knee, squeezing a brown rubber doll. For a little while she made a rocking horse of him They she scratched her head and yawned. Barclay undressed her and put her in the crib.

"Betsy and me and our social position." That social position! Alone he brooded, moody, unreasonable. Resentment gripped his heart. He hated his love of Rhoda's mouth. He hated the flat and his pitiable "social position." He hated fatherhood. He resented the sleeping child.

"Betsy and me and——" Should he go on forever like that? Round the circle of the Eastern field? New York, Boston, Buffalo, Pittsburgh, Harrisburg, Washington, Baltimore, Philadelphia, again New York.

Forever? Getting off nowhere?

Forever fated to the lifelong tasks of the unimaginative? Why was he, a West Indian peasant boy, held prisoner within the huge granite-gray walls of New York? Dreaming of tawny tasseled fields of sugar cane, and silver-gray John-tuhits among clusters of green and glossy-blue berries of pimento. The husbands and fathers of his village were not mechanically driven servant boys. They were hardy, independent tillers of the soil or struggling artisans.

What enchantment had lured him away from the green intimate life that clustered round his village—the simple African-transplanted life of the West Indian hills? Why had he hankered for the hard-slabbed streets, the vertical towers, the gray complex life of this steel-tempered city? Stone and steel! Steel and stone! Mounting in heaven-pursuing magnificence. Feet piled upon feet, miles circling miles, of steel and stone. A tree seemed absurd and a garden queer in this iron-gray majesty of man's imagination. He was a slave to it. A part of him was in love with this piling grandeur. And that was why he was a slave to it.

From the bedroom came a slight stirring and a sleepy murmur of child-language. Barclay was lost in the past. Step by step he retraced his life. . . . His fever-like hunger for book knowledge, for strange lands and great cities. His grand adolescent dream.

The evening of his departure from the village came back star-blue and clear. He had trudged many miles to the railroad with his bright-patterned carpet bag on his shoulder. For three years in the capital of his island he had worked in a rum warehouse. Happy. On the road to his beautiful dream. Later he had crossed over to Santiago in Cuba. And at twenty-five he had reached New York, found his strange land—a great city of great books.

Two years of elevator-running and switchboard-operating had glanced by like a magic arrow against the gaunt gray walls of the city. Time was a radiant servant working for his dream.

His dream, of course, was the Negro university. Now he remembered how he turned green cold like a cucumber when he was told that he could not enter the university course. Two years preparatory work was needed. Undaunted, he had returned to New York and crammed for a year. And the next fall he swept through the entrance examinations.

For Barclay then the highroad to wisdom led necessarily by way of a university. It had never occurred to him that he might have also attained his goal in his own free, informal way.

He had been enchanted by the words: University, Seat of Learning. He had seen young men of the insular island villages returned from the native colleges. They all brought back with them a new style of clothes, a different accent, a new gait, the exciting, intoxicating smell of the city—so much more intriguing than the ever-fresh accustomed smell of the bright-green hill-valley village. Style and accent and exotic smell—all those attractive fruits of college training, fundamental forms of the cultural life. Home study could not give him the stamp. . . . His disillusion had not embittered him. . . .

My college days were happy, he reflected. A symmetrical group of buildings, gray walls supporting in winter stout, dark-brown leafless creepers. An all-Negro body of students—men and women—of many complexions, all intensely active. The booklore was there, housed in a kind of Gothic building with a projecting façade resting on Grecian pillars. The names of Aristotle, Solon, Virgil, Shakespeare, Dante, and Longfellow were cut in the façade. The building was one of the many symbols, scattered over America and the world, summing up the dream of a great romantic king of steel.

Barclay found no romance in textbooks, of course. But he found plenty of it in the company of the jolly girls and chummy chaps of his widened acquaintance. And the barbaric steps of the turkey-trot and the bunny-hug (exciting dances of that period) he had found more enchanting than the library. He was amorously touched by the warm, intimate little dances he attended—the spontaneous outburst of group-singing when the dancers were particularly drunk on a rich, tintinnabulating melody.

Then one day he was abruptly pulled up in his fantastic steps. No more money in the box. He had to wheel round about and begin the heavy steps of working his way through college.

The next fall he met Rhoda. It was at one of those molasses-thick Aframerican affairs that had rendered university life so attractive to him, at the home of a very generous fawn-brown widow who enjoyed giving a few students a nice time at her flat. The widow entertained her guests in a free kind of way. She did not belong to the various divisions that go to the making of nice Negro society, for she was merely the widow of a Pullman porter, who had saved up his tips and paid up on a good insurance policy. She had been too fine for the non-discriminating parlor-social sets, and too secular for the prayer-meeting black ladies. So she had cleverly gone in for the non-snobbish young intellectuals—poor students who could not afford to put on airs.

Barclay recalled the warm roomful of young Negro men and girls. Copper and chocolate and fine anthracite, with here and there a dash of cream, all warmly dancing. One night he was attracted to Rhoda. He danced with her all the time and she was warm to him, loving to him. She was the first American girl with whom he began a steady intimacy. All the ardors of him were stirred to her, and simply, impetuously he had rushed into deep love, like a bee that darts too far into the heart of a flower and unable to withdraw, dies at the bottom of the juice.

Rhoda, who had been earning her own living as a teacher, helped him, and the problem of money was lifted from his mind. Oh, he was very happy then! Books and parties and Rhoda. . . .

In the middle of his junior year she told him she was with child. They discussed whether she should have the child or operate it away. If she had it without being married, she would lose her job. He remembered a school-teaching girl of his village who had tried to conceal her pregnancy and died under an operation in the city.

The other girls, the free peasant girls, always bore their children when they were gotten with child. Perhaps it was better that way.

Rhoda was pleased that Barclay wanted the thing to develop in the natural way. She desired a child. She was at that vague age when some women feel that marriage is more than the grim pursuit of a career. So they went to New York together and got married.

But Barclay did not fully realize the responsibility, perhaps could not, of marriage. Never fully understood its significance.

Barclay remembered now that he was as keen as Rhoda for the marriage. Carried away by the curiosity to take up a new role, there had been something almost of eagerness in his desire to quit the university. And it had seemed a beautiful gesture. Rhoda had helped him when he was in great need, and he felt splendid now to come to her support when she was incapacitated for work. He would have hated to see her drop down to menial tasks. As a Jack-of-all-trades he had met many refined colored girls having a rough time, jammed at the bottom of the common scramble to survive.

He had been happy that Rhoda was not pushed to leave Betsy in one of those dime dumps where poor colored children were guarded while their mothers worked, happy that from his job on the railroad he was earning enough for the family to live simply and comfortably.

About that job he had never taken serious thought. Where was it leading him? What was it making of his character? He had taken it as if he were acting in a play rather than working at a job. It met the necessary bill of being in love. For he was really in love with Rhoda. The autumn-leaf mellowness of her body. Her ripe-ripe accent and richness of laughter. And her mouth: the full form of it, its strength and beauty, its almost unbearable sweetness, magnetic, drawing, sensuous, exquisite, a dark pagan piece of pleasure. . . . How fascinated and enslaved he had been to what was now stale with chewing gum and banal remarks on "social position."

Barclay's attitude to the railroad was about the same toward the modern world in general. He had entered light-heartedly into the whirl and crash and crush, the grand babel of building, the suction and spouting, groaning and whining and breaking of steel—all the riotous, contagious movement around him.

He had entered into the rough camaraderie of the railroad with all the hot energy of youth. It was a rugged, new experience that kindled his vagabonding mind and body. There was rude poetry in the roar and rush and rattle of trains, the sharp whistle of engines and racing landscapes, the charm of a desolate mining town and glimpses of faces lost as soon as seen. He had even tried to capture some of those fleeting piled-up images. Some he had read to his workmates, which they appreciated, but teased him for writing:

We are out in the field, the vast wide-open field,
Thundering through from city to city
Where factories grow like jungle trees
Yielding new harvests for the world.
Through Johnstown glowing like a world aflame,
And Pittsburgh, Negro-black, brooding in iron smoke,
Philly's Fifteenth street of wenches, speakeasies, and cops.
Out in the field, new fields of life
Where machines spin flowers like tropic trees
And coal and steel are blazing suns—
And darkly we wonder, night-wrapped in the light.

The steel-framed poetry of cities did not crowd out but rather intensified in him the singing memories of his village life. He loved both, the one complementing the other. Against the intricate stone-and-steel flights of humanity's mass spirit, misty in space and time, hovered the green charm of his village. Yellow-eyed and white-lidded Spanish needles coloring the grassy hillsides, barefooted black girls, straight like young sweet-woods, tramping to market with baskets of mangoes or star-apples poised unsupported on their heads. The native cockish liquor juice of the sugar cane, fermented in bamboo joints for all-night carousal at wakes and tea meetings. Heavy drays loaded with new-made sugar, yams, and plantains, rumbling along the chalky country road away down and over the hills under the starshine and the hot-free love songs of the draymen.

He remembered all, regretting nothing, since his life was a continual fluxion from one state to another. His deepest regret was always momentary, arising from remaining in a rut after he had exhausted the experience.

Rhoda now seemed only another impasse into which he had drifted. Just a hole to pull out of again and away from the road, that arena of steel rushing him round and round in the same familiar circle. He had to evade it and be irresponsible again.

But there was the child and the Moral Law. The cold white law. Rhoda seemed more than he to be subject to it with her constant preoccupation about social position.

Spiritually he was subject to another law. Other gods of strange barbaric glory claimed his allegiance, and not the grim frock-coated gentleman of the Moral Law of the land. The Invisible Law that upheld those magnificent machines and steel-spired temples and new cathedrals erected to the steel-flung traffic plan of man. Oh, he could understand and love the poetry of them, but not their law that held humanity gripped in fear.

His thought fell to a whisper within him. He could never feel himself more than a stranger within these walls. His body went through the mechanical process, but untamed, for his spirit was wandering far. . . .

Rhoda at the party and the child asleep. He could hear her breathing and wondered if it were breath of his breath. For he had often felt to himself a breath of his own related to none. Suppose he should start now on the trail again with that strange burning thought. Related to none.

There were the Liberty Bonds in his trunk. Rhoda would need them. He remembered how he had signed for them. All the waiters herded together in one of the commissary rooms and lectured by one of the special war men.

"Buy a bond, boys. All you boys will buy a bond because you all believe in the Allied cause. We are in the war to make the world safe for Democracy. You boys on the railroad are enjoying the blessings of Democracy like all real Americans. Your service is inestimable. Keep on doing your part and do your best by buying a bond because you believe in the Allied cause and you want America to win the war and the banner of Democracy to float over the world. Come on, take your bond."

For the Moral Law. Buy a bond.

Well it was all right; he had subscribed. One way of saving money, although the bonds were worth so much less now. There was the bankbook with a couple hundred dollars. Leave that, too. Insurance policies. Forget them.

He thought he heard the child stir. He dared not look. He clicked the door and stepped out. Where? Destination did not matter. Maybe his true life lay in eternal inquietude.

What do you think?

1. Explain what conditions prevail that urge Barclay to be a "dutiful black boy" on his job but a "man in Harlem." Explain why (in view of the way Barclay is treated by those whom he serves) he says that it's better that he should feel "like an irresponsible boy." Why do you agree or disagree with his thinking on this?
2. In general, do you agree with Barclay's opinion that with automatic serving, there is no place for "true human service"? Are there exceptions where people are served in good style? If so, speculate on why this is the case in these particular circumstances.
3. Is Barclay's difficulty in being regular and responsible typical of Americans? Give reasons for your response.
4. What does Barclay mean when he says he'll get nowhere in his job? Why does he say this? Is the explanation for this thought in his lack of ambition or in the very character of the job? Explain your answer.
5. Why would you agree or disagree with Barclay's comment that it would be preferable to be a struggling artisan than to be a dining car waiter?
6. In what ways is Barclay's character being affected by his job? Explain, in general, how a job can positively or negatively affect a person's character.
7. How would you describe Barclay's feelings about himself, his wife, and his little girl? Explain why he should or should not be condemned for leaving his family. Can you account for each of the factors that causes him to leave?
8. In a sentence or two explain what comment about city living is being expressed in the following observations made by Barclay:
   (a) How the subway riders appear to him.
   (b) How the granite-gray walls of New York hold him captive.
   (c) That the city is an iron-gray majesty of man's imagination.
   How is it possible that Barclay feels positive and negative things about the city?

Suggestions for writing

1. Imagine that you are a judge in the court where Rhoda has filed for divorce on grounds of desertion. Write your judgment, that is, whether or not the divorce is granted, and the reasons for it in a short paper (500 words).
2. Some writers argue that certain jobs—such as garbage collection—can have detrimental effects on the opinion a person has of himself. They suggest that such jobs be eliminated and machinery be developed which accomplishes the same end. Write a paper in which you describe a job which you think is unsuitable for human beings. Explain why you hold that opinion and what the best solution(s) to the dilemma is.

THE UPSTAGING OF PISTOL PETE

William F. Reed

"The Upstaging of Pistol Pete" by William F. Reed. From *Sports Illustrated,* March 30, 1970. © 1970 Time Inc.

At the end of his nine-day stay in New York City, Pistol Pete Maravich was ready to go home. He had come to town eager to justify his title as basketball's Mr. Showtime, and he could hardly wait to get out there under the bright lights of Madison Square Garden, before a full house, and fire off the leaping, twisting shots that had made him college basketball's alltime scoring leader. He'd show those city dudes Pistol Pete the magician, scrambling down the floor on a fast break, his long hair flopping, his old gray sweat socks drooping, the basketball dancing through his legs and around his back. As he said before taking his first dribble in the National Invitation Tournament, "I've always insisted that basketball is an entertainment, and New York is where the fans love basketball. Either we will swallow New York—or New York will swallow us."

Well, it turned out to be something like mutual heartburn. New York loved Pete's act, but Marquette's team and its star, Dean Meminger (*opposite*), upstaged him in the end and won the tournament. After his NIT adversaries had come at him with their aggressive, gang-up defenses, Maravich looked—and felt—as if he had been worked over by a mugger in Central Park. At one point, besides a severely upset stomach that caused him to lose 10 pounds, Pete had a knot on his head, a bruised hip, a strained ligament in his leg and a sprained ankle. Although LSU won two games and finished fourth, his brilliant passes were few and far between. And after his team was beaten in the semis, Maravich decided to sit out Saturday's consolation game with Army.

"I didn't want to risk hurting myself further," he said. "I wanted to come here and win for my dad [the LSU coach], but everything was a disaster. Man, I've had enough of this place."

While Maravich was having his troubles, Coach Al McGuire and his hungry, angry urchins from Milwaukee showed why they were the tournament favorites. The Warriors hounded a limping Maravich into uselessness and beat LSU 101–79 in the semifinals. And on Saturday afternoon they easily disposed of McGuire's alma mater, St. John's, to win the final 65–53.

"We're a great little team," said McGuire, whose usual snappy attire was surpassed in brilliance only by his team's black-and-gold striped uniforms. "We thought we would win—and we did."

All season, of course, the Warriors had been pointing not for the NIT but for an at-large berth in the big tournament, the NCAA. After finishing with a fine 22–3 record, Marquette got an NCAA bid all right, but to the Midwest Regional in Fort Worth instead of the Mideast at Dayton, Ohio. This was not the first time that the NCAA had asked a team to switch regions in order to fit in all the best independents, but McGuire balked, fumed and finally said phooey—the Warriors would go to New York and the NIT.

"We were unjustly kept out of the Mideast," said McGuire. "I didn't want to go to Texas. I have nothing against longhorns, but that's 1,500 miles away. What could I get down there—maybe two cheerleaders."

Of course, the NIT was delighted to acquire the Warriors. Usually the tournament has to make do with 16 of the NCAA's rejects and also-rans, so a team like Marquette brought substantial class to the field. Moreover, the Warriors' best players—Meminger and Ric Cobb—are products of New York playgrounds and high schools. So, as the NIT got under way, the smart money liked St. John's in the upper bracket and Marquette in the lower. Neither favorite, despite the local appeal, captivated audiences the way Maravich did.

When they arrived in New York—on Friday the 13th—Maravich and his teammates were taken to the New Yorker Hotel, and right away, as Pete told it later, there was trouble. "We had to wait to get our rooms," he said, "because there had been some kind of shooting and they were still cleaning up." The story was denied by both the New York police and the hotel, but it was fun to tell and Pete always likes to entertain, on or off court. Shortly he was describing how he was stuck on one of the hotel's elevators:

"Here I was, 36 floors up, with this elevator bobbing up and down. Man, I'm saying my life's over—I was going crazy. I kept punching buttons and it kept bobbing between 36 and 37. Then all of a sudden the doors opened and there was nothing but a wall there. I said 'Oh, no' and punched another button. Finally it went up to 40 and I got off. Man, I *walked* down to the lobby."

The next night one of Pete's fans—Al Hirt—invited the team to attend his concert at Carnegie Hall, where he called the players up on stage and introduced them. At about 2:30 a.m. Maravich was sound asleep in his room ("It was so small I had to put my suitcases in the bathroom") when he was awakened by a soft knocking on the door.

"Some girl had gotten outside in the hall," he said, "and she was calling, 'P-e-e-te, P-e-e-te.' I lay there for a few minutes just listening to her. I couldn't believe it. And then, just as I was getting ready to get up, somebody came along and ran her off."

On Sunday afternoon, LSU's opening game was televised nationally; since the New York area was not blacked out Garden attendance was a mere 16,000, more than the size of capacity crowds at the NCAA. But Maravich noticed the empty seats as soon as he jogged out on the floor. "It wasn't packed and I realized that," he said. "When I first went out there, I was scared—I was afraid everybody thought the game was being played somewhere else. The more people there are in the stands the better I like it." One other possible reason for the empty seats is that LSU was supposed to have an easy time with its opponent, Georgetown, an idea that was quickly dispelled.

The first time he put his hands on the ball in a game at the Garden, Pistol Pete gave the crowd what it wanted to see. With only eight seconds gone, he whipped a pass behind his back into a crowd of players jostling under the basket. Although the pass was right in his hands, Maravich's receiver was so surprised, or nervous, that he blew the shot. But nobody in the crowd seemed to mind. After letting out a loud ooooh, the fans settled back, ready to be entertained some more. Showtime was here.

But Georgetown was ready for The Pistol. The Hoyas assigned Guard Mike Laska—"best defensive player in the country," according to his coach—to cling to Maravich, and they had two more players running at him whenever he tried to maneuver into shooting territory. At halftime Pete was only 1 for 4 from the field. "I saw two men on me all the time and I thought, well, hell, I'll just throw the ball around and we'll score that way," said Pete.

He began taking more shots in the second half and in one period hit three long jumpers in a row. "I was starting to wonder how good he was about then," said Laska, "but when he hit those I knew he could have been doing it all day." What really turned on the crowd was a pass Maravich made on one of the few fast breaks LSU was able to generate. With a defensive man planted only steps in front of him as he charged up the middle, Maravich took a pass from his left and zipped it to his right all in the same motion, setting up an easy basket. His two free throws in the closing seconds enabled the Tigers to win 83–82, but Pete was not pleased. In his New York debut he had a modest 20 points—making six of 16 shots—and for the first time this season he was outscored by a teammate. Dark, husky Danny Hester, a 6′ 8″ senior forward, had 30.

"I was pitiful, I was terrible, I stunk," said Pete. "It was one of my worst, no doubt about it. How many shots did I take? Sixteen? That's about 90 under my average, but I had nowhere to go. When I play that bad, I try to forget it. I'll just go hide in my little corner." The corner turned out to be Mr. Laffs, one of the swinging East Side bars.

Pete's best NIT performance—and also his roughest experience—came Tuesday night against Oklahoma in the quarterfinals, and this time there was a full house in the Garden. Showtime fans saw Pistol Pete score 37 points and again hit two free throws in the closing seconds, giving LSU a 97–94 victory. They also saw Pete get hit in the face going for a rebound, scrape his shin diving for a loose ball and twist his ankle while trying to drive between two Oklahoma defenders. After the game his stomach and ankle were troubling him enough so that he turned down an invitation to appear on the Dick Cavett show, which was just as well because his dad was fuming over the team's extracurricular activities anyway.

"We played like a bunch of fifth-graders," said his father. "These kids have been up till all hours of the night. I know they're up watching TV until 2 or 3 in the morning—you have 17,000 channels up here! They get up in the morning and they look like they've been on a seven-day drunk."

After the game a stranger walked up to Lou Carnesecca, the effervescent little coach who was winding up his career at St. John's to take over the New York Nets of the ABA, and pointed out that Maravich had made 14 floor errors. Said Carnesecca, "So what? Michelangelo ruined a few pieces of marble, too."

Had Maravich been well, LSU's game with Marquette might have been the best of the tournament. After working hard to get past Massachusetts 62–55 in the first round, the Warriors had put their game together and whipped a good Utah team 83–63 in the quarterfinals. In addition to Meminger, a smiling, gum-chewing guard who was to become the tournament's Most Valuable Player, they had three excellent rebounders in Cobb, Joe Thomas and Gary Brell. They made up in jumping ability and aggressiveness what they lacked in size. And, of course, they had McGuire, who kept his team sequestered in a small hotel while LSU was gadding about town.

Early on, the game was close. The Warriors came out pressing LSU all over, a revolving double-team concentration on the ball handler, but Maravich was able to dribble or pass his team up the floor for a while. Late in the first half, however, Thomas and Cobb established their rebounding superiority over LSU's Hester and Al Sanders, and the Tigers began to get into foul trouble. Normally, LSU would have started working exclusively to Maravich, but Pete was bottled up by the efficient trapping tactics of Meminger and Guard Jeff Sewell, and he was limping noticeably.

In the second half the game was no contest. Maravich struggled almost 19 minutes without a field goal, and when he finally hit a jumper with 1:12 remaining to make the score 96–73 the Marquette fans gave him a derisive cheer.

"I didn't want to beat Maravich and lose to LSU," said McGuire. "I think that in college ball today, any one man can be stopped. Put a triangle and two on him and where's he going to go?"

Said Maravich, "I know I'm going to have some bad games, and I'm not worried about it. You have to take the good with the bad, and right now I'm taking the bad. But there will be good—I guarantee you that." Later Maravich and Sanders went to look for some of the good at Bachelors III.

With Pete gone, the final game would have been an anticlimax to New Yorkers except for the presence of so many locals on both sides. His last St. John's team had been good to Carnesecca, winning close ones in their bracket against Georgia Tech (56–55) and Army (60–59), but Marquette was too quick and its press too upsetting. Double-teaming the ball and recovering quickly when St. John's found the open man, the Warriors forced errors and bad shots. Against a man-for-man defense in the first half Meminger drove almost at will, and Jeff Sewell was remarkably accurate from outside. As McGuire put it later, "Dean puts the other team into a zone, and Jeff pulls them out of it." The margin of superiority remained at a level throughout: Marquette led by 10 at the half and by 12 at the finish.

Naturally, McGuire was asked how he thought his team would have done in the NCAA. "I haven't seen UCLA, but we're quicker than Jacksonville," he said. "Aw, let's drop it. I'm not looking for comparisons. I have enough trouble without taking on the world."

As for Pete Maravich, he also took time for some reflection before saying goodby to New York. Before he drove a hansom cab around Central Park he sat in the dark, quiet bar at the Plaza Hotel, sipping a bourbon and Coke. Now that his college career is over, Pete is fair game for the warring pro leagues. Would he sign with the Carolina Cougars of the ABA? Or, unlike some of his All-America contemporaries, would he wait for the NBA draft?

"Aw, man, the pressure is just beginning," he said. "I tell you, everybody thinks I've got it made but, you know, it's not worth it. There is so much pressure, and people—every day, every day. You know when I've had the most fun? When I went to Daytona all by myself last year and just took it easy. Nobody knew me. Sometimes I wish I could be an accountant or something, man, so I could live right for a change.

"I haven't even started thinking about the pros yet but I don't think what happened in the NIT makes any difference. I don't care if I only made one point or one assist. You don't base an entire lifetime of basketball on one game or tournament. Nothing has gone right for me here, but it's all over now."

World-weary at 21, already enough of a veteran to look back on a college career as a lifetime, Pete is undoubtedly right that his only fair NIT show will not affect the bids from the pros. He'll get his million, or more. And he has another offer that seriously tempts him. If he'd like, Pistol Pete can make a short, lucrative exhibition tour as the first white man to play *with* the Harlem Globe-trotters. After all, they seldom play in New York.

What do you think?

1. Much of this article is about "Pistol Pete" Maravich. What are the strongest impressions of him that you get?
2. What impressions do you get of New York City? Is it described as an enjoyable and safe place to visit? Why do you think the writer treats that city as he does?
3. Pete gets injured many times while playing basketball. Should a participant in a sport that is *not* a body-contact one tolerate injuries? Is it to be expected? Does it diminish or increase the "excitement" of the game?
4. What difference might it make in "Pistol Pete's" performance that his father is coach of the LSU team? Explain your answer. Are there greater differences or similarities between the feelings that motivate Tom (in the short story, "The Store," p. 9) when his father pulls him up by his hair and the feelings Pete might have about his father?
5. A number of reasons for LSU's losing the NIT Tournament can be found in the article. Name as many as you can. Then examine them in the following way:
   (a) Is each of them reasonable?
   (b) Is there evidence to support the explanations the author accepts?
   (c) Does the author seem to favor some explanations over others?
   (d) Why are some explanations stated openly and others only hinted at?
   (e) Is the author possibly stressing the wrong reasons and overlooking others? Do you agree with the author's thinking? Completely? In part? Not at all?
6. *Hyperbole* is the technical term for a statement that is a deliberate exaggeration. What is the author's point in writing the following exaggerated comments:
   "You have 17,000 channels up here." (Line 178)
   "They look like they've been on a seven-day drunk." (Line 179)
7. In line 263, "Pistol Pete" says, "Sometimes I wish I could be an accountant or something, man, so I could live right." How does this sentiment compare to that implied by Flick in the poem, "Ex-Basketball Player" (page 15)? How do you account for the difference in attitude? What does Pete mean by "live right"? Does Pete feel the same way Flick does about applause? About its absence? Explain.
8. The feeling of the article could be described as light and humorous. What features of the way in which it's written contribute to that quality? Name as many of them as you can. On the other hand, if you think that the feeling is serious, explain what features contribute to that.

Suggestions for writing and reading

1. Many sports develop their own terminology to describe—sometimes vividly, sometimes vaguely—the activities involved in the game. In this article, for example, there are expressions unique in basketball, such as "free throw" or "16 shots."
   Select some game you're familiar with and list as many terms as possible which seem unique to that game. Put the terms that are vivid ones in one column and those that are obscure in another:

Descriptive	*Obscure*
Rebound	Let-serve
Service	Love score

   During class discussions, you may discover disagreement as to whether you've put terms in the best category. But that doesn't matter; the object of this exercise is to remind you of the special ways language is used in sports.

2. If you are unfamiliar with the unusual basketball team called The Harlem Globetrotters, look them up in magazine articles by referring first to the reference book, *The Reader's Guide to Periodical Literature.* What is some of the criticism of this team that originates from the Afro-American community? Is it justified? Should the matter of race enter into sports? Does it? How?
3. This article touches on problems such as the use of violence in sports and the development of a self-concept though participation in sports. If you want to learn more about both these topics, Read: "What a Way to Make a Living: Pro-Football," *Sports Illustrated* Magazine, November 16, 1970; and "Danger as a Way of Joy: Risk-Action Sports," *Sports Illustrated* Magazine, January 27, 1969.

THE JOB

Ben Caldwell

Personnel interviewer, white
Applicant #1, negro woman
Applicant #2, negro man
Applicant #3, negro man
Applicant #4, negro woman
Applicant #5, negro man
Applicant #6, black man
Applicant #7, negro man (latecomer)

Scene 1. Bright lighted office interior. 8:45 A.M. is the time on the wall clock. A large white sign hangs from the light green wall, reading, "NEW YORK OFFICE FOR N.O.," in foot-high letters. Underneath, half the size, is "PROJECT NEGRO OPPORTUNITIES." A blonde, blue-eyed male is seated at a grey steel desk. There is an unoccupied chair beside the desk. A tall file cabinet is close by. Six people stand in single file line. Pink filled-out application forms in their hands. First in line is a pretty dark-complexioned young lady. Straightened hair gleaming. She wears a blue imitation leather coat, a brown skirt, a pink blouse. Her facial expression is sad. Behind her, a young man of about 20. He has on a black leather coat, white shirt, dark tie, green corduroy trousers, brown suede shoes. He is trying so hard to give the impression that he's cool, unconcerned, that he looks tense. Like he's braced against a stiff wind. Behind him is a "cat" who would be considered "clean" in the slang sense. His processed hair sparkles electrically. He wears an olive green, continental cut, entertainer's suit. Black patent leather shoes. The cuffs of his clean yellow shirt hang far beneath his jacket sleeves. Large cuff links. Every now and then he hums the melody of a current popular R & B tune, ("Cool Jerk") and does a little step to relieve his boredom. Behind is a woman of about 35. She has on a fur collared black wool coat, a printed scarf is tied on her head. She looks bored, tired, disgusted. Behind her is a slumped negro man who looks tired from years of hard life and working. He has worked in the clothes he's wearing. Behind him is a tall black man. His hair long, bushy. His black sports coat is much too small. His much-washed khaki trousers are too short. He has dirty white sneakers on his big feet, he wears no sox. He carries a musical instrument case (saxophone). Maybe he just seems big because the clothes are not his. The line faces the blonde blue-eyed male. He examines and files some papers and cards from atop the desk. He then looks up, nods, signaling the first applicant to come forward. She walks to, and stands beside, the desk. The blonde stands to greet her, extending his hand.

INTERVIEWER. Good-morning. Welcome to N.O. My name is Mr. Foster. Won't you sit down. *They both sit. She hands him her application.* Before we begin I'd like to ask you some questions, and tell you a little about N.O. Did the Welfare refer you to N.O.?

1, *southern accent.* Yes.

INTERVIEWER. Good. Now Project N.O. is a government sponsored program designed to fill some of the gaps in our welfare programs. *Broad smile.* We realize that just to offer financial assistance does not solve or eliminate the problem. We realize that some of us have difficulty finding jobs because of educational limitations. The N.O. program tackles both problems. We offer assistance—financial—and training

so that you may qualify for a better paying job. And with your newly acquired skills you also achieve job security. Would you give me your name, please?
1. May-ree Free-mun.

INTERVIEWER, *writing.* How old are you, Mary?
1. 20.

INTERVIEWER. Are you married, Mary?
1. No.

INTERVIEWER. Do you have any children, Mary?
1. *Slightly indignant.* No, I don't.

INTERVIEWER. Do you live alone or with your folks, Mary?
1. I live with my folks.

INTERVIEWER. How far did you go in school?
1. I graduated.

INTERVIEWER. You mean from high school?
1. Yes.

INTERVIEWER. Where was that—I mean where did you go to school?
1. In Georgia.

INTERVIEWER. What part of Georgia? And the name of the school?
1. Backwoods, Georgia. And I went to Freeman Gosden-Charles Corell High.

INTERVIEWER. Oh, yes, I understand that's a very good school. Did you like going to school, Mary?
1, *shrugging shyly.* It was all right.

INTERVIEWER. Well, did you take any special courses?
1. No.

INTERVIEWER. What are some of your interests, Mary?
1, *puzzled. No answer.*

INTERVIEWER. I mean is there something you like to do more than anything else?
1. I like to cook. And sew. I used to want to be a artist.

INTERVIEWER, *scribbing in his note pad.* Oh, that's nice. What kind of work have you done in the past?
1. Factory.

INTERVIEWER. Did you like working in a factory?
1, *shrugs. Indecisive.*

INTERVIEWER. Do you like to work, Mary?
1. Yes, but the jobs didn't pay much money—and they was always layin' off.

INTERVIEWER. I see. Now what we're going to try to do for you is, first, have you tested. Then we're going to see if we can send you to a school—to learn how to cook and sew—so you can get a good job cooking or sewing. Something that you like to do. How does that sound to you?
1. Well, I already can sew good enough to get a job, I just wan . . .

INTERVIEWER. Wait a minute. While you're going to school the government will pay you a salary until you graduate. Ah, you're smiling. I guess it makes you happy to know that things aren't so hopeless after all! *Big Smile.* Yes, N.O. is here to give hope to the hopeless. To give you a second chance for that chance you missed. *Pause.* Now, Mary, I want you to sign these two papers.

He waits while she signs. Meanwhile, on the line, the woman looks, impatiently, at her watch. Asks an unheard question of the man in front of her. The strange man on the end of the line (#6) drops a wrapped object, accidently. It makes a loud metallic ring. He picks it up, unzips the instrument bag, and places the object inside . . .

INTERVIEWER. Now I want you to take this card and go to this address, tomorrow, 9 A.M., to be tested. Then you come back here to see me Wednesday. I hope we've helped you on the way to an everlasting job. Good luck!
1. Thank you.

She gets up to leave. Her disposition changed from the earlier gloom. The men turn to watch her walk out. One of the men makes a remark to her as she passes. She conspicuously ignores him. The INTERVIEWER *writes and files. Then signals the next applicant to come forward.*

Scene 2. The INTERVIEWER *is finishing with the next-to-last applicant. The wall clock states 11:40.*

INTERVIEWER. Now I'm sure that once you finish the training and get a good job—a good *steady* job—you and your wife won't fight, and she won't have to call the cops on you. Ha, ha, ha, ha, ha! Okay, Sam?
5. Ha, ha. Yeah, OK. Thank you fo' everything, Mr. Foster.

INTERVIEWER, *standing as the applicant does—extending his hand.* I want you to keep this job, Sam, so you can stay out of trouble. Okay?
5. Okay.

INTERVIEWER. Okay. Glad we could help you. Best of luck, Sam. *Sam nods his head and leaves.* INTERVIEWER *takes some papers to the file. Files them. Returns to desk to answer the phone.* Yes? Oh, hi Stan. No, not quite. So far only four or five. Got one more to go. Oh, you know, the usual. Yeh. What did you expect? Just another way of keeping them in line. Ha ha ha. Where're you having lunch? Oh, good, I'll meet you there in about 20 minutes. All right, bye.

He looks at the last applicant apprehensively, and motions him forward. He stands to greet him. Into the blonde's extended hand 6 shoves the application. They both sit.

INTERVIEWER. I'm sorry you had to wait so long, sir.
6. That's all right. We've waited so long a few more minutes don't matter.

The INTERVIEWER *looks puzzled at this reply, and more so when he looks at the application. He smiles a nervous smile. He gestures.*

INTERVIEWER. Sir, you haven't filled out your application.
6. I know.

INTERVIEWER. Why is that, sir?
6. There is no reason to fill it out.

INTERVIEWER. Aren't you looking for a job?
6. No. I have a job.

INTERVIEWER, *further puzzled and at a loss for words. The applicant's intense glare unnerves him even more. He makes a "conversation piece" of the instrument case.*

INTERVIEWER. You have a job? Oh! Are you a musician?
6. Yes.
INTERVIEWER, *trying to sound interested instead of uneasy.* Oh! What do you play?
6. I play the truth.

INTERVIEWER. The truth? Is that an instrument? I don't understand! . . . What is this? Is this some sort of joke?
6, *just stares at him.*

We're here to help you. There's no information on this application and there's nothing I can do if . . .
6. I don't want you to do anything. Or I should say *"we."* I have a job. I'm doing what all my people should be doing.

INTERVIEWER. I don't understand you, but I have a job to do. What's your name, sir?
6. Just call me Black Nigger—that's what you'd like to do, Whitey!

INTERVIEWER, *excited.* I thought so! One of those "black nationalist" characters! Look here, I can understand your anger, and even your bitterness—and I sympathize—but what you're doing is unreasonable. You're doing nothing to help yourself or your people. We're here to help *you* people. We're doing all we can to change the shameful conditions that have existed for too long. People like you make things worse. Now if you came here for a job, good—if not . . .
6. *During the speech he places his instrument case on his lap and opens it. He places his hands on the instrument.* I told you I didn't come here to get a job. I have a job. I came to do a job. I FEEL LIKE PLAYING! *He rises, quickly, and swings the instrument, striking the* INTERVIEWER *on the head, it makes a loud thump. The* INTERVIEWER *screams, loudly. Blood is running down his face, onto his white shirt. He runs to the file cabinet and frantically rummages through the cards.*

INTERVIEWER, *hysterical.* Wait! Wait! I know I can find you something! A good job! A good paying, steady, job! You don't have to do this!
6. Yeah! I feel like playing! Like swinging! How you like this JAZZ!?

The applicant swings again, striking him on the arms and hands. He sounds like a preacher preaching a sermon. We should have done this long time ago! *All* niggers should be doing this! Instead of begging and being killed. Kiss your ass when they should be kicking your ass! And trying to be like you! Hoping you'd treat us as men. Hoping you'd stop killing us. Hoping you'd accept us! But all you offer is jobs! We want our freedom and all you offer is jobs and integration! You've turned us wrong-side out! You forced me into this role! Your clothes don't fit me! Your ways don't fit me! I'm not myself! I'm not a killer. *Whop!* I can't be myself till the world is free of you! *Whop! His blow knocks the* INTERVIEWER *to his knees.* I tried and I waited. But all you want is for us to be your slaves! That's all you want! I won't be your slave! *Whop!* I must save myself!

INTERVIEWER, *bubbling, babbling, gurgling, blood-choked sounds!* Oh, god, don't let them kill me! Don't let them kill me! Please don't kill me. *Trying to move away, on his knees.*
6. God ain't gon' answer you—your god is dead!

INTERVIEWER. AAaaaaaaaaaaaaaaaaaaalp! Please, god!
6. Understand how it feels to be beaten! *Whop!* Understand how it feels to beg! *Whop!* Understand how it feels to hope when there's no hope! *Whop!* So many of us died waiting and hoping! Placing faith in your lies and promises! So many of us never ever had reason to hope! They shoulda been doing this! *Whop!* Understand how it feels to have your life taken from you! *WHAM!* There's no hope for you! There's no hope for you now!

He strikes again just as the phone rings. He pulls the desk in front of the apparently dead body. He puts his instrument back into the case. The phone continues to ring. He hurries to leave and bumps into a young man entering.

7. Oh! Excuse me! Is anybody here?
6. There's no one here! There's no one here!
7, *looking around.* Must be out to lunch! I guess I'll wait. I don't have anything to do. And I need a job, bad!

6 exits. 7 stands waiting.

Curtain.

Recorded music: Charlie Parker's "Now is the Time."

What do you think?

1. What reasons can you give for the playwright casting a white person as the personnel interviewer in a project designed for Negroes?
2. The interviewer assures Mary that they'll try to find her a job doing the things she likes: cooking and sewing. Does your concept of the function of a job agency include this kind of consideration? Mention other functions that are, in your opinion, of equal or greater importance.
3. What explanations can you give for the interviewer changing the manner in which he refers to the applicants. That is, in his second speech he uses the word "us" in talking to Mary, whereas, he uses "you" in his response to Black Nigger. Is he trying to accomplish different ends in each case? What might they be?
4. What special significance do you find in the fact that Black Nigger kills the interviewer with a musical instrument?
5. Comment by explaining why you agree or disagree with each of these remarks made by Black Nigger:
   (a) "All niggers should be doing this." (page 136)
   (b) "You've turned us wrongside out!" (page 136)
   (c) "You forced me into this role." (page 136)
6. Explain why you think that any or each or none of the statements above expresses the *central idea of the play.*

Suggestions for writing and listening

1. At one point the interviewer states that "black nationalists" make things worse. Argue for or against this point of view in a paper (1000 words). It will be useful to make clear at the beginning of your paper exactly what kind of person you consider a "black nationalist."
2. Rewrite the play segment in which the interviewer interacts with Black Nigger. Concentrate on the speeches of the interviewer; try to make them more sensitive and informed, so that the play ends without the interviewer being murdered. That is, permit the play to end in an open-ended fashion.
3. Explain in a fairly lengthy paper (1500 words) the logic or senselessness in Black Nigger's statement, "We want our freedom and all you offer is jobs and integration."
4. "Ain't No Ambulances for No Nigguhs Tonight" (Flying Dutchman: FDS 105) combines music and poetry reading in a recording that discusses the effects of contacts between Afro-Americans and whites. Available from Flying Dutchman Productions, 65 W. 55th Street, New York, N.Y.

THE LIMITS OF WALTER HORTON

John Seymour Sharnik

One Sunday morning, led to the piano by an unexplainable impulse, Walter Horton sat down and played the whole of the Chopin B minor sonata. The performance was quite flawless from the standpoint of both technique and interpretation. It was otherwise remarkable in that Horton had never played the piano before in his life.

Until that moment, as a matter of fact, he wasn't aware that he was capable of playing *any* sort of musical instrument. Nor had he ever felt the slightest desire to do so. He listened to music only when waiting for the hourly news summary on the radio, and then with no more effect than if the program had been, say, a speech to some Indonesian patriotic group in their native tongue.

The presence of the piano in the Horton household was his wife's responsibility: ever since their marriage, nine years before, she had talked about resuming the music lessons she had discontinued when she was sixteen. Walter himself was indifferent to his wife's unfulfilled intentions and to the instrument itself. He considered it more or less in the category of furniture, an article that filled a certain space in the living room of their apartment—about as adequately and not much more expensively than a cabinet and a couple of occasional chairs might have done.

When Mrs. Horton discovered that the music was not, as she had assumed, coming from the radio, she was dumfounded. Her husband's explanation of the performance was hardly plausible—if it was an explanation at all.

"I don't know, dear," he said. "I just woke up this morning with a kind of hankering to play the thing. I came in and started to run my hands over the whatchamacallit—"

"The keyboard," she supplied, patiently.

He nodded. "The keyboard. And . . . well. . . ." shrugged.

Mrs. Horton turned and went back to fixing breakfast. If her husband had known how to play the piano all these years, or if he had learned quite recently, why had he made such a point of secrecy? It occurred to her that he might have been nurturing, through the years of their marriage, some inarticulate and peculiarly male resentment of her own musical interests, modest as they were. Now, perhaps, she was being made the victim of a grim attrition, such as quiet and self-contained men are sometimes given to. She felt a twinge of guilt through the quavers of uncertainty.

Craftily, yet sympathetically, she asked, as she set down her husband's orange juice, "What else can you play, dear?"

Horton looked up at her with an expression of surprise. Still absorbed as he was in the phenomenon that had just taken place, the question hadn't even occurred to him. The truth was that he didn't even know what he had played—neither that the music was Chopin's nor, much less, that it was a particular sonata keyed in B minor.

When he tried to explain this, his wife turned, tight-lipped with bafflement, and left the room. Horton lazily left the table, returned to the piano, and amused himself the rest of the morning with the Mozart *Sonata in C,* the *Fireworks* prelude of Debussy and some Liszt waltzes.

Although the music itself meant little to him, he was quite charmed with his suddenly acquired talent, and the next day he postponed going to his office until he had run through two or three Chopin études and a Brahms capriccio. The day after that he stayed home from the office altogether and spent the entire morning and much of the afternoon at the piano. He was almost reluctant to leave it at all, for fear that by the time he returned, his strangely bestowed gift would have been lost.

But there was no apparent diminution of his powers. If anything, he seemed to play more and more prolifically. Each phrase was perfectly formed at his touch. He never repeated himself; in fact, he seemed to be quite incapable of doing so. The music passed through him as if on some endless recording tape. Once he had played any composition, it was lost to time, his part in it having been achieved.

One day, after a few weeks, Mrs. Horton came home in midafternoon from a shopping trip to find him at the piano. It had become almost the only place she ever saw him. Leaving her packages on the bench in the foyer, she went over and gave him a wifely kiss on the forehead, suppressing her anxiety at finding him home so early. He glanced up at her with an abstracted smile.

Hanging up her coat, her eyes lingering sadly on her husband's spare, square-shouldered form, she noticed how much of a studious, preoccupied cast had overtaken his features. She could almost have believed that she had been living with a stranger—a man bearing an amazing superficial resemblance to her husband but another person beneath the sharply drawn lines of his face and behind the familiar gray eyes.

She straightened herself and said in a tone as briskly matter-of-fact as she could summon, "It's nice to see you home so early, dear."

"Hm?" Horton's voice drifted dreamily through the measured tones of a Bach sonata.

"I said you're home early." She couldn't seem to control the waver in her throat. "An easy day at the office?"

"Oh. Yes." His fingers rested quietly on the last chord. He straightened up, then leaned back on the piano bench. "I'm through with it. I'm selling out."

Mrs. Horton felt the ground shift dangerously beneath her feet. His business had come to represent what little was left of normality, of contact with the past, in their life, and she felt desperately that it must be defended. She began gently, then more and more excitedly, to try to dissuade him.

"But," he answered blandly, "it isn't as if I were giving us up to poverty. We have no debts, we've got a bit in the bank, and. . . . Anyway, you always used to say you hoped some day I'd be able to shake free of the office and retire—"

"Retire, yes," she interrupted bitterly. "But at your age it's . . . why, it's almost indecent. And to give yourself up to such—such whimsical nonsense as this!"

"I really don't see what difference it makes," said Horton. "After all, most men find some other interest when they leave their business. Fishing, or stamp collecting—something of the sort."

Mrs. Horton realized helplessly that her argument was futile. The sounds of the piano, echoing magnificently through the house—now in the rich, dramatic periods of Beethoven, now in the delicate traceries of Couperin or Lully—became more and more infuriating, seemed to fill an ever-widening distance between her and her husband.

Since Horton had been one of the most prominent young members of the town's business community, his retirement evoked more than a little interest. It was understood that he had decided to devote himself to music. This came to the attention of the music critic of the local paper—a man named Farley Gresham.

Gresham was a grave, solitary man who lived restlessly with the knowledge of his own failure. As a would-be composer, he had never succeeded in persuading any musician or conductor that his work was worth a public hearing. The job he'd settled for as a music critic neither satisfied his ambitions nor impressed his neighbors. Consequently, he was always somewhat on the defensive in the community and always on the watch for a possible ally.

Gresham paid a call on Horton one evening, heard what he later referred to as "an absolutely unsurpassed rendering of the *Appassionata,*" and was struck with the inescapable fact that he had discovered a prodigy—one of rather advanced age, as the species goes, but unmistakably a prodigy.

"My dear man," Gresham said, almost tearful with gratitude for the opportunity to patronize, "my dear man, such a talent mustn't be kept concealed. You've got to give a recital."

Horton was startled. He began to protest. "Really, I'm not interested—"

"You owe it to the audience," Gresham insisted. "You owe it to music." He made a gesture of finality. "I'll make the arrangements."

Although he was genuinely taken aback and even a little awe-struck at first by the idea of performing in public, Horton could see no reason, after all, for opposing the project. Then he began to think of the audience—his neighbors, the friends for whom he was able to spare less and less attention. The idea of appearing among them in a new and special guise began to amuse him and finally it excited him. He asked his wife what she thought of the idea, but didn't even hear her weak objections. He stood looking across the music rack, over the top of the piano, into the mirror, picturing himself in white tie and stiff shirt on the auditorium stage, and didn't even notice the trail of muffled tears that his wife left on her way to the bedroom.

The selection of a program, of course, presented something of a difficulty, since Horton didn't know the names of compositions or their composers, nor was he able to predict beforehand what he might play at any given time. He didn't want to try to explain this to Gresham because he knew it would seem ridiculous, if not utterly insane, so he was merely evasive. Gresham shrugged off Horton's reluctance to commit himself as evidence of temperament that merely proved the presence of the artist in Horton. At any rate, he didn't want to press his protégé for fear of losing him, so he arranged the recital without any announcement of the program.

The performance attracted a sizable crowd, most of whom came out of neighborly pride, interest, and curiosity. But among them also were a few well placed city critics and reputable musicians whom Gresham, through his connections in the field, had persuaded to attend. They were, of course, overwhelmed by the quality of Horton's performance and the taste with which his program of Clementi, Chopin, Bartók, and Szymanowski had been "selected." "A discreet combination of scholarship and catholicity," one of the critics remarked in his column the next morning, "performed with faultless judgment and incredible technique."

With this encouragement, Gresham arranged a recital in New York. It proved equally successful. The reviews made considerable point of Horton's unique unprofessional background, and this, along with the unanimously laudatory tone of the reviews, earned him a good deal of publicity. The result was a flood of offers for further engagements.

Within a few months, it became obvious that the only way to satisfy the demands of Horton's public was to send him on a nationwide tour. Gresham took care of the arrangements, and the day the last of the signed contracts arrived in the mail, he walked into the office of his managing editor and, with an air of exhilaration slightly fortified by a self-congratulatory drink, quit his job on the paper. His association with Horton had brought him closer to musical glory than his reviews of orchestra road concerts and performances by the students of the local music school ever had. It also promised to bring him more money than he'd made out of his newspaper job and—who could tell?—perhaps the inspiration, and later the leisure, for another, mature attempt to establish a place for himself in the world of music as a composer.

So, with Gresham as his manager and with Mrs. Horton trailing helplessly but devotedly in his wake, Horton undertook a series of recitals whose uniform brilliance reduced Rubinstein, Horowitz, Arrau, and Gieseking to second rank among modern keyboard musicians. Horton's continued reluctance to announce his programs beforehand aroused some comment at first but, as with Gresham, it was dismissed —if not respected—as an artistic whim.

Attempts were made by the New York Philharmonic and the Boston Symphony to engage Horton as a guest soloist, but of course he was obliged to reject them in view of the fact that he couldn't commit himself to any particular piece of music and it was unlikely that what he played would coincide with what the orchestra was playing. This elusiveness made Horton's services even more attractive. His insistence on playing only works written for the solo instrument even added to his prestige as an artist of intense conviction and integrity.

Mrs. Horton, by now feeling hopelessly out of contact with her husband, had long since given up her struggle to restore him—and their marriage—to the normality of his premusical life. But once, quite by accident, she was given a chance to attack this monstrous change with a new weapon. She was being interviewed, between concert tours, by a woman reporter on her role as the wife of an internationally famous artist.

"I suppose," said the reporter sympathetically, "you feel rewarded for the years of struggle and pain you and your husband must have suffered while he was preparing for his career?"

"Struggle?" Mrs. Horton began to laugh hollowly, then broke off with a gasp. In a moment, she found herself telling for the first time Horton's version of how he had learned to play the piano.

The reporter, assuming that Mrs. Horton was either a wanderer in some mental fourth dimension or was elaborately trying to ridicule her, naturally checked the story with Gresham before doing anything so foolish as putting it on paper.

Gresham, when she broke in on him with her question, was in the midst of a kind of transformation of his own. He had had a month of freedom since Horton's last tour, and in this time he had begun—tentatively, doubtfully—to resume the work he had promised himself he would one day return to. He had spent the whole month at a composition of his own—a sonata based on a simple but strangely magnetic theme that had attached itself to his mind years before but that he had been fearful of trying to capture and reconstruct on paper. But now it flowed from his pen exactly as he had imagined it all those years.

Gresham tossed aside the sheaf of staff paper he was writing on and gave the reporter a generous smile. He listened to her story and, naturally, laughed it off extravagantly. "I've heard Mrs. Horton tell that gag in the company of some of the country's greatest artists," he said, "and you know, my dear, she almost had them believing it. Why, Graustein himself—the magnificent Graustein—sat down on the floor and wept because he'd been practicing nine hours a day since he was knee-high to a cello and hadn't acquired half the technique that—to hear Mrs. Horton tell it—Horton had acquired overnight. Of course, Mrs. Horton was horrified to think Graustein believed her—nearly died of shame." He shook his head admiringly. "Incredible sense of humor that woman has."

The story, of course, never appeared in the papers. It did not fail to impress Gresham, however. For some time, he'd been taking notice of the amazing variety of Horton's programs. He'd noticed also that Horton's refusal to repeat a composition applied not only to his public performances but even to the most casual frittering away of time at the piano in his own living room.

Thinking back over the period of their association, Gresham could not recall having heard Horton play any single composition, nor even so much as a single passage, more than once. Furthermore, he had been struck by a rather odd development in the character of Horton's recent programs. More and more they tended toward the obscure and pedantic—the lesser known compositions of the masters and the works of half-forgotten composers. Just recently, Horton had performed a suite that was unfamiliar even to the *avant-garde* among the reviewers, and a number of them had assumed that it was an original work. Horton, characteristically, had refused either to confirm or deny that he had written the suite—it was widely known and accepted that Horton never deigned to discuss what he had played any more than he'd announce what he was going to play—so the assumption had gone unchallenged. To Gresham the thing had sounded like something by Scriabin. That is, he would have said Scriabin, except that to his knowledge Scriabin had never written any such work. Gresham decided to do a little research.

It took him almost a month to establish that the suite was indeed a work of Scriabin. He traced it to a manuscript in a university music-library collection, but he was puzzled by the curator's insistence that the composition had never been published, nor even previously performed.

Gresham began to wonder seriously about Mrs. Horton's story. Not that the events she'd described to the reporter were the important thing. Even if one accepted Horton's rare talent as the purest sort of inspiration, that didn't explain what was happening. It occurred to Gresham that perhaps he'd been witnessing some phenomenon even more fantastic—a phenomenon that even Horton himself wasn't fully aware of.

Was it possible, Gresham asked himself, that all of the best of music—the greatest works of the whole historical field of musical creation—was being transmitted through Horton, each single work achieving through him its perfect, its ultimate, form? If that were true, then through what accident or what cruel irony had he been selected as its pure instrument? And what were the limits of this process? Time? History itself? Indeed, were there limits at all? Gresham found himself jealous, appalled, shaken with awe and apprehension.

One evening, several months after these questions had first occurred to him, Gresham was seated at the small piano in the study of Horton's New York apartment, snatching a few moment's work at his own manuscript while waiting to see Horton about some details of his next performance. He felt a sense of exhilaration, for he was nearing the end of the sonata now and he had as yet found no reason to give it up. He almost dared to hope it might be worth trying to persuade some young pianist to perform it at one of those small down-town recitals sponsored by groups of experimental-minded amateurs of the arts.

At the large piano in the living room, while Mrs. Horton sat trying to absorb herself in a detective novel, Horton was playing the final movement of one of Prokofiev's recent works. There was a pause as the final, perfectly struck chords of the allegretto died away, and then Horton began to play something else. As the music drifted in through the door of the study, Gresham became aware that the composition was one which he himself had listened to on a television concert only the night before. It was a fantasia by a young California composer named Shorrer. The puzzling thing about it was that it had been introduced on the television show as the first performance of a new work.

It was possible, of course, that Horton himself had heard it and that his ability to repeat it now—note for note, Gresham would have sworn—could be attributed to a hypersensitive musical memory.

But no. Gresham brought himself erect with a start. Horton had been on the stage at Carnegie Hall at the very time Shorrer's work was being performed on television. He couldn't possibly have heard the composition before. Gresham's pencil dropped from his quivering fingers. He arose from his piano, his mind paralyzed by the enormity of what had happened and by the apprehension of what might happen next. He paced the floor of the study, unable to transmit to paper the concluding phrases of his own work which lay, totally formed, in the recesses of his brain. Horton, he knew, had exhausted the past; he had caught up with his own time.

The next evening Gresham stood in the wings of the concert hall as Horton strode across the stage, acknowledged his applause with a nod, and seated himself briskly at the piano. As his fingers poised over the keyboard, a gasp of expectation escaped Gresham's tightened lips.

Horton struck a series of brilliant chords, which dissolved into a delicate and poignant melody. Gradually, it subsided into a throbbing echo, low and ominous, as a new theme developed against it. The counterpoint became more and more intense, mounted to a delirious climax, then fell to a whisper from which issued the slow and ghostly theme of a new movement.

The beauty of his own sonata was almost painful to Gresham and he was so transported by it that it was minutes before he realized that he was witnessing Horton's transition from the past into the immediate present.

As he listened almost hypnotically to the mathematical symbols that he had so painfully written materializing into exquisite sound at Horton's touch, Gresham felt a surge of triumph. For to have been transmitted through Horton—didn't this mean that the sonata had been given a place, alongside all the other works which the pianist had unwittingly performed, in the history of great music? Tears of fulfillment and gratitude began to dim Gresham's eyes.

Then, almost as quickly as it had risen in him, triumph began to ebb. For the whispers among the few other onlookers in the wings and the excited glances in the front rows of the audience told him something that he hardly dared to believe but knew he must face: The sonata would be credited to Horton! And Horton, he knew, would never disown it! Nor could anyone deprive him of it—except by explaining the truth that was too fantastic, too obviously an insane figment of jealousy, to be believed.

Gresham started away in disappointment, but one thought consoled him and drew him back. For he had not given the whole of his work to Horton after all. The sonata was unfinished—its concluding passages had not yet been committed to form but existed only as ideas which lay unwritten in Gresham's mind. And when Horton, having exhausted both past and present, reached the boundaries of the future—what could he do? Gresham stood waiting, a bitter smile on his lips.

He listened as the music rolled to a thunderous climax. Horton's hands hung over the keyboard, gestured uncertainly and fell. The echo of a chord faded into the excruciating silence of the hall.

Gresham felt a quick lift of hope, which turned in the same instant to horror, as Horton's hands fluttered, then inexorably returned to the keyboard. The knowledge struck Gresham sickeningly that he would no more be able to stop himself from creating such music than he could stop Horton from playing it as his own, and he thought of all the years of music that would pour, as quickly as he conceived it, from his own mind into Horton's waiting fingers.

Transfixed and helpless, he stood listening as the music resumed and Horton played the concluding bars of the sonata.

What do you think?

1. How is your opinion of Walter Horton affected when he first postpones going to work, then doesn't go at all, in order to play the piano?
   (a) In general, do you consider practicing or performing on a musical instrument a form of work? Why or why not? Is it, in the words of Mrs. Horton, "whimsical nonsense"? Explain.
2. We're told that Farley Gresham settled on being a music critic once he realized that he couldn't be a successful composer. What is your opinion of a person who compromises in this fashion? Is he a failure in any sense?
3. Gresham attributes Walter Horton's refusal to announce what compositions he will perform to artistic temperament. Do you recognize a stereotype in operation? Is there any truth to it? Who benefits most from perpetuation of the stereotype? Comment in some detail.
4. How would you describe Mrs. Horton's relationship to her husband? Support your description by outlining her behavior throughout the story. What stereotype of feminine behavior does she fit?
5. What reasons can you give for Gresham's dismissing Mrs. Horton's honest explanation for her husband's mastery of the piano? Be prepared to defend your reasons.
6. In your own words, explain exactly what Walter Horton's limits are. In the light of your response, would you consider this story comic? Tragic? Science fiction? Give reasons for your answer.
7. Does the theme of the story violate a sense of fairness which is basic to American values, that is, that men should *earn* fame and fortune? For example, how would you describe the general attitude toward persons who inherit large sums of money or positions of power? If the truth about Walter Horton's ability to perform were widely known, speculate on how it would affect his reputation. Why?
8. What is your explanation for the fact that we learn very little about *how* Walter Horton felt about what was happening to and through him? Did he appear to change in any significant ways? Support your opinion by explaining what you consider "significant."

Suggestions for research and writing

1. Farley Gresham can serve as a model for the phenomenon of persons who aspire to be in one profession but switch to another out of fear of failure or because of actual failure to achieve. What are other professions that are traditionally considered second choice and what were the first choices in each case? Confer with friends and your family in order to make your list as exhaustive as possible.
2. Look up the word "work" in a collegiate dictionary and in a specialized one such as *The Encyclopedia of the Social Sciences.* Would Walter Horton's practicing come under the heading of work? Would it be considered as work in other cultures such as those of the American Indian?
3. Crucial to Walter Horton's success as a performing artist is the willingness of his public and the critics to provide their own romantic explanations for his irregular behavior. Write a short paper (500 words) in which you speculate on why they do this. Then make some general observations about other instances in which the public explains (rather than honestly tries to analyze and understand) a particular person and his behavior or a group and its behavior.

LAGOD JUST AN AMATEUR ON SCENT OF PRO JACKPOT

Marvin Weinstein

Jerome Lagod is an amateur in a world of professionals. He's confident he has a place there.

Lagod, a 30-year-old mechanical engineer from Barrington, is an amateur sports car racer who is determined to make his mark with the professional U.S. Auto Club and the Trans-American Sedan series, one of the pro branches of the Sports Car Club of America.

Racing is a hobby right now for Lagod, but he admits he'd like nothing better than to race full time.

"I've always been interested in racing," Lagod said. "I started in drag racing. After I got out of school I became interested in sports car racing and built a couple of modifieds for club races."

That changed look

After three years of sports car competition, "I purchased a 1968 Camaro, completely reassembled the car and built it into a Trans-Am racer. It took me a year."

Last year Lagod won his division title for A Sedans in the SCCA world, earning him a berth in the nationals at Daytona Speedway in Florida. "Daytona Beach is the fastest I've ever driven," he recalled. "I was clocked at 178 m.p.h. in the traps." He finished third nationally.

This year he hopes to run all the Midwest Trans-Am races, plus the USAC road course events and some sports car meets.

"I ran the USAC road race in Claremont, Ind., and got sixth place, which isn't too bad considering we were strictly amateurs running against the big boys. We were the first pony car to finish.

"The only USAC races I intend to run are road races. I've never tried ovals but I'd like to."

Lagod is running pro races instead of sports cars because of the cost. "We spend $100 or $125 on a weekend running for nothing. In a pro race if you just qualify you can recover the entry fee. I think anyone who goes into racing to make money is kidding himself."

Preparation and practice are the keys to racing success, Lagod believes.

"Normally, I spend 50 to 100 hours preparing a car for a race. Practice is the most important thing. Just getting out there and running."

Preparation is fun

"My wife and I prepare the car completely ourselves. She's quite a help to me. I think she enjoys the preparation more than the actual races. But I guess she is concerned when I'm on the track."

"I mainly just hand him tools," Linda Lagod demurred. "I just keep him company."

Mrs. Lagod enjoys the excitement of racing and meeting new people. She handles the administrative details for the team. The Lagods have been married 1½ years and have a six-month old son intrusted to the care of grandparents on race weekends.

Linda admits, though, it's not all fun on race day.

"Usually I'm out there with a stopwatch on him. When he's a couple of seconds off on the stopwatch I get kind of worried when I don't see him come around. This is the worst part."

What do you think?

1. Carefully reread the headline. What prejudice is implied in it? Why are you in agreement or not with that prejudice?
2. What are the qualities that distinguish professionals from amateurs? For whom is this division between amateur & professionals most important? Explain why. Are professionals more skilled than amateurs? Name the sports you are referring to in your answer?
3. Is there a contradiction between what we ordinarily mean by the term "job" and the circumstance of a person actually enjoying what he does for a living? Explain your response.
4. If a person can't make money in professional auto racing, why would he continue to do it? What seems to motivate Lagod?
5. Isn't preparation and practice the key to success in *any* sport? Give reasons for your answer.
6. Does the involvement of Mrs. Lagod in racing help or harm their marriage? Explain your answer.

Suggestion for writing

1. Write a short paper in which you compare the unappealing facts (such as spending 50 to 100 hours preparing a car) that lie behind a sports figure's public performance, and the glamorous picture that most people have.

THE HAPPIEST MAN ON EARTH

Albert Maltz

"The Happiest Man on Earth" by Albert Maltz. By permission of Albert Maltz.

Jesse felt ready to weep. He had been sitting in the shanty waiting for Tom to appear, grateful for the chance to rest his injured foot, quietly, joyously anticipating the moment when Tom would say, "Why of course, Jesse, you can start whenever you're ready!"

For two weeks he had been pushing himself, from Kansas City, Missouri, to Tulsa, Oklahoma, through nights of rain and a week of scorching sun, without sleep or a decent meal, sustained by the vision of that one moment. And then Tom had come into the office. He had come in quickly, holding a sheaf of papers in his hand; he had glanced at Jesse only casually, it was true—but long enough. He had not known him. He had turned away. . . . And Tom Brackett was his brother-in-law.

Was it his clothes? Jesse knew he looked terrible. He had tried to spruce up at a drinking fountain in the park, but even that had gone badly; in his excitement he had cut himself shaving, an ugly gash down the side of his cheek. And nothing could get the red gumbo dust out of his suit even though he had slapped himself till both arms were worn out. . . . Or was it just that he *had* changed so much?

True, they hadn't seen each other for five years; but Tom looked five years older, that was all. He was still Tom. God! was *he* so different?

Brackett finished his telephone call. He leaned back in his swivel chair and glanced over at Jesse with small, clear blue eyes that were suspicious and unfriendly. He was a heavy, paunchy man of forty-five, auburn-haired, rather dour looking; his face was meaty, his features pronounced and forceful, his nose somewhat bulbous and reddish-hued at the tip. He looked like a solid, decent, capable business man who was commander of his local branch of the American Legion—which he was. He surveyed Jesse with cold indifference, manifestly unwilling to spend time on him. Even the way he chewed his toothpick seemed contemptuous to Jesse.

"Yes?" Brackett said suddenly. "What do you want?"

Elihu M. Williams

His voice was decent enough, Jesse admitted. He had expected it to be worse. He moved up to the wooden counter that partitioned the shanty. He thrust a hand nervously through his tangled hair.

"I guess you don't recognize me, Tom," he said falteringly, "I'm Jesse Fulton."

"Huh?" Brackett said. That was all.

"Yes, I am, and Ella sends you her love."

Brackett rose and walked over to the counter until they were face to face. He surveyed Fulton incredulously, trying to measure the resemblance to his brother-in-law as he remembered him. This man was tall, about thirty. That fitted! He had straight good features and a lank erect body. That was right too. But the face was too gaunt, the body too spiny under the baggy clothes for him to be sure. His brother-in-law had been a solid, strong young man with muscle and beef to him. It was like looking at a faded, badly taken photograph and trying to recognize the subject: the resemblance was there but the difference was tremendous. He searched the eyes. They at least seemed definitely familiar, gray, with a curiously shy but decent look in them. He had liked that about Fulton.

Jesse stood quiet. Inside he was seething. Brackett was like a man examining a piece of broken-down horse fiesh; there was a look of pure pity in his eyes. It made Jesse furious. He knew he wasn't as far gone as all that.

"Yes, I believe you are," Brackett said finally, "but you sure have changed."

"By God, it's five years, ain't it?" Jesse said resentfully. "You only saw me a couple of times anyway." Then, to himself, with his lips locked together, in mingled vehemence and shame, What if I have changed? Don't everybody? I ain't no corpse.

"You was solid looking," Brackett continued softly, in the same tone of incredulous wonder. "You lost weight, I guess?"

Jesse kept silent. He needed Brackett too much to risk antagonizing him. But it was only by deliberate effort that he could keep from boiling over. The pause lengthened, became painful. Brackett flushed. "Jiminy Christmas, excuse me," he burst out in apology. He jerked the counter up. "Come in. Take a seat. Good God, boy"—he grasped Jesse's hand and shook it—"I *am* glad to see you; don't think anything else! You just looked so peaked."

"It's all right," Jesse murmured. He sat down, thrusting his hand through his curly, tangled hair.

"Why are you limping?"

"I stepped on a stone; it jagged a hole through my shoe." Jesse pulled his feet back under the chair. He was ashamed of his shoes. They had come from the Relief originally, and two weeks on the road had about finished them. All morning, with a kind of delicious, foolish solemnity, he had been vowing to himself that before anything else, before even a suit of clothes, he was going to buy himself a brand new strong pair of shoes.

Bracket kept his eyes off Jesse's feet. He knew what was bothering the boy and it filled his heart with pity. The whole thing was appalling. He had never seen anyone who looked more down and out. His sister had been writing to him every week, but she hadn't told him they were as badly off as this.

"Well now, listen," Brackett began, "tell me things. How's Ella?"

"Oh, she's pretty good," Jesse replied absently. He had a soft, pleasing, rather shy voice that went with his soft gray eyes. He was worrying over how to get started.

"And the kids?"

"Oh, they're fine. . . . Well, you know," Jesse added, becoming more attentive, "the young one has to wear a brace. He can't run around, you know. But he's smart. He draws pictures and he does things, you know."

"Yes," Brackett said. "That's good." He hesitated. There was a moment's silence. Jesse fidgeted in his chair. Now that the time had arrived, he felt awkward. Brackett leaned forward and put his hand on Jesse's knee. "Ella didn't tell me things were so bad for you, Jesse. I might have helped."

"Well, goodness," Jesse returned softly, "you been having your own troubles, ain't you?"

"Yes." Brackett leaned back. His ruddy face became mournful and darkly bitter. "You know I lost my hardware shop?"

"Well sure, of course," Jesse answered, surprised. "You wrote us. That's what I mean."

"I forgot," Brackett said. "I keep on being surprised over it myself. Not that it was worth much," he added bitterly. "It was running down hill for three years. I guess I just wanted it because it was mine." He laughed pointlessly, without mirth. "Well tell me about yourself," he asked. "What happened to the job you had?"

Jesse burst out abruptly, with agitation, "Let it wait, Tom, I got something on my mind."

"It ain't you and Ella?" Brackett interrupted anxiously.

"Why no!" Jesse sat back. "Why however did you come to think that? Why Ella and me—" he stopped, laughing. "Why, Tom, I'm just crazy about Ella. Why she's just wonderful. She's just my whole life, Tom."

"Excuse me. Forget it." Brackett chuckled uncomfortably, turned away. The naked intensity of the youth's burst of love had upset him. It made him wish savagely that he could do something for them. They were both too decent to have had it so hard. Ella was like this boy too, shy and a little soft.

"Tom, listen," Jesse said, "I come here on purpose." He thrust his hand through his hair. "I want you to help me."

"Damn it, boy," Brackett groaned. He had been expecting this. "I can't much. I only get thirty-five a week and I'm damn grateful for it."

"Sure, I know," Jesse emphasized excitedly. He was feeling once again the wild, delicious agitation that had possessed him in the early hours of the morning. "I know you can't help us with money! But we met a man who works for you! He was in our city! He said you could give me a job!"

"Who said?"

"Oh, why didn't you tell me?" Jesse burst out reproachfully. "Why as soon as I heard it I started out. For two weeks now I been pushing ahead like crazy."

Brackett groaned aloud. "You come walking from Kansas City in two weeks so I could give you a job?"

"Sure, Tom, of course. What else could I do?"

"God Almighty, there ain't no jobs, Jesse! It's a slack season. And you don't know this oil business. It's special. I got my Legion friends here but they couldn't do nothing now. Don't you think I'd ask for you as soon as there was a chance?"

Jesse felt stunned. The hope of the last two weeks seemed rolling up into a ball of agony in his stomach. Then, frantically, he cried, "But listen, this man said *you* could hire! He *told* me! He drives trucks for you! He said you *always* need men!"

"Oh! . . . You mean *my* department?" Brackett said in a low voice.

"*Yes,* Tom. That's it!"

"Oh, no, you don't want to work in my department," Brackett told him in the same low voice. "You don't know what it is."

"Yes, I do," Jesse insisted. "He told me all about it, Tom. You're a dispatcher, ain't you? You send the dynamite trucks out?"

"Who was the man, Jesse?"

"Everett, Everett, I think."

"Egbert? Man about my size?" Brackett asked slowly.

"Yes, Egbert. He wasn't a phony, was he?"

Brackett laughed. For the second time his laughter was curiously without mirth. "No, he wasn't a phony." Then, in a changed voice: "Jiminy, boy, you should have asked me before you trekked all the way down here."

"Oh, I didn't want to," Jesse explained with naïve cunning. "I knew you'd say 'no.' He told me it was risky work, Tom. But I don't care."

Brackett locked his fingers together. His solid, meaty face became very hard. "I'm going to say 'no' anyway, Jesse."

Jesse cried out. It had not occurred to him that Brackett would not agree. It had seemed as though reaching Tulsa were the only problem he had to face. "Oh, no," he begged, "you can't. Ain't there any jobs, Tom?"

"Sure, there's jobs. There's even Egbert's job if you want it."

"He's quit?"

"He's dead!"

"Oh!"

"On the job, Jesse. Last night if you want to know."

"Oh!" . . . Then, "I don't care!"

"Now you listen to me," Brackett said. "I'll tell you a few things that you should have asked before you started out. It ain't dynamite you drive. They don't use anything as safe as dynamite in drilling oil wells. They wish they could, but they can't. It's nitroglycerin! Soup!"

"But I know," Jesse told him reassuringly. "He advised me, Tom. You don't have to think I don't know."

"Shut up a minute," Brackett ordered angrily. "Listen! You just have to *look* at this soup, see? You just *cough* loud and it blows! You know how they transport it? In a can that's shaped like this, see, like a fan? That's to give room for compartments, because each compartment has to be lined with rubber. That's the only way you can even *think* of handling it."

"Listen, Tom—"

"Now wait a minute, Jesse. For God's sake just put your mind to this. I know you had your heart set on a job, but you've got to understand. This stuff goes only in special trucks! At night! They got to follow a special route! They can't go through any city! If they lay over, it's got to be in a special garage! Don't you see what that means? Don't that tell you how dangerous it is?"

"I'll drive careful," Jesse said. "I know how to handle a truck. I'll drive slow."

Brackett groaned. "Do you think Egbert didn't drive careful or know how to handle a truck?"

"Tom," Jesse said earnestly, "you can't scare me. I got my mind fixed on only one thing: Egbert said he was getting a dollar a mile. He was making five to six hundred dollars a month for a half a month's work, he said. Can I get the same?"

"Sure, you can get the same," Brackett told him savagely. "A dollar a mile. It's easy. But why do you think the company has to pay so much? It's easy—until you run over a stone that your headlights didn't pick out, like Egbert did. Or get a blowout! Or get something in your eye, so the wheel twists and you jar the truck! Or any other God damn thing that nobody ever knows! We can't ask Egbert what happened to him. There's no truck to give any evidence. There's no corpse. There's nothing! Maybe tomorrow somebody'll find a piece of twisted steel way off in a cornfield. But we never find the driver. Not even a finger nail. All we know is that he don't come in on schedule. Then we wait for the police to call us. You know what happened last night? Something went wrong on the bridge. Maybe Egbert was nervous. Maybe he brushed the side with his fender. Only there's no bridge any more. No truck. No Egbert. Do you understand now? That's what you get for your God damn dollar a mile!"

There was a moment of silence. Jesse sat twisting his long thin hands. His mouth was sagging open, his face was agonized. Then he shut his eyes and spoke softly. "I don't care about that, Tom. You told me. Now you got to be good to me and give me the job."

Brackett slapped the palm of his hand down on his desk. "No!"

"Listen, Tom," Jesse said softly, "you just don't understand." He opened his eyes. They were filled with tears. They made Brackett turn away. "Just look at me, Tom. Don't that tell you enough? What did you think of me when you first saw me? You thought: 'Why don't that bum go away and stop panhandling?' Didn't you, Tom? Tom, I just can't live like this any more. I got to be able to walk down the street with my head up."

"You're crazy," Brackett muttered. "Every year there's one out of five drivers gets killed. That's the average. What's worth that?"

"Is my life worth anything now? We're just starving at home, Tom. They ain't put us back on relief yet."

"Then you should have told me," Brackett exclaimed harshly. "It's your own damn fault. A man has no right to have false pride when his family ain't eating. I'll borrow some money and we'll telegraph it to Ella. Then you go home and get back on relief."

"And then what?"

"And then wait, God damn it! You're no old man. You got no right to throw your life away. Sometime you'll get a job."

"No!" Jesse jumped up. "No. I believed that too. But I don't now," he cried passionately. "I ain't getting a job no more than you're getting your hardware store back. I lost my skill, Tom. Linotyping is skilled work. I'm rusty now. I've been six years on relief. The only work I've had is pick and shovel. When I got that job this spring I was supposed to be an A-1 man. But I wasn't. And they got new machines now. As soon as the slack started they let me out."

"So what?" Brackett said harshly. "Ain't there other jobs?"

"How do I know?" Jesse replied. "There ain't been one for six years. I'd even be afraid to take one now. It's been too hard waiting so many weeks to get back on relief."

"Well you got to have some courage," Brackett shouted. "You've got to keep up hope."

"I got all the courage you want," Jesse retorted vehemently, "but no, I ain't got no hope. The hope has dried up in me in six years' waiting. You're the only hope I got."

"You're crazy," Brackett muttered. "I won't do it. For God's sake think of Ella for a minute."

"Don't you *know* I'm thinking about her?" Jesse asked softly. He plucked at Brackett's sleeve. "That's what decided me, Tom." His voice became muted into a hushed, pained whisper. "The night Egbert was at our house I looked at Ella like I'd seen her for the first time. *She ain't pretty any more, Tom!*" Brackett jerked his head and moved away. Jesse followed him, taking a deep, sobbing breath. "Don't that tell you, Tom? Ella was like a little doll or something, you remember. I couldn't walk down the street without somebody turning to look at her. She ain't twenty-nine yet, Tom, and she ain't pretty no more."

Brackett sat down with his shoulders hunched up wearily. He gripped his hands together and sat leaning forward, staring at the floor.

Jesse stood over him, his gaunt face flushed with emotion, almost unpleasant in its look of pleading and bitter humility. "I ain't done right for Ella, Tom. Ella deserved better. This is the only chance I see in my whole life to do something for her. I've just been a failure."

"Don't talk nonsense," Brackett commented, without rancor. "You ain't a failure. No more than me. There's millions of men in the identical situation. It's just the depression, or the recession, or the God damn New Deal, or . . . !" He swore and lapsed into silence.

"Oh, no," Jesse corrected him, in a knowing, sorrowful tone, "those things maybe excuse other men. But not me. It was up to me to do better. This is my own fault!"

"Oh, beans!" Brackett said. "It's more sun spots than it's you!"

Jesse's face turned an unhealthy mottled red. It looked swollen. "Well, I don't care," he cried wildly. "I don't care! You got to give me this! I got to lift my head up. I went through one stretch of hell but I can't go through another. You want me to keep looking at my little boy's legs and tell myself if I had a job he wouldn't be like that? Every time he walks he says to me, 'I got soft bones from the rickets and you give it to me because you didn't feed me right.' Jesus Christ, Tom, you think I'm going to sit there and watch him like that another six years?"

Brackett leaped to his feet. "So what if you do?" he shouted. "You say you're thinking about Ella. How's she going to like it when you get killed?"

"Maybe I won't," Jesse pleaded. "I've got to have some luck sometime."

"That's what they all think," Brackett replied scornfully. "When you take this job your luck is a question mark. The only thing certain is that sooner or later you get killed."

"Okay then," Jesse shouted back. "Then I do! But meanwhile I got something, don't I? I can buy a pair of shoes. Look at me! I can buy a suit that don't say 'Relief' by the way it fits. I can smoke cigarettes. I can buy some candy for the kids. I can eat some myself. Yes, by God, I want to eat some candy. I want a glass of beer once a day. I want Ella dressed up. I want her to eat meat three times a week, four times maybe. I want to take my family to the movies."

Brackett sat down. "Oh, shut up," he said wearily.

"No," Jesse told him softly, passionately, "you can't get rid of me. Listen, Tom," he pleaded, "I got it all figured out. On six hundred a month look how much I can save! If I last only three months, look how much it is—a thousand dollars—more! And maybe I'll last longer. Maybe a couple years. I can fix Ella up for life!"

"You said it," Brackett interposed. "I suppose you think she'll enjoy living when you're on a job like that?"

"I got it all figured out," Jesse answered excitedly. "She don't know, see? I tell her I make only forty. You put the rest in a bank account for her, Tom."

"Oh, shut up," Brackett said. "You think you'll be happy? Every minute, waking and sleeping, you'll be wondering if tomorrow you'll be dead. And the worst days will be your days off, when you're not driving. They have to give you every other day free to get your nerve back. And you lay around the house eating your heart out. That's how happy you'll be."

Jesse laughed. "I'll be happy! Don't you worry, I'll be so happy, I'll be singing. Lord God, Tom, I'm going to feel *proud* of myself for the first time in seven years!"

"Oh, shut up, shut up," Brackett said.

The little shanty became silent. After a moment Jesse whispered: "You got to, Tom. You got to. You got to."

Again there was silence. Brackett raised both hands to his head, pressing the palms against his temples.

"Tom, Tom—" Jesse said.

Brackett sighed. "Oh, God damn it," he said finally, "all right, I'll take you on, God help me." His voice was low, hoarse, infinitely weary. "If you're ready to drive tonight, you can drive tonight."

Jesse didn't answer. He couldn't. Brackett looked up. The tears were running down Jesse's face. He was swallowing and trying to speak, but only making an absurd, gasping noise.

"I'll send a wire to Ella," Brackett said in the same hoarse, weary voice. "I'll tell her you got a job, and you'll send her fare in a couple of days. You'll have some money then—that is, if you last the week out, you jackass!"

Jesse only nodded. His heart felt so close to bursting that he pressed both hands against it, as though to hold it locked within his breast.

"Come back here at six o'clock," Brackett said. "Here's some money. Eat a good meal."

"Thanks," Jesse whispered.

"Wait a minute," Brackett said. "Here's my address." He wrote it on a piece of paper. "Take any car going that way. Ask the conductor where to get off. Take a bath and get some sleep."

"Thanks," Jesse said. "Thanks, Tom."

"Oh, get out of here," Brackett said.

"Tom."

"What?"

"I just—" Jesse stopped. Brackett saw his face. The eyes were still glistening with tears, but the gaunt face was shining now, with a kind of fierce radiance.

Brackett turned away. "I'm busy," he said.

Jesse went out. The wet film blinded him but the whole world seemed to have turned golden. He limped slowly, with the blood pounding his temples and a wild, incommunicable joy in his heart. "I'm the happiest man in the world," he whispered to himself. "I'm the happiest man on the whole earth."

Brackett sat watching till finally Jesse turned the corner of the alley and disappeared. Then he hunched himself over, with his head in his hands. His heart was beating painfully, like something old and clogged. He listened to it as it beat. He sat in desperate tranquillity, gripping his head in his hands.

What do you think?

1. What significant things do we learn about Brackett or Fulton from the following?
   (a) Brackett's failure to recognize Fulton.
   (b) Fulton's willingness to hitchhike the 214 miles from Kansas City to Tulsa.
   (c) Fulton's growing anger over Brackett's staring at him unbelievingly.
   (d) Fulton's intention to buy a pair of shoes before any other item of clothing.
2. Brackett says that although the hardware store wasn't much and was losing money for three years, ". . . I just wanted it because it was mine." Is this an unusual reason for wanting to own something? What are the advantages and disadvantages of owning a small business such as a hardware store? List as many as possible.
3. Brackett admits that they don't know how Egbert was killed. Yet in explaining how accidents happen he says, "It's easy—until you run over a stone that your headlights didn't pick out, like Egbert did." Which story is true? What might motivate Brackett to tell the latter story?
4. Do you believe Jesse's story about why he and his family were on relief? Is he merely making excuses or has he done everything possible to support them? What clues in the story do you base your answer on?
5. Jesse describes himself as hopeless. Are there other characters in this book whom you would describe that way? What about the businessmen in the cartoon on page 116? Why or why not? Is the state of hopelessness the worse state a person can be in? Explain your answer.
6. Brackett denies that Jesse is a personal failure, explaining that the circumstances in the country are the reason for his being out of work. What is your opinion of his explanation? Are people sometimes *not* responsible for the painful situations they get into? Explain.
7. Isn't it presumptuous for anyone to call himself the "happiest man in the world"? What do we learn about Jesse when he describes himself that way?
8. Do the names of the three men—Egbert, Fulton, and Brackett—fit their personalities or situations? Explain your answer.
9. Later in their conversation, Brackett implies that if business were better he might be able to get him a nontruck-driving job because his Legion friends are in the oil business. Is the practice of hiring friends a common one? Is it fair to the friends? Is it fair to the person who has the skills and motivation but isn't a friend?
10. The story can be described as *ironic* in feeling. What does that term mean? Why is it suitable?

Suggestions for reading and writing

1. The system of relief is mentioned in the story. Relief may be called something different in your community. Check any newspaper or magazine articles you can find on the system to discover whether a Jesse Fulton could have been removed from its rolls because he found a job but then could not be reinstated when he and his family were starving. In class discussion, share with the class any unfair features (inflexibility, unreasonable stipulations, and so on) that the relief system in your community has.
2. Question 6 raises the problem of how responsible we are for the situations we sometimes find ourselves in. Write a short paper (500 words) in which you describe a situation in which you can point to other factors or persons who were primarily responsible for its development.
3. Write a short paper (500 words) in which you explain just how much control a person has over his own life. Give concrete examples wherever possible to support your explanation.
4. The lengths or depths to which desperation can drive a person are not always as dramatic as what we witness in this story. Have you heard of an experience or suffered through one that was motivated by desperation? If so, write a paper (1000 words) describing the experience. Be certain to make clear how the person you describe was forced to act in a desperate fashion.

Burk Uzzle/Magnum Photos

BROWN EYED CHILDREN OF THE SUN

Pedro Contreras

Up to California from Mexico you come,
to the Sacramento Valley to toil in the sun.
Your wife and seven children, they're workin', every one;
and what will you be givin' to your brown eyed children of the sun.

Your face is lined and wrinkled and your age is 41.
Your back is bent from picking, like your dying time has come.
Your childrens' eyes are smiling, their life is just begun;
and what will you be givin' to your brown eyed children of the sun?

You are bending and you're picking with your back and your arms in pain;
Your wife and seven children they never do complain.
"Oh Jesus, can't you help us, can't you shade us from this sun?"
and what will you be givin' to your brown eyed children of the sun?

Your hands can feel the soil as you're working in the field;
You can feel the richness in it, you can see the crops it yields.
You're tired and you're hungry and your day is almost done,
and what will you be givin' to your brown eyed children of the sun?

You have marched on Easter Sunday, to the capital you came;
and you've fought for union wages and your fight has just begun.
You are proud men and you're free men and this heritage is one
that you can be givin' to your brown eyed children of the sun.

Pedro Contreras
La Guardia
June, 1970
Vol. 1, No. 6

La Burrdia Ltd.
805 South Fifth Street
Milwaukee, Wisconsin
53204

What do you think?

1. The physical description of the father could easily fit someone considerably older. What explanations can you provide for his early aging?
2. How do you account for the fact that the first observation in the poem about a positive feature has to do with the soil? In what way is this in keeping with the orientation of the subjects of the poem?
3. In what sense are the men in the poem enslaved? In what sense are they free? How would you evaluate the importance of these two contradictory states?
4. Explain in what way the heritage that the children of these workers will acquire is a mixed one (having positive and negative elements).
5. What effect does the poet have on you by repeating the question, ". . . and what will you be givin' to your brown eyed children of the sun?"
6. What is the dominant feeling that the poet seems to have for the children and parents in the poem?

Suggestions for writing and reading

1. Imagine that you are either a community organizer who wants to change the living and working conditions of the migrant worker or that you are a grower who wants to maintain conditions just as they are. Write a short paper (200 words) in which you outline steps you would take to assure that your objectives would be reached.
2. The march referred to in the fifth verse occurred in California in 1966. Anyone curious about that event can read the following selections which give details about the demonstration and its background:
   Life Magazine: "March of Migrants" April 29, 1966.
   New Republic: "Grape Pickers' Strike" January 29, 1966.
   La Raza: Forgotten Americans. Ed. Julian Samora (1966). Pages 84-90 describe the march.
3. The conditions under which thousands of migrant workers across the nation work and live have been described in books such as the following:

   The Ground is Our Table by Steve Allen (1966) includes a chapter on Mexican-Americans in the United States.

   They Harvest Despair by Dale Wright (1965). The contents was originally published as newspaper articles.

   Wandering Workers by Willard Heaps (1968). Consists of interviews with migrant workers. The book was written especially for young adults.

THE APOSTLE

Hoyt Fuller

"The Apostle" by Hoyt Fuller from *Beyond the Angry Black* reprinted by permission of Cooper Square Publishers.

As Clyde Hedger wheeled his Chevrolet sedan onto the expressway and sped southward in the stream of morning traffic, he felt downright gay. The project on which he was embarking was so simple—even *natural*—that it now seemed incredible he had never thought of it before. He was driving across town for an appointment with the famous ("Infamous, really," he chuckled to himself) Apostle, an interview which might very well prove the key to his advancement to a vice presidency of Keene and Associates Advertising Company, Inc. At twenty-eight, and after only three years as a junior executive at the firm, Mr. Hedger already stood at the very portals of that high-ranking post, and only a brilliant stroke like signing the Apostle was needed to bring it off. It was no secret at the agency that Mr. Keene, deeply enmeshed in emotional and litigious involvements with two beautiful women, one of them his wife, leaned with increasing weariness on the sturdier shoulders of the more singular-minded Mr. Hedger. And Mr. Hedger more than justified this reliance with new accounts and spectacular production. Within the past few months, for instance, he had conceived and directed a project for Summit Meat Products which had almost doubled that firm's city-wide sales. He had accomplished this by persuading two public idols—the star catcher of the city's baseball team and the city's most popular disc jockey—to endorse Summit meats. With some 700,000 or 800,000 Negroes in the city (nobody seemed to be able to come up with a more exact number) still to be directly influenced, corraling the Apostle was not merely an opportunity, it was a duty. That the man was an outright charlatan was beside the point. After all, he wasn't supporting the man; he was merely going to exploit him, for a price, just as he had the ballplayer and the disc jockey. Smiling roguishly, Mr. Hedger recalled his secretary's sarcastic summation of the Apostle and his cult. "The Apostle's secretary says he has over a million followers

Elihu M. Williams

all over, but was rather vague about the number locally," Miss Henderson had droned. "The church, she says, holds over a thousand, and it's always full. As a round figure for local followers, she gave two hundred thousand. Inflation, of course. They don't keep a membership list, only of disciples. Disciples, sometimes called 'lambs,' are inner-circle cultists, and they number about ten thousand. All round numbers, you see. That gal had it down like a circus spieler, and it all sounds like hokum." Old Dora and her prejudices, Mr. Hedger thought cheerily. Well, all he cared about was that—when the Apostle spoke—the South Side listened.

The idea of signing up the Apostle had come to him suddenly Sunday afternoon, three days earlier. He and Janice were lounging around the living room, as they usually did on Sundays, and he was still thumbing through the papers. Jan was beginning to grow restless, having finished the society and entertainment sections, the only pages that interested her. She flipped on the television control, remarking with no particular enthusiasm that there was an old Marilyn Monroe movie on, and then she flopped down beside him. Neither of them had bothered to change the dial, or the volume, and the face and voice which flared forth from the screen were worlds away from the sexy movie star.

Mr. Hedger laughed out loud recalling the shock on his wife's pretty face. She actually went bone-white. There filling the twenty-three inch screen was the slate-black, swollen featured face, fantastically crowned, of a ranting Negro, his pit-deep voice so loud that it shook the apartment. Janice Hedger physically recoiled, her hands automatically flew to her face. Well, to be honest, Mr. Hedger admitted that he also momentarily froze at the sight.

The face was wet with sweat and, in the heat and glare of klieg lights, glittered like moonlit water. The eyes were small and bulbous, the eyebrows wispy, but the nose and lips, spread across the broad face, were as emphatically sculptured as cast-iron. An embroidered white turban arched over the brow and rose into the unseen beyond the borders of the screen. ". . . I will show you the way to salvation, my lambs," the great plowing voice promised. "I am the Apostle. Follow me. The Kingdom of Heaven has a training ground here on earth, and it is here, right here in this very building, this temple of the Divine Supremacy . . ."

By this time Mrs. Hedger had recovered equilibrium enough to stalk across the room and switch the dial. "Holy Moses!" she said adjusting the sound to normal room volume. "What a monster!" But Mr. Hedger's agile mind was dancing. There were all those stories and jokes about the Apostle. It was said that the man performed black magic, that he conjured up apparitions, that he sold lottery numbers and seduced wealthy old widows. He had a fleet of Cadillacs, a couple dozen servants in livery, enough furs and finery to outfit a harem, more jewelry than Babs Hutton . . . Mr. Hedger recalled the night, months earlier, he had driven through the South Side on the way to visit his parents in the suburbs. Approaching the old Apollo Theatre he had noticed mobs of Negroes under the marquee and spilling over into the street. The red flashers of police cars enflamed the sky, and the officers scurried around on foot trying to keep the street open to traffic. He had asked one of the offices, a tall, prizefighter type who reminded him of the young Joe Louis, what was going on at the theatre. "That's not a theatre anymore, mister, that's the Apostle's church," the policeman told him. "There's a near-riot there everytime the doors open. Everybody wants to get inside." Glancing up at the marquee, Mr. Hedger had noted that, indeed, the words "The Apostle" gleamed where "Apollo" had once been.

Mr. Hedger's blossoming scheme demanded that he retrieve the lost program and, against his wife's protests, he switched the dial back to the Apostle. "This character is going to mean money in the bank for us." It was an irresistible argument. Mrs. Hedger cuddled up beside her husband and was quiet.

". . . We have such great strength, and we waste it," the Apostle said. He spoke in a sorghumy, insinuating tone which—like an intraracial attic—seemed stored with old and bitter memories. "We have such wonderful power, and we fritter it away. Children, I tell you, my lambs, we have such unheard of wealth, and we are poor. I will show you how to be strong, my lambs. I will show you how to use your power. I will show you how to be truly rich . . ." He beamed a benevolently monarchial smile, raised a flared sleeve into camera range, and mopped his black face with a huge white handkerchief. He shook his head and rumbled, "Ah, yes, it's true, my lambs," and flashed the kingly smile. "My lambs, my children, there is so much evil around us, it's everywhere you turn. Evil people. You must fight this evil. Come to me and I will show you how. I am with you. You people out there in the television audience, I come to you because our glorious temple is just not big enough to accommodate everybody. Then, too, so many of you have requested to visit me privately, but there is room for only a few at a time at my little place. Paradise, my little home. And I must have rest. So, you understand, my lambs, if I can't see you all. And it's expensive, my lambs, to bring you this television message of your salvation. You can help me do it. Will you help me? For I must fight evil. Evil is ugly, and I don't like ugly. God don't like ugly, and the Apostle don't like ugly, my lambs. Remember that. I don't like ugly, I just don't like ugly. . . ."

On that repetitive refrain, the sound gradually diminished until the hypnotic voice was inaudible. The cameras simultaneously retreated from the Apostle's face, drawing away until his full figure was visible in the center of a stage. He wore a gorgeous gown of bright shimmering material which swept the floor. Behind him, arrayed over the width of the stage against a curtain backdrop, stood a robed choir of dark-faced men and women. The Apostle raised an arm and, abruptly, the chorus filled the theatre with rousing jazz-beat song. Again the sound faded, and the scene shifted to the television studios, focusing on the white, cinematically serene face of an announcer. The man's cool, measured tone pealed into the room like chimes on the tail of a dirge. Mrs. Hedger said, "What a phony!" in obvious relief, but Mr. Hedger's attention remained fastened on the screen. The announcer said, "The preceding telecast was a presentation of the Commonwealth of the Triumph of the Divine Supremacy," a smirk crowding the edges of his professionally poker expression.

It was Mrs. Hedger who turned the set off. "Now I believe all I've ever heard about that guy," she said in disgust.

Mr. Hedger remained pensive. "He's a big man on the South Side, Jan. Thousands of followers. They'll do anything he says."

"It's frightening!"

"No, you don't understand." Mr. Hedger began to display his excitement. "It's a great opportunity. Look, all the Apostle's followers eat meat. With the Apostle telling them to buy Summit, the factory won't be able to make the stuff fast enough!"

Mrs. Hedger murmured something about the Apostle taking advantage of ignorant people and prating about salvation, but Mr. Hedger emphasized the man's power. "He can elect the mayor, Jan," he said. She was unimpressed. "He kept saying, 'I don't like ugly, I don't like ugly,' as if he never looked in a mirror. Why, he's ugly enough to shut down a clock factory." Mr. Hedger ignored her. "We can confine the campaign to the South Side, use throw-aways, billboards and ads in the Negro papers," he said. "It will be a breeze."

Miss Henderson, the secretary Mr. Hedger had inherited from Mr. Keene and on whom he depended for seasoned advice, had seen the immediate possibilities of his plan. She proceeded to quote statistics relative to the Negro market ("Negroes in this country have a bigger annual income than the whole of Canada. Just imagine that! And they have the gall to complain about conditions.") and to warn against the pitfalls of religion ("With this Apostle fellow there might be problems. You have to be so careful with these sects and cults, honey."). Miss Henderson obviously was not fond of Negroes and never hesitated to say so ("They're as slippery as eels, honey"), and she did not hesitate now. "Personally, I wouldn't go near the critter for any amount of money, but it's your funeral, honey," she said. Mr. Hedger resented facile expressions of racism and considered challenging Miss Henderson's remarks, but he settled for a mild, "And why not, Dora, what's so different about him?" Mr. Hedger sometimes, as a moral duty, lectured to skeptical friends about their racial prejudices. Negroes are like anybody else, he would tell them. It gave him a sense of maturity and authority to be able to isolate and squelch racial myths. After all, he knew from experience. He had sat in classes with Negroes in college and bunked next to them in the Army. However, he was in too lighthearted a mood for arguing now, so he settled for some ungallant observations of Miss Henderson. Wrinkles showed through the heavy make-up on her long face, he noted, and her dyed red hair, pulled back from her face like a mane, gave her the appearance of a rouged horse. He wondered whatever had attracted Mr. Keene to the woman in the first place. Mr. Hedger gave Miss Henderson a bland little smile and asked her to get background information on the Apostle and the Commonwealth of the Triumph of the Divine Supremacy, plus Negro population figures. He needed the facts for presentation to Mr. Keene. She promised a report within the hour, and Mr. Hedger knew she would have it. Dora Henderson *was* efficient. "I just hope you can handle the coon," she said as she opened the door to leave. Mr. Hedger drily told her he could.

The entire project was all but wrapped up that very morning. Mr. Keene, as expected, approved the plan, and a call to Dave Koscinski at Summit brought enthusiastic support. "We've been thinking about moving out in the Black Belt for some time," Mr. Koscinski said. "We do pretty well out there as it is, but naturally we can do a lot better. Those people eat more meat than we do, you know. Especially pork. They thrive on it. So go right ahead, Clyde. Summit is one hundred percent behind you." A little later, Miss Henderson announced that the Apostle had agreed to receive Mr. Hedger at nine-thirty Wednesday morning. Mr. Hedger was so pleased with himself that he felt like lighting up a cigar but, having none available, he settled for a cigarette. Things couldn't have been going better.

As he turned his car up the ramp leading off the expressway, Mr. Hedger hummed merrily. He checked his notes for the Apostle's address and headed for the street. The Apostle's Paradise was situated in a part of the city rarely visited by Mr. Hedger. The neighborhood once had been elegant, inhabited by some of the state's richest and most highly placed people. As a child, he often had driven with his parents along the wide boulevards, marvelling at the landscaped gardens and wondering about the life behind the forbidding walls. But the neighborhood in recent years had been a battle-ground in the seemingly interminable racial war of living areas. In this warfare, it was the pattern of conflict that Negroes were the aggressors, constantly storming and over-running the bastions of the embattled whites. As the whites withdrew, establishing new positions behind new Maginot lines, the Negroes spilled over into the freshly evacuated territory, pausing only to solidify their occupation before plunging forth in the next assault. The Apostle had been in the vanguard of this army of occupation, and his billet, the three-story graystone Soderheim mansion (thirty rooms, indoor swimming pool, gymnasium), was a truly worthy spoil. Mr. Hedger, having imagined in the ankle regions of his mind that the Apostle's place of residence would match his flamboyant television image (possibly with neon signs announcing "This is Paradise"), was mildly disappointed to find the mansion virtually as staid as in its more respectable past. There was a touch of individuality in the vertical blinds at the front windows and in the blue and white striped awning over the stoop, but these girlish additions to the dowager building were less than sensational.

Mr. Hedger arrived at the mansion at nine-twenty and, finding no parking space in the block, double-parked in front of the sprawling lawn. Someone was sure to emerge from one of the surrounding buildings and move a car. He surveyed the block. On both sides of the boulevard the houses sat rods from the street, the doorways reached by cement walks that wound over grounds once uniformly green and manicured but now mostly pocked and scabbed like mangy hides. Some of the buildings towered four stories, as tall as apartment buildings which most, in fact, had become. There were tales that many of the high-ceilinged old bedrooms now housed whole families, and this, Mr. Hedger concluded, accounted for the bumper-to-bumper crop of cars at the curbs.

Two middle-aged, comfortably heavy Negro women, dressed in smock-like dresses, approached on the sidewalk. One of them, brown, comely, with a sly, motherly face suggesting a roguish madonna, stopped suddenly, threw her head back and laughed lustily. The other woman, darker and more gentle, regaled her with some delicious story. A third woman walked toward them. Though the approximate age of the morning gossipers, this one was their opposite in appearance. She was corseted to slimness and impeccably dressed. She walked rapidly, head high, her narrow high heels tapping the pavement. As she passed the two women, she smiled an impersonal apology and stepped off the sidewalk onto the Apostle's lawn to avoid brushing the woman nearest her. The gossipers stopped talking, fixed their attention on the passing woman and glared at her. The darker woman made a mocking face, tossed her head and pranced like a clumsy drayhorse. Her friend howled uproariously at this performance, slapping the actress on the back like a logger in a barroom.

The laughter was infectious and Mr. Hedger found himself chuckling. Then he glanced at his watch and grew panicky. It was past nine-thirty. A motor turned over behind him, and he saw that the well-dressed Negro woman was at the wheel of the Cadillac at the curb. She adroitly maneuvered the big car into the street and, as she drove past Mr. Hedger, smiled warmly at him. Mr. Hedger gratefully smiled back, then hurriedly deposited his car in the vacated space.

Hugging his briefcase under his arm, Mr. Hedger hustled up the S-shaped walk to the canopied doorway and rang the bell. The door was opened immediately by a small, wiry man the color of brandy, wearing a royal blue uniform replete with brass buttons and a broad snaggle-toothed grin. He had an open, small-featured face that reflected all the hazards of some fifty years of living. "Good morning, sir," he said, his voice redolent of cotton fields and drafty cabins. "Can I help you, sir?"

"I have an appointment with the . . . with . . . with Mr. Apostle." The realization that he did not know the appropriate manner of addressing the Apostle brought Mr. Hedger a moment of alarm. The doorman, bowing, invited Mr. Hedger into a reception hall furnished with delicate, velvet-cushioned chairs that looked ancient and unused and ornate Oriental vases almost as tall as the doorman. Across a hallway a wide, richly carpeted stairway curved upwards. The doorman lifted a telephone from the table beside him. "What is the name, sir?"

"Hedger. Mr. Clyde Hedger of Keene and Associates."

"Yessir."

He dialed a number and, when a voice answered, announced, "Mr. Hedger to see His Goodness."

"Yes, mam, Miss Shell, I'll send him right in." The doorman replaced the telephone and clicked on his jigsaw smile. "His Goodness will see you now, sir." He stepped into the areaway and pointed a bony finger. "At the end of the hall, sir. Miss Shell will take you in. Last room down the hall."

Mr. Hedger started off, then hesitated. "Excuse me, but how is the Apostle usually addressed by visitors?"

"Well, we lambs of the Commonwealth always call him His Goodness, but other folks usually just say Apostle Lovett. Just Apostle Lovett, sir."

"Thank you very much," Mr. Hedger said. "I never met Apostle Lovett before, and I wanted to be sure."

"Yessir, Apostle Lovett will be allright, sir."

"Thank you."

"A pleasure, sir."

Mr. Hedger strode down the padded and dark-paneled hallway. Having suppressed the impulse to add "lamb" to his "thank you," he now steadied himself for business by recalling data about the Apostle and his sect. "The Commonwealth of . . ." He stopped, found Miss Henderson's memo in his pocket and checked it. "Real name: Jesse Lovett. Cult: Commonwealth of the Triumph of the Divine Supremacy. Place of worship: Temple of the Divine Supremacy. Home: Paradise ('Hallelujah!' Miss Henderson had interpolated). Marital status: Uncertain, don't mention . . ."

Conscious of a presence, Mr. Hedger looked up. The doorway was open in front of him and a slim, youthful figure filled it. When his eyes lifted to her face he saw that she was as young and as comely as her figure and that she was smiling at him. She had curly black hair, worn like a tiara, green-gray eyes, lips that were full and very red, and skin the color of gold. Mr. Hedger slipped the memo in his pocket and uttered an embarrassed "Good morning." He decided that Miss Shell looked more like a night club hostess than a preacher's Girl Friday. "Good morning, Mr. Hedger," she said smokily. "Please come in."

He walked past her into an ante-chamber furnished with desk and typewriter, telephone, filing cabinet, chair and small leather couch. A wide window overlooked a garden, and a breeze from it wafted Miss Shell's perfume into Mr. Hedger's nostrils. He followed her into the adjoining room.

There he almost gasped in astonishment. He had visualized the Apostle surrounded by plush and gilt and outrageously luxurious trappings. Instead, the ballroom-sized room was practically bare. A magnificent window at the rear, its heavy wine-colored draperies half-drawn, admitted a rectangle of light into the otherwise unlighted vastness. The shaft of light fell across a desk no bigger nor handsomer than Miss Shell's and on an ordinary looking leather desk chair behind it. At an angle to the desk, just out of the light, was a leather lounge chair, apparently reserved for visitors. The room, like the hallway, was completely paneled in dark wood and the floor covered by a thick carpet of burnished burgundy. It seemed to Mr. Hedger, under the circumstances, as perversely austere as a monk's cell.

But if the room was a surprise, the man Mr. Hedger found there was a shock. It was hardly the same man he had seen on television. That man had been homely, yes, but with a certain attractiveness in his flaring features and deep, resonant voice. He had seemed as tall and as masterful as a Watusi prince in the dramatic headpiece and the flowing robe. But the man who met Mr. Hedger in the center of the great room now was remarkable only for his surpassing ugliness. The Apostle stood just over five feet and was shaped like an egg. His rough ebony skin seemed as tough as a crocodile's hide, and that portion of his head that had hidden under the turban was absolutely bald and glittered like polished glass. The nose and mouth which had seemed heroic on the screen seemed in person only grossly distorted. He extended a hand, grinning up at his visitor like a well-tailored but over-fed pygmy. "Good morning, Mr. Hedger."

Mr. Hedger realized, as he shook hands, that not even the Apostle's voice was the same. The under-plowing, Robesonian quality was there, sounding incongruous now in such an unimpressive person, but the intraracial, honey-slow, gospel-and-blues accent was gone. "It's a pleasure to have you here," the Apostle said, his diction as precise as a British don's. "Please come and sit down."

Mr. Hedger followed the Apostle to the desk and, after the cultist was seated, settled in the lounge chair. Then he saw that the Apostle, framed like some gnomish deity in the window light, looked down on him from behind the desk. The Apostle now seemed fully two heads taller than he had been standing, and Mr. Hedger decided that the Apostle's chair was not so ordinary after all. It did better than equalize the Apostle's height: it was raised to give him an advantage. And it was impossible not to look up to him. There was nothing else on which to focus attention. The Apostle sat primly, the welcoming grin unchanged on his face.

"I want to apologize for being late, Apostle Lovett," Mr. Hedger began. "I had a little trouble finding a parking space outside."

"Yes, we have quite a parking problem on our street," the basso voice replied. "We're rather crowded on this side of town, Mr. Hedger."

"Well, the parking situation is kind of bad all over. It's no better where I live. I guess we're a nation with too many cars."

Mr. Hedger immediately regretted his words. They had been innocent enough, but he remembered that the Apostle was supposed to own several limousines and station wagons. If the Apostle was offended, however, he gave no indication. "Could be, Mr. Hedger," he said, still grinning amiably.

Abruptly the Apostle clasped his fingers together on the polished desktop as in supplication. It was, it turned out, a misleading gesture. He had a point to press. "You were obviously surprised to find me in a business suit rather than in ceremonial robes, Mr. Hedger . . ."

"Well, I was a little surprised," Mr. Hedger admitted warily.

"The costumes are for my followers, Mr. Hedger. The fancy clothes remind them that their ancestors were once kings, long ago, back in the days of Solomon and Sheba. The Mali Empire. The kingdom of Benin. They like to be reminded of such things . . ."

Mr. Hedger was silent. He did not know where the Apostle's recitation was leading.

"I'm in the public service, Mr. Hedger," the Apostle continued. "The public I serve likes pageantry and frills because it also brings a bit of glamor to their lives. They work hard, and life is not easy for them. I try to help lift their morale and give them a little hope."

Mr. Hedger shifted uneasily. He hoped the Apostle would not feel it necessary to convince him of his piety, but he listened dutifully, studying the black face. He noticed that the small eyes actually were lashless and red as if bloodshot, and that a smudge the color of Miss Shell's lipstick covered one corner of the mouth. The Apostle finished his little speech and reared back in the elevated chair, the grin intact. "I do want to make things clear," he said.

"I understand, sir," Mr. Hedger said, not understanding at all. He decided to get to the point without further delay. "As my secretary indicated, my firm, Keene and

Associates, represents the Summit Meat Products Company. They produce a wide assortment of quality meats—sausages, lunch meats, that sort of thing. Perhaps you're familiar with some of them?"

"Yes, I know . . ."

"Well, if you've tried them, it might help my cause if you liked them," Mr. Hedger said brightly. But it was impossible to know if this intended humor amused the Apostle because the face merely held the same grin.

The Apostle shook his shiny head. "I'm sorry, Mr. Hedger, but I never ate any of your products. I've seen them advertised. That's all."

"Well, we're remedying that at once. We're having a special assortment delivered to you this afternoon."

"That is kind of you."

"Well, we certainly hope you'll like them, Apostle Lovett. You see, we're asking you to endorse our products."

The grin contracted for a fleet moment then settled again in its groove. "Why me, Mr. Hedger?"

Mr. Hedger smiled shyly. "Well, frankly, because you're one of the most popular personalities in town, and if you think our products are all right, that'll be good enough recommendation for a whole lot of people."

The Apostle unclasped and reclasped his fingers. He considered a moment. "Perhaps you overestimate my influence, Mr. Hedger. People believe in me because I tell them good things. I tell them things to help them. That doesn't mean they will necessarily do what I do, or even what I want them to do . . ."

"You're being modest, Apostle Lovett. Your followers would do anything you asked them."

The Apostle shook his head again, manipulating his fingers like a fan. "Perhaps. Perhaps. People are kind to me as you can see, Mr. Hedger. They have provided me with many of life's material comforts—this nice house here, for example—and it gives me great spiritual comfort to feel I am of some help to them. I'm grateful to them. But they have faith in me only because they know I will not deceive them."

"Well, in endorsing Summit meats you certainly wouldn't be deceiving anybody." Mr. Hedger was aware of the hollow sound of this claim and added quickly: "And we're prepared to make a substantial contribution for your endorsement."

"How substantial?"

The alert response heartened Mr. Hedger. "Well, we have two contracts. The first offers five hundred dollars, the second a thousand . . ."

"Substantial, Mr. Hedger?"

Mr. Hedger stared blankly at the Apostle. He had not imagined the man might consider a thousand dollars inconsequential. He recalled Miss Henderson's warnings with annoyance and directed his irritation at the Apostle's ineradicable grin. "This is a local company," he said. "We've never paid anyone more than a thousand dollars for an endorsement of this kind. We sometimes get endorsements from prominent people for a year's supply of meats, or even less than that . . ."

"I don't think a thousand dollars is a very substantial sum of money, Mr. Hedger."

Mr. Hedger sank back in the lounge chair. "I wish somebody would offer *me* a thousand dollars just for the use of *my* name and picture!"

"I wish that for you also, Mr. Hedger. However, *I* am not *you*."

Mr. Hedger fumbled in his pockets and brought out his cigarettes. It gave him something to do with his hands while mute epithets marched through his head. Then, realizing that the Apostle might object to his smoking, he asked if he could.

"Yes, of course, Mr. Hedger." The Apostle pushed an ashtray toward his guest.

"Would you care for a cigarette, sir?"

"No, thank you."

Mr. Hedger lighted the cigarette and inhaled deeply, averting his eyes from the face across the desk. His glance fell on his briefcase lying unopened at his feet with all the brochures and illustrations of Summit meats inside. There had been no opportunity to disply them, and now it was perhaps just as well. He raised his eyes and said: "Then we can't do business?"

The Apostle's grin for once broadened. He even laughed softly. "I didn't say that, Mr. Hedger."

"But you said . . ."

"I said I didn't think a thousand dollars a substantial sum of money. That's what I said." He leaned forward over his clasped hands. "Mr. Hedger, there are dozens of objects inside this house that cost over a thousand dollars."

"But will you consider endorsing our products? We can't offer more."

"I *am* considering it, Mr. Hedger. Money is very useful."

Mr. Hedger sighed, relieved. He decided to press forward. "Well, this is rather urgent, Apostle Lovett. I mean, we're trying to get our posters and ads placed before Memorial Day and the start of the vacation season. Do you think you could let us know in a few days? Say, a week?"

"I can let you know this morning, Mr. Hedger."

"Oh, splendid! That would be splendid!"

Mr. Hedger scooped up his briefcase and extracted the illustrations, spreading them across the desk. "These are actual photographs taken in Summit's test kitchens. Samples of all these meats will be delivered to you this afternoon."

The Apostle rummaged through the slick colored sheets perfunctorily. Then he pushed them aside and reclasped his hands, fixing Mr. Hedger with the inscrutable grin.

"Would you like to go over the contracts?" Mr. Hedger said, excited by the possibility of concluding negotiations at once. He drew the contracts from the briefcase and, selecting the thousand dollar one, proceeded to explain it. "With this contract, Apostle Lovett, we agree to pay you a thousand dollars for your signed endorsement of Summit meats and the right . . ."

"Mr. Hedger . . ."

". . . Yes?"

"Just one question, Mr. Hedger, if you don't mind . . ."

". . . Yes?"

"Does the Summit Meats Products Company employ Negroes?"

Mr. Hedger felt suspended, as if the floor had been whisked from beneath his feet. "Well, I don't know for sure, but they're a very progressive and fair-minded company, and I'm sure they have nothing against employing Negroes . . ."

There was a twinkle in the Apostle's muddy eyes. "Would you find out, Mr. Hedger?"

Mr. Hedger swallowed. "I sure will," he said. "I'll find out as soon as I get back to the office . . ."

The Apostle shook his head. "Now, Mr. Hedger. Would you find out now?"

Once in the third grade Clyde Hedger had been caught throwing chalk across the classroom. To punish him, the teacher had led him to the office and made him telephone his mother and tell her what he had done. Now, staring at the telephone, he had the same sensation of helplessness and doom. He picked up the receiver and, when Miss Shell's voice responded, gave her Summit's number. A moment later he had his connection. "Give me Mr. Koscinski, please."

Waiting for Mr. Koscinski's voice, Mr. Hedger forced himself to look at the Apostle. The imperturbable grin suddenly reminded him of the disembodied leer of the Cheshire cat. The malicious thought eased his frustration.

Then Mr. Koscinski spoke and Mr. Hedger braced himself, keeping his voice casual. "Clyde Hedger, Mr. Koscinski . . . I'm at Apostle Lovett's now . . . Could you tell me offhand how many Negroes work at Summit?"

He listened sinkingly as the other voice, hesitant, embarrassed at the question and at the inevitable answer, evaded a direct reply, explaining, "We've often considered hiring some of them, Clyde, but, well, the regular people would object . . . They wouldn't want to work with them . . . And we have to avoid trouble . . ."

"Yes, thank you, Mr. Koscinski."

Mr. Hedger lowered the phone from his ear and slowly—while Mr. Koscinski's voice was still audible, making some further explanation—replaced it in its cradle. He did not look at the Apostle, his eyes might have been closed. He felt defeated—and resentful. The grinning face mocked and accused him, lumped him among the conspirators in a plot for which he shared no responsibility. At last he raised his eyes to meet the Apostle's in a gesture of lost defiance. "They don't hire Negroes," he said.

The Apostle made no immediate response. He sat Buddha-still. But after a moment he unclasped his fingers and, shrugging his narrow shoulders, spread his hands in an expression of regret. "Then we *can't* do business, Mr. Hedger."

Although he knew this would be the answer, a blood-scalding sensation burned Mr. Hedger's skin. His temples throbbed and his pulse raced. Nevertheless, he calmly swept up his papers and stuffed them in his briefcase. "Well, thank you for your time," he said, standing up.

"It was nothing, Mr. Hedger," the Apostle said. "I wish I could have helped you. As I explained to you, I find money very useful. But I'm a discreet man. I keep faith with my followers."

"Yes, of course."

Mr. Hedger turned to go, wanting to avoid further confrontation with the ugly face, but the Apostle's voice pulled him around again. "Mr. Hedger . . ."

". . . Mr. Hedger, I won't agree to endorse your meats," the voice said. "But then, I will make no mention of the fact that your company has a white-only employment policy. In that way, I will be helping you still."

The two-pronged blade of spite and condescension cut deeply into Mr. Hedger's composure. A flaming, unfamilar emotion raged inside him. To the black man behind the desk he said a curt, "Good day," and walked away.

"Goodby, Mr. Hedger," the now-hated voice came after him.

Mr. Hedger crossed the shadowed room to the door, opened and closed it behind him without looking back. Miss Shell was sitting cross-legged on the couch. He nodded at her, leaving her low-pitched, "Goodby Mr. Hedger," unacknowledged, letting himself into the hallway. The major-domo in the blue suit jumped to attention, flashing the wide smile as he held open the door. "Good morning, sir." Mr. Hedger nodded, thinking, "That goddam tribal grin!"

As Mr. Hedger walked toward his car, an airplane roared overhead, gaining altitude on its journey to some other city. He watched it glittering in the sun and tried to read the insignia on its side. At the sidewalk, he almost collided with someone and, turning automatically to apologize, saw that it was a little boy.

The boy, no higher than Mr. Hedger's elbow, had the face of an elf and the color of ginger bread. He stood just beyond Mr. Hedger's reach, staring at him with eyes as big and dark as a calf's. Under his arm he cradled a loaf of bread, holding it so tightly that it bulged perilously at each end.

Mr. Hedger's apology died unspoken. He met the boy's unwavering gaze, standing as still as stone. The boy, aping Mr. Hedger, froze motionless too. After a moment, though, he drawled, "Good morning, white man," and walked back slowly, alerted for flight. He stretched his mouth in a mocking grin and began to chant, "Good morning, Mr. White Man, Good Morning, Mr. White Man, Good Morning, Mr. White Man," the tempo rising with his backward speed. Finally, he whirled around and, still singing the ridiculous greeting, sprinted along the sidewalk and across the littered lawn of one of the big houses.

Mr. Hedger watched the boy vanish into the building, and the dark emotion that had been rioting in him discovered its catharsis. "The grinning little nigger!" he said out loud, the words pouring forth deliciously.

Mr. Hedger climbed into his car and drove northward toward the crosstown expressway. He made a mental note to have Miss Henderson cancel the delivery of Summit meats to the Apostle. He wondered what she would say.

What do you think?

1. Specifically, what techniques does the author use throughout the story to make us aware of things that Hedger is unaware of?
2. Judging from the following observations of Mrs. Hedger, what does the narrator want us to think of her:

   (a) That she reads only the society and entertainment sections of the Sunday paper?
   (b) That her first reaction to the Apostle on television is to call him a "monster"?
   (c) That she stops complaining about watching the Apostle when her husband says he may result in his making more money?
3. Mrs. Hedger says that the Apostle is a phony and that he takes advantage of ignorant people. Explain how this is or is not true. Explain whether that description would fit her husband.
4. What do the following remarks suggest about the nature of the relationship between the Negro community and the white one in the city in which the story takes place?
   (a) "nobody seemed to be able to come up with a more exact number" (of the Negroes in the city). Page 160, line 19.
   (b) "We can confine the campaign to the South Side. . . ." Page 162, line 124.
   (c) "We're rather crowded on this side of town." Page 166, line 304.
5. What is the point of the vignette about the Negro women passing one another on the sidewalk in front of the Apostle's home? How does it add to or distract from the main story about Hedger and the Apostle?
6. Why does the doorman's smile *click* on? In what way is his smile similar to the Apostle's? Does he say "sir" excessively?
7. Recount the mistakes that Hedger makes in his interview with the Apostle. How do you account for his making them? Describe the Apostle's attitude throughout the interview. How do you account for it?
8. What kinds of hand movements do both the Apostle and Mr. Hedger use during the interview? Explain why the narrator focuses on their movements.
9. What is the "plot" in which Hedger feels he shares no responsibility? Is he correct in that opinion? Why or why not?
10. Name the key differences between the kind of prejudice Miss Henderson has and that of Mr. Hedger. If you were Negro, which of them would you prefer to work with? Why?
11. At one point in the story, Hedger recalls the stories he's heard about what things the Apostle owns. Do you believe any, all, or none of those stories? Why do you think such stories are created about outstanding people? Who creates them?
12. In your own words, explain what kind of person the Apostle really is.
13. Are there certain professions in which a person must be deceptive or evasive in order to be successful? What are they? Do they do damage to the person's sense of right or wrong? Should such jobs be abolished? Explain.

Suggestions for writing, reading, and viewing

1. At one point, Miss Henderson says that Negroes are as slippery as eels. What other stereotypes of Negroes have you heard? Are any of them contradictory? Make a list of them.
2. Rewrite the scene in which the Hedgers are watching the Apostle on television. Substitute a Negro couple who are followers of his. Carefully rewrite

the dialogue so that the kind of faith and admiration that you think followers would have comes through dramatically.

3. In a very short paper (300 words), comment on the accuracy of the opinion that "Advertising is the fine art of persuading people to buy what they do not need or want." You might use what you learn about advertising from this story as an example in the paper.
4. Is the narrator's description of the competition between Negroes and whites over living areas as "warfare" accurate? Explain your viewpoint in a paper (750 words).

"The Hangman" is a short (10 min.) color film using surrealistic animated stills that dramatize the poem by Maurice Ogden of the same name. The film provokes questions about the rightness or wrongness of a person's job and whether others ought to interfere with his performance as executioner.

WORK AND THE SELF

Everett Hughes

"Mistakes at Work" by Everett C. Hughes. First published in *Canadian Journal of Economics and Political Science,* Vol. XVII, August 1951, pp. 320-327. Used by permission of Everett C. Hughes and Canadian Political Science Association.

NOTE: Because of the length of the essay and the nature of its ideas, it's divided into two parts. Accordingly, the instructor might wish to make the reading of it two assignments.

I

There are societies in which custom or sanctioned rule determines what work a man of given status may do. In our society, at least one strong strain of ideology has it that a man may do any work which he is competent to do; or even that he has a right to the schooling and experience necessary to gain competence in any kind of work which he sets as the goal of his ambition. Equality of opportunity is, among us, stated very much in terms of the right to enter upon any occupation whatsoever. Although we do not practice this belief to the full, we are a people who cultivate ambition. A great deal of our ambition takes the form of getting training for kinds of work which carry more prestige than that which our fathers did. Thus a man's work is one of the things by which he is judged, and certainly one of the more significant things by which he judges himself.

Many people in our society work in named occupations. The names are a combination of price tag and calling card. One has only to hear casual conversation to sense how important these tags are. Hear a salesman, who has just been asked what he does, reply, "I am in sales work," or "I am in promotional work," not "I sell skillets." Schoolteachers sometimes turn schoolteaching into educational work, and the disciplining of youngsters and chaperoning of parties into personnel work. Teaching Sunday School becomes religious education, and the Y.M.C.A. Secretary is in "group work." Social scientists emphasize the science end of their name. These hedging statements in which people pick the most favorable of several possible names of their work imply an audience. And one of the most important things about any man is his audience, or his choice of the several available audiences to which he may address his claims to be someone of worth.

These remarks should be sufficient to call it to your attention that a man's work is one of the more important parts of his social identity, of his self; indeed, of his fate in the one life he has to live, for there is something almost as irrevocable about choice of occupation as there is about choice of a mate. And since the language about work is so loaded with value and prestige judgments, and with defensive choice of symbols, we should not be astonished that the concepts of social scientists who study work should carry a similar load, for the relation of social-science concepts to popular speech remains close in spite of our efforts to separate them. The difference is that while the value-weighing in popular speech is natural and proper, for concealment and ego-protection are of the essence of social intercourse —in scientific discourse the value-loaded concept may be a blinder. And part of the problem of method in the study of work behavior is that the people who have the most knowledge about a given occupation (let us say medicine), and from whom therefore the data for analysis must come, are the people in the occupation. They may combine in themselves a very sophisticated manipulative knowledge of the appropriate social relations, with a very strongly motivated suppression, and even repression, of the deeper truths about these relationships, and, in occupations of higher status, with great verbal skill in keeping these relationships from coming up for thought and discussion by other people. This is done in part by the use of and insistence upon loaded value words where their work is discussed.

My own experience in study of occupations illustrates the point that concepts may be blinders. My first essay into the field was a study of the real estate agents in Chicago. These highly competitive men were just at that point in their journey toward respectability at which they wished to emphasize their conversion from business-minded suspicion of one another to the professional attitude of confidence in each other coupled with a demand for confidence from the public. I started the study with the idea of finding out an answer to this familiar question, "Are these men professionals?" It was a false question, for the concept "profession" in our society is not so much a descriptive term as one of value and prestige. It happens over and over that the people who practice an occupation attempt to revise the conceptions which their various publics have of the occupation and of the people in it. In so doing, they also attempt to revise their own conception of themselves and of their work. The model which these occupations set before themselves is that of the "profession"; thus the term profession is a symbol for a desired conception of one's work and, hence, of one's self. The movement to "professionalize" an occupation is thus collective mobility of some among the people in an occupation. One aim of the movement is to rid the occupation of people who are not mobile enough to go along with the changes.

There are two kinds of occupational mobility. One is individual. The individual makes the several choices, and achieves the skills which allow him to move to a certain position in the occupational, and thus—he hopes—in the social and economic hierarchy. His choice is limited by several conditions, among which is the social knowledge available to him at the time of crucial decision, a time which varies for the several kinds of work.

The other kind of occupational mobility is that of a group of people in an occupation, i.e., of the occupation itself. This has been important in our society with its great changes of technology, with its attendant proliferation of new occupations and of change in the techniques and social relations of old ones. Now it sometimes happens that by the time a person has the full social knowledge necessary to the smartest possible choice of occupations, he is already stuck with one and in one. How strongly this may affect the drive for professionalization of occupations, I don't know. I suspect that it is a motive. At any rate, it is common in our society for occupational groups to step their occupation up in the hierarchy by turning it into a profession. I will not here describe this process. Let me only indicate that in my own studies I passed from the false question "Is this occupation a profession?" to the more fundamental one, "What are the circumstances in which the people in an occupation attempt to turn it into a profession, and themselves into professional people?" and "What are the steps by which they attempt to bring about identification with their valued model?"

Even with this new orientation the term profession acted as a blinder. For as I began to give courses and seminars on occupations, I used a whole set of concepts and headings which were prejudicial to full understanding of what work behavior and relations are. One of them was that of the "code of ethics," which still tended to sort people into the good and the bad. It was not until I had occasion to undertake study of race relations in industry that I finally, I trust, got rid of this bias in the concepts which I used. Negro industrial workers, the chief objects of our study, performed the kinds of work which have least prestige and which make least pretension; yet it turned out that even in the lowest occupations people do develop collective pretensions to give their work, and consequently themselves, value in the eyes of each other and of outsiders.

It was from these people that we learned that a common dignifying rationalization of people in all positions of a work hierarchy except the very top one is, "We in this position save the people in the next higher position above from their own mistakes." The notion that one saves a person of more acknowledged skill, and certainly of more acknowledged prestige and power, than one's self from his mistakes appears to be peculiarly satisfying. Now there grow up in work organizations rules of mutual protection among the persons in a given category and rank, and across ranks and categories. If one uses the term "code of ethics" he is likely not to see the true nature of these rules. These rules have of necessity to do with mistakes, for it is in the nature of work that people make mistakes. The question of how mistakes are handled is a much more penetrating one than any question which contains the concept "professional ethics" as ordinarily conceived. For in finding out how mistakes are handled, one must get at the fundamental psychological and social devices by which people are able to carry on through time, to live with others and with themselves, knowing that what is daily routine for them in their occupational roles may be fateful for others, knowing that one's routine mistakes, even the mistakes by which one learns better, may touch other lives at crucial points. It is in part the problem of dealing routinely with what are the crises of others. The people in lower ranks are thus using a powerful psychological weapon when they rationalize their worth and indispensability as lying in their protection of people in higher ranks from their mistakes. I suppose it is almost a truism that the people who take the larger responsibilities must be people who can face making mistakes, while punctiliousness must remain in second place. But this is a matter which has not been very seriously taken into account, as far as I know, in studies of the social drama of work.

Of course, the rules which people make to govern their behavior at work cover other problems than that of mistakes. Essentially the rules classify people, for to define situations and the proper behavior in situations one has to assign roles to the people involved. Among the most important subject matter of rules is the setting up of criteria for recognizing a true fellow-worker, for determining who it is safe and maybe even necessary to initiate into the in-group of close equals, and who must be kept at some distance. This problem is apt to be obscured by the term "colleagueship," which, although its etymology is perfect for the matter in hand, carries a certain notion of higher status, of respectability. (In pre-Hitler Germany the Social-Democratic workers called one another "Comrade." The Christian trade-unions insisted on the term "Colleague.")

Allow me to mention one other value-laden term which may act as a blinder in study of the social psychology of work, to wit, "restriction of production." This term contains a value assumption of another kind—namely, that there is someone who knows and has a right to determine the right amount of work for other people to do. If one does less, he is restricting production. Mayo[1] and others have done a good deal to analyze the phenomenon in question, but it was Max Weber[2] who—forty years ago—pointed to "putting on the brakes," as an inevitable result of the wrestling match between a man and his employer over the price he must pay with his body for his wage. In short, he suggested that no man easily yields to another full control over the amount of effort he must daily exert. On the other hand, there is no more characteristically human phenomenon than determined and even heroic effort to do a task which one has taken as his own. I do not mean to make the absurd implication that there could be a situation in which every man would be his own and only taskmaster. But I think we might better understand the social interaction which determines the measure of effort if we keep ourselves free of terms which suggest that it is abnormal to do less than one is asked by some reasonable authority.

[1] Mayo, Elton, W. *Human Problems of an Industrial Civilization.* New York, 1933.

[2] Weber, Max, "Zur Psychophysik der industriellen Arbeit," in *Gesammelte Aufsätze zur Soziologie und Sozialpolitik.* Tübingen, 1924. Pp. 730-770.

You will have doubtless got the impression that I am making the usual plea for a value-free science, that is, for neutrality. Such is not my intention. Our aim is to *penetrate more deeply* into the personal and social drama of work, to understand the social and social-psychological arrangements and devices by which men make their work tolerable, or even glorious to themselves and others. I believe that much of our terminology and hence, of our problem setting, has limited our field of perception by a certain pretentiousness and a certain value-loading. Specifically we need to rid ourselves of any concepts which keep us from seeing that the essential problems of men at work are the same whether they do their work in some famous laboratory or in the messiest vat room of a pickle factory. Until we can find a point of view and concepts which will enable us to make comparisons between the junk peddler and the professor without intent to debunk the one and patronize the other, we cannot do our best work in this field.

Perhaps there is as much to be learned about the high-prestige occupations by applying to them the concepts which naturally come to mind for study of people in the most lowly kinds of work as there is to be learned by applying to other occupations the conceptions developed in connection with the highly-valued professions. Furthermore, I have come to the conclusion that it is a fruitful thing to start study of any social phenomenon at the point of least prestige. For, since prestige is so much a matter of symbols, and even of pretensions—however well merited—there goes with prestige a tendency to preserve a front which hides the inside of things; a front of names, of indirection, of secrecy (much of it necessary secrecy). On the other hand, in things of less prestige, the core may be more easy of access.

In recent years a number of my students have studied some more or less lowly occupations: apartment-house janitors, junk men, boxers, jazz musicians, osteopaths, pharmacists, etc. They have done so mainly because of their own connections with the occupations in question, and perhaps because of some problem of their own. At first, I thought of these studies as merely interesting and informative for what they would tell about people who do these humbler jobs, i.e., as American ethnology. I have now come to the belief that although the problems of people in these lines of work are as interesting and important as any other, their deeper value lies in the insights they yield about work behavior in any and all occupations. It is not that it puts one into the position to debunk the others, but simply that processes which are hidden in other occupations come more readily to view in these lowly ones. We may be here dealing with a fundamental matter of method in social science, that of finding the best possible laboratory for study of a given series of mechanisms.

II

Let me illustrate. The apartment-house janitor is a fellow who, in making his living, has to do a lot of other people's dirty work. This is patent. He could not hide it if he would. Now every occupation is not one but several activities; some of them are the "dirty work" of that trade. It may be dirty in one of several ways. It may be simply physically disgusting. It may be a symbol of degradation, something that wounds one's dignity.

Finally, it may be dirty work in that it in some way goes counter to the more heroic of our moral conceptions. Dirty work of some kind is found in all occupations. It is hard to imagine an occupation in which one does not appear, in certain repeated contingencies, to be practically compelled to play a role of which he thinks he ought to be a little ashamed. Insofar as an occupation carries with it a self-conception, a notion of personal dignity, it is likely that at some point one will feel that he is having to do something that is *infra dignitate.* Janitors turned out to be bitterly frank about their physically dirty work. When asked, "What is the toughest part of your job," they answered almost to a man in the spirit of this quotation: "Garbage. Often the stuff is sloppy and smelly. You know some fellows can't look at garbage if it's sloppy. I'm getting used to it now, but it almost killed me when I started." Or as another put it, "The toughest part? It's the messing up in front of the garbage incinerator. That's the most miserable thing there is on this job. The tenants don't co-operate—them bastards. You tell them today, and tomorrow there is the same mess over again by the incinerator."

In the second quotation it becomes evident that the physical disgust of the janitor is not merely a thing between him and the garbage, but involves the tenant also. Now the tenant is the person who impinges most on the daily activity of the janitor. It is the tenant who interferes most with his own dignified ordering of his life and work. If it were not for a tenant who had broken a window, he could have got his regular Sunday cleaning done on time; if it were not for a tenant who had clogged a trap, he would not have been ignominiously called away from the head of his family table just when he was expansively offering his wife's critical relatives a second helping of porkchops, talking the while about the importance of his job. It is the tenant who causes the janitor's status pain. The physically disgusting part of the janitor's work is directly involved in his relations with other actors in his work drama.[3]

By a *contre coup,* it is by the garbage that the janitor judges, and, as it were, gets power over the tenants who high-hat him. Janitors know about hidden love-affairs by bits of torn-up letter paper; of impending financial disaster or of financial four-flushing by the presence of many unopened letters in the waste. Or they may stall off demands for immediate service by an unreasonable woman of whom they know from the garbage that she, as the janitors put it, "has the rag on." The garbage gives the janitor the makings of a kind of magical power over that pretentious villain, the tenant. I say a kind of magical power, for there appears to be no thought of betraying any individual and thus turning this knowledge into overt power. He protects the tenant, but, at least among Chicago janitors, it is not a loving protection.

Let your mind dwell on what one might hear from people in certain other occupations if they were to answer as frankly and bitterly as did the janitors. I do not say nor do I think that it would be a good thing for persons in all occupations to speak so freely on physical disgust as did these men. To do so, except in the most tightly closed circles, would create impossible situations. But we are likely to overlook the matter altogether in studying occupations where concealment is practiced, and thus get a false notion of the problems which have to be faced in such occupations, and of the possible psychological and social by-products of the solutions which are developed for the problem of disgust.

Now the delegation of dirty work to someone else is common among humans. Many cleanliness taboos, and perhaps even many moral scruples, depend for their practice upon success in delegating the tabooed activity to someone else. Delegation of dirty work is also a part of the process of occupational mobility. Yet there are kinds of work, some of them of very high prestige, in which such delegation is possible only to a limited extent. The dirty work may be an intimate part of the very activity which gives the occupation its charisma, as is the case with the handling of the human body by the physician. In this case, I suppose the dirty work is somehow integrated into the whole, and into the prestige-bearing role of the person who does it. What role it plays in the drama of work relations in such a case is something to find out. The janitor, however, does not integrate his dirty work into any deeply satisfying definition of his role that might liquidate his antagonism to the people whose dirt he handles. Incidentally, we have found reason to believe that one of the

[3] Gold, Ray, "Janitors vs. Tenants; a status-income Dilemma," *The American Journal of Sociology,* LVII (March, 1952), pp. 487-493.

deeper sources of antagonisms in hospitals is the belief of the people in the humblest jobs that the physician in charge calls upon them to do his dirty work in the name of the role of "healing the sick," although none of the prestige and little of the money reward of that role reaches them. Thus we might conceive of a classification of occupations involving dirty work into those in which it is knit into some satisfying and prestige-giving definition of role and those in which it is not. I suppose we might think of another classification into those in which the dirty work seems somehow wilfully put upon one and those in which it is quite unconnected with any person involved in the work drama.

There is a feeling among prison guards and mental-hospital attendants that society at large and their superiors hypocritically put upon them dirty work which they, society, and the superiors in prisons and hospitals know is necessary but which they pretend is not necessary. Here it takes the form, in the minds of people in these two lowly occupations, of leaving them to cope for twenty-four hours, day in and day out, with inmates whom the public never has to see and whom the people at the head of the organization see only episodically. There is a whole series of problems here which cannot be solved by some miracle of changing the social selection of those who enter the job (which is the usual unrealistic solution for such cases).

And this brings us to the brief consideration of what one may call the social drama of work. Most kinds of work bring people together in definable roles; thus the janitor and the tenant, the doctor and the patient, the teacher and the pupil, the worker and his foreman, the prison guard and the prisoner, the musician and his listener. In many occupations there is some category of persons with whom the people at work regularly come into crucial contact. In some occupations the most crucial relations are those with one's fellow-workers. It is they who can do most to make life sweet or sour. Often, however, it is the people in some other position. And in many there is a category of persons who are the consumers of one's work or services. It is probable that the people in the occupation will have a chronic fight for status, for personal dignity with this group of consumers of their services. Part of the social psychological problem of the occupation is the maintenance of a certain freedom and social distance from these people most crucially and intimately concerned with one's work.

In a good deal of our talk about occupations we imply that the tension between the producer and consumer of services is somehow a matter of ill-will or misunderstandings which easily might be removed. It may be that it lies a good deal deeper than that. Often there is a certain ambivalence on the side of the producer, which may be illustrated by the case of the professional jazz-musicians. The musician wants jobs and an income. He also wants his music to be appreciated, but to have his living depend upon the appreciation does not entirely please him. For he likes to think himself and other musicians the best judges of his playing. To play what pleases the audience—the paying customers, who are not, in his opinion, good judges—is a source of annoyance. It is not merely that the listeners, having poor taste, demand that he play music which he does not think is the best he can do; even when they admire him for playing in his own sweet way, he doesn't like it, for then they are getting too close—they are impinging on his private world too much. The musicians accordingly use all sorts of little devices to keep a line drawn between themselves and the audience; such as turning the musicians' chairs, in a dance hall without platform, in such a way as to make something of a barrier.[4] It is characteristic of many occupations that the people in them, although convinced that they themselves are the best judges, not merely of their own competence but also of what is best for the people for whom they perform services, are

[4] Becker, Howard S. "The Professional Dance Musician and his Audience," *The American Journal of Sociology*, LVII (September, 1951), pp. 136-144.

required in some measure to yield judgment of what is wanted to these amateurs who receive the services. This is a problem not only among musicians, but in teaching, medicine, dentistry, the arts, and many other fields. It is a chronic source of ego-wound and possibly of antagonism.

Related to this is the problem of routine and emergency. In many occupations, the workers or practitioners (to use both a lower and a higher status term) deal routinely with what are emergencies to the people who receive their services. This is a source of chronic tension between the two. For the person with the crisis feels that the other is trying to belittle his trouble; he does not take it seriously enough. His very competence comes from having dealt with a thousand cases of what the client likes to consider his unique trouble. The worker thinks he knows from long experience that people exaggerate their troubles. He therefore builds up devices to protect himself, to stall people off. This is the function of the janitor's wife when a tenant phones an appeal or a demand for immediate attention to a leaky tap; it is also the function of the doctor's wife and even sometimes of the professor's wife. The physician plays one emergency off against the other; the reason he can't run right up to see Johnny who may have the measles is that he is, unfortunately, right at that moment treating a case of the black plague. Involved in this is something of the struggle mentioned above in various connections, the struggle to maintain some control over one's decisions of what work to do, and over the disposition of one's time and of one's routine of life. It would be interesting to know what the parish priest thinks to himself when he is called for the tenth time to give extreme unction to the sainted Mrs. O'Flaherty who hasn't committed a sin in years except that of being a nuisance to the priest, in her anxiety over dying in a state of sin. On Mrs. O'Flaherty's side there is the danger that she might die unshriven, and she has some occasion to fear that the people who shrive may not take her physical danger seriously and hence may not come quickly enough when at last her hour has come. There may indeed be in the minds of the receivers of emergency services a resentment that something so crucial to them can be a matter of a cooler and more objective attitude, even though they know perfectly well that such an attitude is necessary to competence, and though they could not stand it if the expert to whom they take their troubles were to show any signs of excitement.

What do you think?

1. In the opening paragraph the author says that this country espouses "equality of opportunity" but does not always provide it. Can you find examples that support his opinion? What long-range effect might this kind of hypocrisy have upon people—both those who espouse the idea and those who know from experience that it isn't true?
2. The author says, ". . . for there is something almost as irrevocable about choice of occupation as there is about choice of a mate." How accurate or significant is this comparison when you consider the fact that a person can change jobs or get a divorce? Explain your answer.
3. What are some of the psychological and social reasons why a person would adopt language and concepts about his work the author calls "blinders"? Give as many reasons as you can. How many of these particular "blinders" are applicable to your job:
   (a) the title
   (b) the rationalization of mistakes
   (c) the production restriction
4. Use your own experience if you have a part-time or full-time job to test the author's thought that there is a certain criterion for deciding who can and who must be invited into the "in group." Describe that criterion in as detailed a way as you can.
5. Among the occupations that the author considers low in prestige are some that generally pay well. For example, janitors, pharmacists, and jazz musicians command moderately high salaries. How do you explain this contrast?
6. In this essay, the doctor and the janitor are seen as persons who deal with (and so respond differently to) the duty aspect of their jobs. Are there other occupations that are like the doctor's? The janitor's?

Suggestions for writing, reading, and viewing

1. Sometimes persons in a particular occupation adopt titles for themselves or are given ones that lend prestige. For example, some janitors are called maintenance engineers. List as many other examples as possible.
2. What kinds of things do some jazz artists do that seem designed to keep their audiences at a distance? This kind of information is often included in the liner notes on record jackets and in jazz magazines such as *Downbeat.* Gather pertinent information on at least three different artists.
3. *The Peter Principle* is the title of a paperback that humorously analyzes the problem of incompetence in society, including incompetence on jobs. It is provocative reading for anyone interested in learning some of the reasons which lie behind apparent incompetence.

The short color film "Alf, Fred and Bill" (8 min.) is recommended for stimulating discussion and writing experiences. It is about a man who inherits money and changes his life style with it, only to eventually return to his simpler way of living. (Contemporary Films.)

Also the short color film "The Violinist" (7 min.) is recommended. It looks into a different stereotype surrounding work by poking fun at the old notion that an artist must undergo suffering in order to create great works.

How To Succeed In Business Without Really Trying
From the Broadway Musical "How To Succeed In Business Without Really Trying"
By FRANK LOESSER
With Ambition
Piano
Voice
E♭6 add F
How to ap - ply for a job, How to ad-
C7
Fm add G
vance from the mail room, How to sit down at a desk,
E♭6 add F
D7
Recitative
Gm
How to dic - tate mem - o - ran - dums, How to de - vel - op ex - ec - u - tive style,
colla voca
F402-4
©-Copyright 1961 by FRANK LOESSER
All Rights Throughout the Entire World Controlled by
FRANK MUSIC CORP., 119 West 57th St., New York 19, N.Y.
International Copyright Secured
Made in U.S.A.
All Rights Reserved

"HOW TO SUCCEED IN BUSINESS WITHOUT REALLY TRYING" by Frank Loesser. © 1961 FRANK MUSIC CORP. Used by permission.

3
C7
Ebmaj7
How to com-mute in a three but-ton suit, with that wea-ry ex-ec-u-tive smile.
mp
First Tempo
Eb6 add F
This book is all that I need,
mf
sfz
G7add Bb
Bbm6
Bb6
C
C7
How to, how to suc - ceed.
sfz
f
mf
F6add G
How to ob - serve per-son-nel, How to se-
sfz
mf
F 402 - 4

4
D7
Gmadd A
lect whom to lunch with, How to a - void pet - ty friends,
sfz mf
sfz
F6 add G
E7
Am
How to be - gin mak - ing con - tacts, How to walk
sfz mf
sfz mf
G
D
in - to a con - fer - ence room with an i -
f
G
D7
G
dea, Bril - liant bus - 'ness i - dea,
F 402 - 4

5
D7 Fm7 Bb7 Fm7 Bb7 E
that-'ll make your ex - pense ac-count zoo - oom.
F6 add G
This book is all that I need,
A7add C Cm6 C6 D6 add E
How to, how to suc - ceed.
mp ff sfz mf f
F 402 - 4

HOW TO SUCCEED IN BUSINESS WITHOUT REALLY TRYING

Lyrics by Frank Loesser

How to apply for a job,
How to advance from the mail room,
How to sit down at a desk,
How to dictate memorandums,
How to develop executive style,
How to commute in a three button suit,
With that weary executive smile.

This book is all that I need,
How to, how to succeed.

How to observe personnel,
How to select whom to lunch with,
How to avoid petty friends,
How to begin making contacts,
How to walk into a conference room with an idea,
Brilliant bus'ness idea,
That'll make your expense account zoo-oom.

This book is all that I need,
How to, how to succeed.

What do you think?

1. How would you describe the general nature of the advice offered in this song? What type of person do you think is offering it? Explain in some detail.
2. How does the advice here compare with the kind you think would be given by instructors in the Business Department of your school?
3. Most of the specifics in the song have to do with social contacts not with job performance. Has your experience with jobs indicated that this is the best way to "succeed"? Give details from your experiences in answering.
4. In what job situations, other than a business such as the one in this song, would the recommended behavior help a person "succeed"? Explain how and why you think it would be helpful. Would this behavior be beneficial to an individual in a blue collar situation such as a factory? Give reasons for your response.
5. What definition of "success" is being used in this song? Are there others which are appropriate to a job?
6. What is meant by "executive style"? Can everyone develop it? Is it innate? Explain your answer.

Suggestions for writing and listening

1. Write a paper of approximately 1000 words in the form of a debate in which you have a successful employee arguing in favor of the kinds of behavior recommended in the song and a successful employer arguing against it. Make the arguments of each as strong and attractive as possible. Probably your own attitude will result in your giving one of the debaters a more persuasive argument than the other.
2. There are other popular songs that describe a work situation. Locate one by checking in current and back issues of magazines that publish song lyrics. Compare the attitude toward work performance in any one of them with the attitude expressed in this song. In a short paper, analyze and describe these attitudes indicating which you think is most likely to be satisfying for the individual employee.

"This is a bright mundo, *my streets, my barrio de noche. With its thousands of lights, hundred of millions of colors. Mingling with noises, swinging street sounds of cars and curses. Sounds of joys and sobs that make music. If anyone listens real close, he can hear its heart beat."*

from Down These Mean Streets
by Piri Thomas, 1967. Reprinted by
permission of Alfred A. Knopf, Inc.

PART 4

"THIS IS A BRIGHT MUNDO, MY STREETS, MY BARRIO DE NOCHE."

Demographers have made some interesting observations about the dominant American living patterns. For example, a disproportionate percentage—one-sixth—of the total population is crowded along the northeast coast between Washington, D.C. and Boston. And, since 1965, an average of 900,000 Americans have moved from cities to suburbs each year. This marks the third major population shift this country has experienced. The first was the move westward, and the second was the move from rural areas into cities.

Despite these general, common features, America stands for many different living styles. In many cases, the styles are influenced by the immediate physical environment. Certainly, the farmer's day-to-day living pattern could not be transported to Cleveland, Ohio, without undergoing change. Neither could the San Franciscan move to a small town without making changes in his way of life.

The thrust of this section is to invite the student to examine his own environment and the myriad ways in which it affects his own lifestyle. One of the selections describes a Puerto Rican newly arrived in New York City who misses the fresh air and green spaces of home. There is another contrast offered, this time within the same city: two boys living only two blocks apart virtually live in two different worlds when one considers the vast differences in services, cleanliness, noise, and congestion marking their neighborhoods.

Several poems widen our view beyond communities as the poets discuss America as a society. The section ends with song lyrics about the meaning of a tenement room to a boy whose dreams carry him away from its smells and sounds.

John Wesley, *Service Plaque for a Small Legion Post* 1962.
Courtesy of Robert Elkon Gallery, New York

Claes Oldenburg, *Flag Fragment* 1961. Photo by Robert R. McElroy

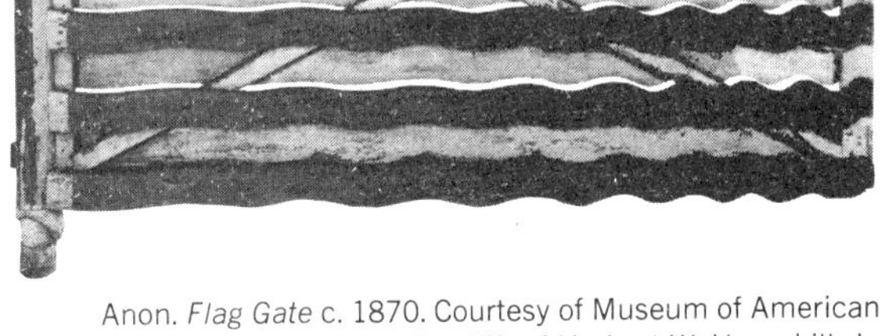

Anon. *Flag Gate* c. 1870. Courtesy of Museum of American Folk Art, Gift of Herbert W. Hemphill, Jr.

Hugh Roberts/Monkmeyer

What do you think?

1. Describe your emotional reaction to viewing these pictures of the flag.
2. Which picture most closely symbolizes your feelings about America? Explain why.

Suggestion for writing

1. Sketch a version of the flag that expresses your opinion of and attitude about America. Write a brief (250 words) explanation of what feelings you are expressing in your sketch.

I, TOO, SING AMERICA

Langston Hughes

I, too, sing America.

I am the darker brother.
They send me to eat in the kitchen
When company comes,
But I laugh,
And eat well,
And grow strong.

Tomorrow,
I'll sit at the table
When company comes.
Nobody'll dare
Say to me,
"Eat in the kitchen,"
Then.

Besides,
They'll see how beautiful I am
And be ashamed—

I, too, am America.

What do you think?

1. When the poet says "I too" in the first line, he means in addition to whom or what? Who are the "they" that send him to eat in the kitchen?
2. Throughout this poem, can you imagine that Hughes is really referring to more than the one situation he explicitly talks of? If so, what other situations come to mind?
3. What is the significance of the phrase, ". . . when company comes"? How does our behavior, manner, or expectations change when there is company?
4. Hughes doesn't give reasons *why* he thinks he will be treated differently "tomorrow." *When* exactly is he referring to? Can you give any reasons why the situation might or will improve? Be as specific and concrete as possible.
5. What will "they" be ashamed of?
6. Explain why the last line differs from the first. Also, explain why the poem is more effective or ineffective because Hughes has not used names but only pronouns.

Suggestion for research

1. Depending on how you interpret this poem, you may view it as quite literal or as one in which figurative meaning predominates. However, it may be necessary for you to do some research before coming to a conclusion. What, for example, does the term *figurative language* mean? Do you use it in your everyday speech? Do you know the names of each of the figures of speech that you use? Of some of them? Make a list of the kinds of figures of speech that you use and share it with the person sitting nearby. Do you learn anything new by looking at the other person's list?

POEM, OR BEAUTY HURTS MR. VINAL

e. e. cummings

take it from me kiddo
believe me
my country, 'tis of

you, land of the Cluett
Shirt Boston Garter and Spearmint
Girl With The Wrigley Eyes(of you
land of the Arrow Ide
and Earl &
Wilson
Collars)of you i
sing: land of Abraham Lincoln and Lydia E. Pinkham,
land above all of Just Add Hot Water And Serve—
from every B. V. D.

let freedom ring

amen. i do however protest, anent the un
-spontaneous and otherwise scented merde which
greets one(Everywhere Why)as divine poesy per
that and this radically defunct periodical. i would

suggest that certain ideas gestures
rhymes, like Gillette Razor Blades
having been used and reused
to the mystical moment of dullness emphatically are
Not To Be Resharpened. (Case in point

if we are to believe these gently O sweetly
melancholy trillers amid the thrillers
these crepuscular violinists among my and your
skyscrapers—Helen & Cleopatra were Just Too Lovely,
The Snail's On The Thorn enter Morn and God's
In His andsoforth

do you get me?)according
to such supposedly indigenous
throstles Art is O World O Life
a formula: example, Turn Your Shirttails Into
Drawers and If It Isn't An Eastman It Isn't A
Kodak therefore my friends let
us now sing each and all fortissimo A-
mer
i
ca, I
love,
You. And there's a
hun-dred-mil-lion-oth-ers, like
all of you successfully if
delicately gelded(or spaded)
gentlemen(and ladies)—pretty

littleliverpill-
hearted-Nujolneeding-There's-A-Reason
americans(who tensetendoned and with
upward vacant eyes, painfully
perpetually crouched, quivering, upon the
sternly allotted sandpile
—how silently
emit a tiny violetflavoured nuisance:Odor?

ono.
comes out like a ribbon lies flat on the brush

What do you think?

1. What aspect of American society does Cummings concentrate on? Does he approve or disapprove of what he's talking about? Are the values and preferences of Americans reflected positively or not in what he says about these American products?
2. Why does Cummings use the lyrics of "My Country 'Tis of Thee" as the framework for his own observations? What effect does this have on the song?
3. Why does Cummings rank "Just Add Hot Water and Serve" higher than the others? Do you agree with what seems to be his underlying reason?
4. What contribution did Lydia E. Pinkham make to America that would justify her inclusion here? (Look this information up in the library if necessary.)

Suggestions for research and writing

1. Find an advertising slogan like "Just Add Hot Water and Serve" which you think catches the spirit or nature of America. Use it as the title of a short paper (500 words). In the paper, explain the ways in which you think the slogan mirrors America.
2. Build a montage by clipping parts of advertisements and pasting them in overlapping fashion on a sheet of $8\frac{1}{2} \times 11$ inch paper. Try to find conflicting claims made by producers of different or even the same products. You might elect to write a short paper (500 words) on what can be said about Americans in light of the conflicting goals and procedures mentioned in the advertisements.
3. Read several magazine articles on the American artist Andy Warhol who has used advertising extensively in his work. Comment in either a short paper or in a verbal report to the class on whether you think Mr. Warhol approves or disapproves of advertising.
4. If you have already read the short story, "The Apostle" (page 160), write a short paper (500 words) in which you imagine the reaction Mr. Hedger would have to E. E. Cummings' poem.

THE IMAGE OF SUBURBIA

Robert C. Wood

SUBURBIA AS LOOKING GLASS

Strictly speaking, suburbs are places and suburbanites are people. Even more strictly speaking, suburbs are places in the country immediately outside a city and suburbanites are the inhabitants of that country. Suburbs depend upon the special technological advances of the age: the automobile and rapid transit line, asphalt pavement, delivery trucks, septic tanks, water mains, and motor-driven pumps. Suburbanites have habits which distinguish them more or less sharply from other Americans: they are commuters, they tend to own their own homes, which have at least some access to open space, and they have more children than the average American family. These definitions and characteristics indicate in concrete ways what suburbs and suburbanites are.

They do not, however, explain *why* suburbs exist, or, aside from simple progress, what accounts for the extraordinary explosion of our large cities into the countryside. To understand the underlying motives and aspirations which gave momentum to the massive shift of population another definition is necessary. We have to explain an abstraction, a concept of the mind, with elusive and subtle connotations. We have to explain "suburbia."

The most fashionable definition of suburbia today is that it is a looking glass in which the character, behavior, and culture of middle class America is displayed.

Rogers/Monkmeyer

When we look at suburbs we see our homes; when we look at suburbanites we see ourselves. Suburbia, according to this interpretation, reflects with fidelity modern man, his way of living, his institutions and beliefs, his family and his social associations. Because forty-seven million of us live in suburbs—more than in the cities or in isolated towns or on the farms—the suburbanite is, by statistical definition, the average American. Because over twelve million of us have moved to the suburbs in the last ten years—marking the greatest migration in the shortest time of the nation's history—the suburban trend should typify our contemporary way of life.

Many of the specialists who have looked carefully into the mirror find a man who is not appealing. The old images of national life seem to them to have disappeared; the stern Puritan, the sturdy yeoman, the hard-working capitalist are gone. In their place is a prototype whom it is difficult to idealize: a man without direction or ambition except for his desire for a certain portion of material security, a man so conscious of his fellows that he has no convictions of his own. Lacking the stern code of conduct of the "inner directed" man of the nineteenth century, separated from the Protestant ethic that maintained individuality fifty years ago, the suburbanite seeks direction from a passing parade of "experts" who, in the rapid succession of changing fashions, dictate the design of his house, the education of his children, the choice of his friends, and the use of his income. He willingly turns the direction of community affairs over to others. But since his neighbors are just as uncertain as he is, few real individualists appear to guide civic destinies. In the suburbs, in the opinion of its prominent investigators, the modern American exchanges individuality, privacy, the certain satisfactions of pride of craftsmanship and work well done, for something obscurely defined as the social ethic, being a good fellow, and group cooperation.

In this context, the suburb is the home of the modern man, the big organization on his doorstep. Suburban culture and the pattern of suburban life are designed to intensify the pressures on the individual. They encourage conformity, and subtly rearrange the use of space and time, the relations of the family, the activities of social and political organizations for the higher purpose of "the group." Each characteristic and institution of suburban life bears witness to the fact that David Riesman's lonely crowd is everywhere.

Thus, John Seeley and his associates point out that the suburbanite lives not in a house that expresses his individuality or that blends landscape and architecture to emphasize man's oneness with nature. Instead, he builds a house which expresses values of real estate experts but never his own, or he settles in a big development constructed on too little land. In either case, except for trivial detail, he builds his house as much like his neighbor's as possible. He whistles up the bulldozers, in John Keats' words, "to knock down all the trees, bat the lumps off the terrain, and level the ensuing desolation." He becomes lost in "squads and platoons" of little boxes on concrete slabs each surrounded by "a patch of bilious sod and two rusty dwarf cedars struggling for life beside each identical doorstep." If income permits, the houses are larger, though their lots are proportionately the same, and crammed with mechanical conveniences that testify to a preoccupation with consumption. They are arranged to "stage" elaborate displays of entertainment, built to encourage family and neighborhood sociability, erected as symbols of material well-being. The disappearance of clean styles of architecture, the rise of the modified Cape Cod–ranch type Colonials, their uniform reproduction row on row, the violence done to the natural terrain—all these are taken to document "togetherness," the new social ethic in practice.

The use of time in the suburbs is described as a further indication of the new America. Most observers find an implacable array of schedules which seem to testify to the suburbanite's inability to live as an individual and as he chooses. The commuter schedule for the husband, the nursery and social schedule for the wife, the school day for the growing child, these govern suburban life relentlessly. There are no longer any options, but instead unbreakable patterns for the day, the week, the year, and the generation. Time spent going to and from work, time spent in hauling children, time spent in class, the weekday for work, the weekend for "career maneuvering" or "improving" social status, all are by the clock. To the reporters of Crestwood Heights, one of the suburbs most meticulously observed, time is apparently the master of each and every inhabitant. Endlessly active, constantly harassed, the suburbanite hurries everywhere, caught up in a chain of events never of his own making but from which he cannot withdraw. He is plunged into a "hotbed of participation," an endless circle of meetings, appointments, arrivals, departures, and consultations.

Suburban institutions provide further ammunition for the looking-glass theory. They are shown as monuments of a society in which each member is attuned to the others but never to himself. The school emerges as the all-important focus of existence, and from the school, to children and parents alike, comes the constant message of "life adjustment." As "opinion leaders," teachers strive to inculcate cooperation, belongingness, togetherness. Courses aim at "socializing" the child through a process by which he learns specific skills at the same time that he is taught to use them only in an overtly friendly manner. Competition is subdued; so is individuality; the cry is for a common outlook, and discipline is achieved by indirect measures of ostracism. The generalization has even been made that by the time he gets to college, a suburban student chooses his career in business administration or science, where there are human relations to be cultivated or where there are facts, but where there are never values.

The aim of learning to get along with others, of advancing oneself only as a member of the group, infects, it is said, family life and leisure hours. The commuter-father is no longer the figure of authority; stern measures of discipline are not countenanced, and even if they were, the father is not home enough to use them in the proper time and place. Although family life is "important," and love and constant association are expected, the means for holding the family together are obscure. It is left to the mother and the schools, and the experts on whom both rely, to rear the child and run the suburb. Educated women, wanting motherhood but expecting something more, anxious to put their talents to use beyond the family circle, are in charge. Skipping from one meeting to another, indulging or wanting to indulge in extramarital affairs, ceaselessly expunging their feelings of guilt by overprotecting their children, they rule suburbia. So the desires and demands of children—space for their play, their training, their future careers, their happiness—become the predominant force in suburbia.

The decline of individuality is also found, according to most reports, in adult associations and activities. Suburban friendships are determined, by and large, by the physical layout of the neighborhoods in which they take place, or dictated by career maneuvering necessary in big-organization office politics. In the politics of public life, suburbanites are passive consumers of the national issues of the day or "inside-dopesters" on what the issues really are. On the local scene their political activity is frenzied but ineffective, for suburbanites are always ultimately manipulated by the shrewd, calculating developer, the old residents, or the school superintendent.

From this pattern of character, space, time, and the interaction of these institutions and beliefs, most observers go on to say, has come a new type of culture. Self-consciously friendly, in constant association, afraid or unable to differentiate themselves from their neighbors, the suburban residents form a classless society. Suburbia is a melting pot of executives, managers, white-collar workers, successful or unsuccessful, who may be distinguished only by subtle variations in the cars they drive, the number of bedrooms in their houses, or the tables they set. Their consumption is inconspicuous because they cannot deviate too far from the standards of their neighbors—but for the same reason it has a common quality. It is never ceasing, and for almost all suburbanites, time payments for purchases in an already overextended budget have replaced the savings account.

By this interpretation the life of suburbanites is "outgoing" in the sense that, lacking internal resources, they search for status and reassurance from the group around them, and that life is pathetic in the same sense. A fundamental transformation of American society is in full swing, and since the suburbs are seen to represent the transformation with such fidelity, they should be taken as the symbol and sign of the future.

HOLDOUTS IN SUBURBIA

Intriguing as the looking-glass interpretation is, it cannot be taken as a precise definition of suburbia. It is more a commentary on middle class Americans wherever they live: on the farms now equipped with central heating and television, within the city limits, in Peyton Place, Middletown updated, or the growing Southern town absorbing the second industrial revolution in the United States. As a generalization, the group-man theory is far too sweeping to take into account the suburbs which are not residential. It cannot explain the industrial suburb, where more people work than live, the slum suburb, deserted by the middle class and fallen on evil days, the racetrack suburb, the honky-tonk suburb of night clubs, amusement parks and used-car lots. It deals only with the dormitory suburb, and principally with the better type of dormitory suburb.

Even in the residential suburb, there are limitations to the theory. Against the broad wave of mass culture, mass values, and mass society, there is at least one stubborn holdout. While residential suburban living and individual suburbanites may represent modern character and behavior, their suburban governments do not. They join the other suburban political units around our large cities in clinging persistently to the independence they received when they were isolated villages and hamlets in a rustic countryside. If the suburb is a brand new development taking the place of forest or potato farm, the inhabitants insist on creating governments modeled after their older autonomous neighbors. These rural neighbors, far from acquiescing to the cult of size, turn their backs on progress and resist the influences of modernity. Though they accept the homes of the organization man, they insist on retaining the legal form and the public institutions which are relics of a bygone age.

This superimposition of provincial government on cosmopolitan people provides a strange pattern of incongruity. Within the single economic and social complex we have come to call a metropolitan area, hundreds and hundreds of local governments jostle one another about. Counties overlie school districts, which overlie municipalities, which overlie sanitary and water districts, which sometimes overlie townships and villages. Except for the special-purpose "districts," each suburban government maintains its own police force, its fire station, its health department, its library, its welfare service. Each retains its authority to enact ordinances, hold elections, zone land, raise taxes, grant building licenses, borrow money, and fix speed limits.

The spectacle of these ancient jurisdictions careening merrily on their way is often amusing and more frequently disturbing. By ordinary standards of effective, responsible public services, the mosaic of suburban principalities creates governmental havoc. Across a typical suburban terrain, twenty or thirty or fifty volunteer fire departments buy equipment and, with varying degrees of efficiency, put out fires. A welter of semi-professional police forces, usually poorly equipped and inadequately staffed, jealously compete or lackadaisically cooperate, uncertain of the limits of their jurisdiction. Independent school systems build costly plants, some crammed to capacity, others with excess space. In one municipality the water table dips perilously low; in another, foresighted or fortunate enough to have access to a reservoir, sprinklers turn all summer long. And, always, for suburban governments taken together, there is the extra and apparently unnecessary cost of doing individually what might be done collectively: the additional expense of making separate purchases without benefit of quantity discounts, of administrative and political overhead, of holding local elections and hiring city managers, of reporting, accounting, and auditing these separate activities.

The anachronisms of suburban governments have long been apparent and long decried. For almost half a century, the conditions of inefficiency, confusion, duplication, overlapping and waste have been under fire. . . .

SUBURBIA AS RENAISSANCE

The paradox which suburban government presents to suburban society sharply limits the theory of suburbia as the looking glass and suburbanites as the advance guard of the new America. A social order apparently built upon a commitment to the virtues of large organizations, indoctrinated to the advantages of size and scale, still tolerates tiny, ineffective governments which seem almost willfully bent on producing chaos, and which are still multiplying. As political entities, suburbs represent an order unwilling to join in the change going on about them; they flout the modern ideology attributed to suburban man.

They flout this ideology, moreover, by raising an ancient and honorable standard straight out of American political folklore. The justification of suburban legal independence rests on the classic belief in grassroots democracy, our longstanding conviction that small political units represent the purest expression of popular rule, that the government closest to home is best. The defense of suburban autonomy is that no voter is a faceless member in a political rally, but an individual citizen who knows his elected officials, can judge their performance personally and hold them accountable.

In the suburb, according to the folklore, the school board is likely to be composed of neighbors or friends, or at least friends of friends or neighbors of neighbors. Its members do not come from another part of a large city; they are available and accessible. So are the mayor, the county clerk, the commissioners, the councilmen, and selectmen. So are the chief of police, the water superintendent, the plumbing inspector, and the health officers. In this way, elected officials, bureaucrats, party leaders—the entire apparatus of democratic politics—are exposed to view, recognized and approached as they never are in a great metropolis. In politics, the suburb dwellers hold fast to a conviction that the small organization, run by a group of relatively few individuals, provides the best management of public affairs that is possible. . . .

The strength of this conviction has been powerful enough, at least to date, to blunt the edge of all the reform efforts to bring suburban governments into the twentieth century. In spite of statistics indicating that the metropolitan area in which suburbia exists is actually a single community, in spite of the obvious organizational chaos brought on by this political multiplicity, even the most ardent efficiency expert hesitates to deny the values small governments represent. Instead of recommending outright abolition of suburban jurisdictions, he presents one ingenious scheme after another—federations, special authorities, new systems of representation, new complexities of local government—designed to provide some measure of administrative rationality while still maintaining suburban autonomy. At rock bottom he accepts the value of small size and he works to preserve the suburb as a legal entity even if its powers must be reduced in the face of the realities of the modern world.

So, as yet there is little sign that this array of small municipalities merely represents a cultural lag. On the contrary, the statistics point in exactly the opposite direction, for every census report shows more—and smaller—and more self-consciously independent suburban governments than existed ten years earlier. And those which the looking-glass theory selects as the best examples of the home of modern man are also the ones which exhibit the most independent political institutions.

There are also signs that this renaissance of small-scale autonomy is not confined to suburban governments alone. Even the most confirmed advocate of the New American Character still finds signs of small town behavior throughout the suburbs he studies. So William H. Whyte, Jr., in investigating the organization man at home, discovers two sides to every coin he examines, notes something old as well as something new, remains ambivalent in his judgment of the suburb in a way which contrasts sharply with his indictment of the organizational world in general.

Whyte's residents are, of course, transients, newcomers to the town in which they live, and they are soon to move on to other, better suburbs. Nonetheless, they try to put down roots and they succeed to some degree; even though the roots are shallow. To Whyte there is something admirable in the vigor with which they respond to the advertisements that call their suburb a friendly small town, as contrasted to the lonely big city, and in the way they work to make the advertisement a reality. The suburbanite penchant for joining his neighbors to agitate against the town hall indifference and the developer may be participation for participation's sake, but it also may express citizenship of the highest sort. Small roots are better than none, civic spirit is to be preferred to apathy, and the chance to "chew on real problems" in public affairs is desirable, for it creates allegiances that have purpose.

Whyte does not scorn community affairs then. He approves of the suburbanite's self-conscious efforts to guide his town's future, even though he is only passing through and cannot stay to enjoy it. It is still an indication of older values, however sugar-coated in new jargon, and so is the classlessness of his suburbia. The melting-pot analogy is, after all, another cherished American ideal. It seems a laudable fact that the suburb often promotes better understanding among inhabitants with different ethnic origins, religions, and backgrounds, even though they are all within the middle class, that it helps prevent the emergence of classes and furthers the ideal of equality. It is to be preferred to the jarring hostility of groups wrangling among themselves in the large cities and it is a sign of small town life as it has always been known.

The pattern of inconspicuous consumption, the web of friendship, and the outgoing life that Whyte describes also have something of the flavor of a renaissance. Although "keeping down with the Joneses" may indicate group tyranny, it is still better than keeping up with them. At least it displays disapproval of overt snobbishness and obvious symptoms of city superciliousness; it harks back once again to the frontier spirit of equality. While suburbanites should probably manage their budgets more prudently than they do, at least their desire for improvement and progress is a sturdy American trait. Even suburban friendships have their admirable qualities so far as the observers are concerned. They may be largely determined by the location of play areas, the placement of driveways and lawns, and the size of the living room, and they may impose a surveillance that makes privacy clandestine and the way of the introvert hard. But here are old-time qualities of warmth, helpfulness, and service to others. While Whyte finds pressures for benevolent conformity, he also discovers brotherhood. He sees that the church may have sacrificed theology for acceptance and the school may stress adjustment at the expense of the liberal arts, but he sees also that it is good to have churches and schools. These provide a sense of community, institutions that are socially useful, and it is not surprising that in the end Whyte speaks of his suburbanites as pioneers.

Even more impressive than the fragments of small town culture still persisting in the suburb is the ideal that every analyst of suburbia seems to cherish of what suburbia ought to be. There is a special temper in the rage which the looking-glass philosopher expresses when he uncovers the organization man at home, for to him there is a special irony and incongruity in making the suburb synonymous with modern life.

John Keats sketches the idealized suburb most clearly. Following Mary and John Drone through their weary succession of inadequate, overpriced homes in suburbs inhabited by directionless people who do not know they are unhappy, he is angry not at suburbia but at what has been done to it. He objects not a whit to the popular demand for space, for relatively small neighborhoods, for private homes, for roots, however temporary. He protests only against the degradation of these aspirations by greedy, selfish contractors and by the foolish, undisciplined residents themselves. He describes developments, and he wants communities.

Keats' prescription is not to tear suburbia apart, but to build it better. He wants homes arranged so that the illusions of privacy and aesthetics can be cultivated in small space. He wants suburbanites to join together to build libraries and swimming pools, where truly useful and common purposes are served. He would encourage the flight from the city so long as it is properly done, with taste and recognition of family budgetary limits and with awareness of the public problems to be faced. He would surround with regulations and controls the builder who remains the sturdy nineteenth century individualist and is responsible for the damage suburbs do. What suburbia ought to be, for Keats, is a carefully designed constellation of small towns, each with its own community center, each self-contained, each controlling its local affairs at the local level with polite regard for the larger region to which it belongs.

. . . The small town, the small community, this is what seems good about the suburb to most observers, what needs to be preserved, and what the large organization should not be permitted to despoil. Spontaneous collaboration, voluntary neighborliness, purposeful participation, these are the goals of real suburbanites. And all of the observers seem to cherish the hope that in the suburbs we can re-create the small communities we have lost in our industrial sprawl since the Civil War. The irony they find is that our suburbanites do not discriminate between the type of association a small town can give and that which Madison Avenue promotes. . . .

. . . Thus, while the looking-glass theory protests the onrush of modern culture, it takes comfort in the hope that suburbia can somehow hold out against it. It is encouraged by the possibility that the suburbs may break up the sprawling metropolitan area into discrete units distributing here an industrial area, here a low-income neighborhood, here a retail center, here an exclusive residential area, but everywhere permitting a closer communion within the small localities. It applauds newspaper editorials which warn against making governments and communities "so big that no one counts" and speaks out for "the concept of people working together in identifiable units in a community with a cohesive past and future . . . of which the individual can feel a part and for the life of which he can feel a sense of participation and responsibility."

These hopes are imperfectly realized today, of course; modern circumstances always threaten them and frequently combine to subvert them. But the vision is powerful; it helps move the ordinary citizen to suburbia, the sociologist to protect it, and the political scientist to preserve it. The ancient symbol of the "republic in miniature" persists, and the suburb is its contemporary expression. For all our changes in culture and behavior, for all the heavy price we pay in inadequate local public services, nonexistent metropolitan services, and high taxes, the good life and the good government still come for us in small packages. Although minimum adjustments to the demands of urban life must be made, it seems the job of the suburb, either by social resistance or political compromise, to ensure the preservation of these values.

Suburbia, defined as an ideology, a faith in communities of limited size and a belief in the conditions of intimacy, is quite real. The dominance of the old values explains more about the people and the politics of the suburbs than any other interpretation. Fundamentally, it explains the nature of the American metropolis. It indicates why our large urban complexes are built as they are, why their inhabitants live the way they do, and why public programs are carried out the way they are. If these values were not dominant it would be quite possible to conceive of a single gigantic metropolitan region under one government and socially conscious of itself as one community. The new social ethic, the rise of the large organization, would lead us to expect this development as a natural one. The automobile, the subway, the telephone, the power line certainly make it technically possible; they even push us in this direction.

But the American metropolis is not constructed in such a way; it sets its face directly against modernity. Those who wish to rebuild the American city, who protest the shapeless urban sprawl, who find some value in the organizational skills of modern society must recognize the potency of the ideology. Until these beliefs have been accommodated reform will not come in the metropolitan areas nor will men buckle down to the task of directing, in a manner consonant with freedom, the great political and social organizations on which the nation's strength depends. A theory of community and a theory of local government are at odds with the prerequisites of contemporary life and, so far, theory has been the crucial force that preserves the suburb. There is no economic reason for its existence and there is no technological basis for its support. There is only the stubborn conviction of the majority of suburbanites that it ought to exist, even though it plays havoc with both the life and government of our urban age.

What do you think?

1. The author is critical of what he calls "togetherness." What reasons does he provide for his negative opinion? Do you agree with his opinion and find his reasons for it satisfactory? Explain.
2. The author says that the suburbanite is "caught up in a chain of events never of his own making." How can this be? Who developed the chain? Who or what encouraged him to become enchained?
3. Do you think that nonsuburban schools try consistently to teach students something very different from how to adjust to life? What is the prevailing philosophy of the school you are attending? Explain fully how you arrived at your interpretation of that philosophy.
4. Wood says that the suburban woman and the schools rear the children. This is similar to the comments of some sociologists who claim that in the inner-city the woman, not the man, raises the children. Is America becoming a country where the family head is the mother? Support your answer with reasons and examples.
5. Why doesn't Wood accept the "looking glass theory" as an adequate one for describing society?
6. Wood ends by defining suburbia as an ideology. What does this term mean in this context and why does he state this when the essay began with a different definition?
7. In general, do you agree with Wood's descriptions and criticisms of suburbia? Give reasons for your opinion.

Suggestions for writing and viewing

1. Write a short paper (500 words) in which you compare the portrait of suburbia presented in the short story "Profession: Housewife" with that one of the dormitory suburb in Wood's essay.
2. Using current issues of the reference book, *Readers' Guide to Periodical Literature,* locate and read three or four articles on different kinds of suburbs: working class, middle-income, and affluent ones might be one kind of choice you make. Write a paper (1000 words) comparing the drawbacks or advantages of each in comparison to the particular locale in which you live.
3. *The Fur-Lined Foxhole* (National Educational Television, 1964; 30 min.) depicts a family living in Wheeling, Illinois, a suburb of Chicago, as they talk about some of the social and artistic values and living patterns of people living in suburbia.

BEDFORD'S SURRENDER: WHAT USED TO BE IS GONE

David Murray

In his travels to feel the pulse of America's suburbs, writer David Murray visited his home town of Bedford, Mass., near Boston. Its story is that of many another small American town—swallowed up into megalopolis.

"What Used to Be is Gone" by David Murray. Reprinted with permission from the *Chicago Sun-Times*.

BEDFORD, Mass.—It used to be, a generation ago, that the land from the top of the hill swept away northward nearly uninterrupted, down to Vine Brook and the pond, across the checkered truck-garden farms to the tree-dark horizon.

Now, the town of Bedford, 16 miles northwest of Boston, is a suburb, a bedroom community for Boston and the electronic plants which have blossomed nearby.

Now, the hill where Capt. Jonathan Wilson used to live is crammed with small houses. Capt. Wilson commanded the Bedford Minutemen in the Concord Fight in 1775 and his house still stands, but the 100 or more acres he had have shrunk to two acres. But in Bedford, that is still a large parcel.

The pond, where the pickerel could be taken a generation ago, is a sump now, its banks cluttered with broken stone dumped there by the builders when the new highway went through, replacing the old blacktop road.

DRIVING AROUND the old, winding roads, one finds the names on the proliferated mailboxes new. Paul Little's name is still on one of them, with "Shawsheen River Farms" underneath it, the way it used to be when his father was a farmer here.

The farm is gone, however. Paul Little tried to farm it, but as people moved in they wanted more schools, more roads, more sewers and town water. The taxes got too high for farming, and the competition from the vast agriconomy of California and Florida got too steep.

So Little, pushing 50 now, made his peace with the suburban Visigoths and in 1969 turned his land into a golf course.

"Farming's dead and you've got to face facts," he said after he had exchanged old memories of friends who had scattered, far gone from Bedford.

"Next winter," he said, waving a hand across the once-rich bottomland and dairy pasturage, "I'm putting in a 1,000-foot T-bar and a snowmaker and lights for night skiing. I'll be putting in tennis courts, too. People have got money for recreation, if they don't have it for anything else."

He said he "didn't want to give up the land, but I couldn't farm it any more. Bedford isn't Bedford the way you and I knew it. If I owned the land I used to farm, there sure wouldn't be any houses on it."

SHAWSHEEN RIVER Farms isn't the only thing that has made the transition from agriculture to suburb. But the population growth (from 3,000 in 1940 to 12,500 in 1970) did not alone make Bedford into a suburb. It changed, became something new, because the newcomers brought with them or forged a new mode of living.

A generation ago, for example, everyone in town knew Bedford had sent 77 Minutemen to Concord on that April 19 195 years ago and that the Bedford Flag, aside from being the only one carried at the Bridge, was the oldest American flag.

The thing was that almost no one paid it any great mind. Bedford was dwarfed in the history books by Concord and Lexington, four miles east, where Capt. Dan Parker told his men in the chilly dawn to "stand your ground; don't fire unless fired upon."

In 1964, however, the Bedford company of Minutemen was reactivated apparently for social and ceremonial, rather than political, purposes. The company roster includes such ranks as "Cornet Flag Bearer," "Sergeant Cannoneer" and "Sergeant Armorer." But its officers do not seem to include one name which could be called "old Bedford." Not a Page or a Davis or a Webber in the lot.

THE STATION WAGONS gather in the parking lot of the new shopping center and the newcomers patronize such hallmarks of Suburbia as the Volkswagen agency, the hobby shop and the garden center. There was a plant sale on a recent Saturday on the lawn of the 18th-century Fitch Tavern.

Not far away from the shopping center is a professional building, and one of the three doctors listed on the shingle is an obstetrician, and one of the three dentists is an orthodontist.

There is the Belle Isle Skating School, so the children don't have to wait for the pond at Bedford Springs to freeze over with black ice, ringing under the skate blades in a New England winter. And the mixed smells of the old feed, grain, coal and oil store down by the Boston & Maine tracks have been replaced with the more modern, antiseptic aroma of a paint and hardware store.

The churches are more diversified in denomination. Like most small New England towns, the Unitarians and Congregationalists came first, and Roman Catholics with the immigration from Ireland and Italy. Episcopalians were Tories and always suspect.

Now, there are churches in Bedford for Lutherans and Baptists, and the latter have the Rev. Phillips Brooks Henderson as minister.

THERE IS A COMMUNITY Santa Claus program and on Independence Day, 1968, little Donna Mead, dressed as "Miss Minute Maid," pushing a bunting-decked carriage and carrying a replica of the Bedford Flag, won the town's first official doll-carriage parade.

The following year, the spanking new library was opened, and to help with its funding, the "Friends of the Library," a cross-section of "old" and "new" people, got out "The Bedford Sampler," full of drawings of the old houses few people used to pay much heed to and recipes given by their present owners, recipes for such suburban fare as spinach salad, shrimp casserole and "Yummy Quick Hamburger Dinner."

As Mrs. Stefanelli, who still has the grocery store just across from the green and the first meeting-house, said:

"There aren't many of us left anymore."

What do you think?

1. Is it reasonable or not to expect a town to change in character in the span of a generation? Explain your answer.
2. Is the author most interested in the present or the past character of Bedford? How do you account for his interest?
3. What is the meaning of each of these terms the writer uses:
   (a) bedroom community (column 1, line 7).
   (b) a sump (column 1, line 17).
   (c) agriconomy (column 1, line 30).
   (d) suburban Visigoth (column 1, line 33).

   Are these technical terms? Is the article written, for the most part, from a technical point of view?
4. What is the significance of Murray's mentioning the following?
   (a) The Captain Jonathan Wilson estate.
   (b) The plant sale on the lawn of the 18th-century Fitch Tavern.
   (c) That one of the three dentists is an orthodontist.
   (d) That the Baptist minister's name is Rev. Phillips Brooks Henderson.
5. How would you describe the author's attitude toward the changes which have developed in Bedford? Support your answer with specific passages. Is his attitude justifiable? Explain.
6. Do people with attitudes like Murray's impede progress? Can you imagine the author lying in front of a bulldozer that was preparing to demolish the 18th-Century Fitch Tavern? Would you participate in such an act? Why or why not?

Suggestions for writing and drawing

1. Mr. Murray's observation about rapid and radical change may be applicable to your own community. If so, write a long paper (1000 words) in which you describe how things looked and felt before and after the changes. Select a street, a corner, a tourist spot, or some other such geographically limited area. Like this journalist, do not openly state your attitude about the changes; instead let it come through the particular details which you include.
2. By checking an almanac or a U.S. Atlas in the library, determine whether or not the growth that Bedford realized between 1940 and 1970 is unusual for towns which were less than 5000 in 1940. If so, read some factual data on Bedford in order to explain her growth. If not, do some research to try to discover what shifts in the entire nation can explain these widespread changes in population. Write a short paper (500 words) which presents your findings.
3. Compare the different ways in which three authors use personal names. Carefully note the significance of names in this article, the use of names in "The Apostle" on page 160, and that in "The Happiest Man on Earth" on page 148. How is the use and significance different? How similar?
4. Draw an editorial cartoon or write a short and sharply worded editorial in which Paul Little's experience and attitude is dramatized. Circulate your work among the class. Is there agreement that you succeeded in capturing his essence?

Suggestion for viewing

1. "Suburban Living" is a long, black-and-white film that comes in two parts (40 min. apiece). It has an informal panel discussion format with the discussants noting mostly the virtues of six different innovative developments in suburban housing. It is recommended only for classes interested in the technical aspects of housing such as architecture, landscaping, the relationship of work to play areas, and so on.

TWO BLOCKS APART

Juan Gonzales and Peter Quinn
Charlotte Leon Mayerson, Editor

Juan Gonzales and Peter Quinn, two seventeen-year-old boys, live in the same New York City neighborhood. They are both high school seniors in the same school district, both Catholics in the same parish, both ballplayers with the same parks and school yards at their disposal. That they do not know each other is an urban commonplace; that they are utter strangers in the conditions of their lives, in their vision of what they themselves are, seems a personal illustration of the apparent failure of the American melting pot. . . .

NEIGHBORHOOD

The area in which these boys live contains some of the most beautiful streets in New York and also some of the ugliest. It has a large park, playgrounds and ball fields, a library, a museum, and a narcotics-addiction center. Houses scattered throughout the neighborhood are, from time to time, "raided for dope" or for prostitution. These raids take place around the corner from the many well-kept and sometimes expensive apartment houses of the area. The crime rate here is relatively low for this borough of New York City, although burglaries, muggings, and juvenile complaints have vastly increased over the neighborhood's own formerly low rate. About 30 per cent of the population is classified as "nonwhite."

Sam Falk/Monkmeyer

Juan lives in a New York Housing Authority Low Income Project, which faces on a particularly unattractive commercial area. More than nineteen hundred families live in the nine buildings that comprise the project. To qualify for residence, a family with two children can earn no more than $5,080 a year. Family income is closely checked by Housing Authority employees, who also may inspect individual apartments at will to ascertain that building rules are being complied with.

The area formerly contained small "old law tenements" and "single-room occupancy" dwellings that were condemned for bad repair, dirt, disease, and crime. Juan lived in one of these houses until it was demolished, moved to another neighborhood for a few years, and returned when the project was completed.

Peter lives in a well-kept apartment house that was built on a fairly luxurious scale in the nineteen twenties. The building is on one of the nicer streets of the neighborhood, overlooking a large park. One hundred families live in the house. A doorman is always in attendance in the front lobby and the whole atmosphere seems remarkably friendly and intimate.

JUAN GONZALES

Man, I hate where I live, the projects. I've been living in a project for the past few years and I can't stand it. First of all, no pets. I've been offered so many times dogs and cats and I can't have them because of the Housing. Then there's a watch out for the walls. Don't staple anything to the walls because then you have to pay for it. Don't hang a picture. There's a fine. And they come and they check to make sure.

Don't make too much noise. The people upstairs and the people downstairs and the people on the side of you can hear every word and they've got to get some sleep. In the project grounds you can't play ball. In the project grounds you can't stay out late. About ten o'clock they tell you to go in or to get out. Then . . . there's trouble because they don't want you to hang around in the lobby. They're right about that one thing, because like in good houses, the lobby should be sort of like a show place, I think. You know, then you could have something special.

The elevators smell and they always break and you see even very old people tracking up and down the stairs. That's when the worst thing comes. People are grabbed on the stairs and held up or raped. There was this girl on the seventh floor who was raped and there was a girl on the fourth who was raped and robbed. There was an old man who was hit over the head—about fifty years old—he was hit over the head on the stairs and beat up bad. I don't know, maybe it's not always the people who live there. Maybe there's a party going on in the next-door and there are strangers in the party. You know how it is, not everybody is a relative. And those people come out and they start fights and arguments. Or they go around banging on the doors when they are drunk.

Before, when things happened in the halls, nobody would come out for nothing. When there were muggings, nobody wanted to come out in the halls and maybe have to face a guy with a knife or a gun. Lately, though, it's a little bit more friendly. Like my mother might have somebody come into our house to learn how to make rice and beans and then I tell my mother to go with them and learn how to make some American foods for a change. So now people are beginning to see on our floor that it's better to have someone help you if you are in trouble than to be alone and face the guy.

I guess in some ways the projects are better. Like when we used to live here before the projects, there were rats and holes and the building was falling apart. It was condemned so many times and so many times the landlords fought and won. The building wasn't torn down until finally it was the last building standing. And you know what that is, the last building . . . there's no place for those rats to go, or those bugs, or no place for the bums to sleep at night except in the one building still standing. It was terrible. The junkies and the drunks would all sleep in the halls at night and my mother was real scared. That was the same time she was out of work and it didn't look to us like anything was ever going to get better.

Then they were going to tear the house down. When I was about eleven or so we moved to another neighborhood. Down there I met one of the leaders of a gang called the Athletes, and the funny thing is that even though this boy was the leader, he didn't really want to belong to a gang. He only went into it because he was alone and everybody else was belonging. What could he do? Then I got associated with him and he quit his gang and we walked along together. Finally we had a whole group of us that were on our own. We still know each other. Even now sometimes I go over there or sometimes he comes here. When I was living there, sometimes he'd go away to Puerto Rico and I was always waiting for him to come back. You know, I missed him and he missed me.

My friend kept me from that fighting gang even though he was the leader. And he lived there with us, so we didn't have any trouble on the block because other gangs were afraid to come. We all lived together—Negroes, Puerto Ricans, and Italian kids—and we got along happy before I moved.

But my mother was afraid because the gang wars near the block made the other streets dangerous. You'd have all kinds of war. The Athletes would fight the Hairies. Then the newspaper had it the Hairies were fighting somebody else. My mother wanted to transfer back here, to the old neighborhood we'd lived in before the projects came.

Well, we did. But you know, every time you move you feel like it's not right because you're leaving part of yourself back there. I used to go back down there every weekend because, when we moved back here, everything was different. The projects were up, no more small houses, all twenty-one floors. There were new kids, a new school.

That time, before I knew anyone here on the block, I would have to fight a person to get introduced, and then finally either he'd beat me or I'd beat him. That way we'd get to know each other. I was new, you know. It was my building and my neighborhood, but I was new.

I would fight one guy in front of about twenty kids and I was afraid they were going to jump me. One time I said, "Look out, one guy and all of you gonna jump me. Is that a way to fight?" The guy I was fighting said they wouldn't jump me, and we fought that day and I went home bleeding. And then the next day I didn't get anybody to help me, but I went back and we fought again, and he beat me again. Then one day, I beat him. I proved to him that I had courage and that I could succeed, and then, when the other boys came, this boy I had beaten up told them to lay off me.

Like back then, when I first came back to the neighborhood, my mother didn't want me to go out with all those kids on the street. I'd say to her, "Man, what am I going to do? I don't have any friends here. All I can do is just go out and look at people. You could go crazy." There were like groups of boys around and they stuck together. There were coloreds, Puerto Ricans, and Italian boys all together. But they were all friends with each other and they didn't want anybody crashing in on them. But after those fights we shook, and that was it. From then on, I was in. . . .

White kids don't belong to gangs much. They're usually cowards. Only maybe sometimes, if one white, he lived around a colored neighborhood for a long time, and he proved he's not scared, then they take him in. Me, I'm not afraid of tough kids. It's bad when you're afraid of them. Like a Paddy boy will chicken out if he was alone. Really scared to death, you know. But not me. Oh, I was smeared a lot of times—

smeared is you don't have a chance. I was jumped in the park a couple of times. I was jumped down there once by a group of guys I didn't even know. Those guys jumped on me and started beating the heck out of me, kicking, cursing, using their cigarettes. That time I went to the hospital and they patched me up and took me home. But the thing is I wasn't afraid of them. Why they did so good, what happened, was they just caught me by surprise. I mean I would have caught a couple of them and they wouldn't have been able to hurt me that badly, but the trouble was they caught me by surprise and I didn't have a chance. If I knew them I would kill them afterwards. Do you think I would come home bandaged up, and you think I'm not going to do anything about it? I get riled sometimes when a guy looks at me the wrong way. You think I'm not going to get those that got me? I'll get them one at a time if I'm alone, or all at once if I have a group with me. I'm not scared to walk down the street ever. I can handle myself and I might take on a guy, he's alone, because I've seem him act big when he's with his men and now I want to test him, like alone. But taking on a whole gang, that's another thing.

Going home from school once, there was big trouble like that. On the subway, right on the train when it was moving, some guys grabbed a couple of white school girls . . . and they raped them. I couldn't stand it, right there on the subway and they did it without interference. That's something in my life I'm not proud of.

Man, you believe me? I ran all over that train trying to find a cop. And I wouldn't have minded jumping in and stopping it, no matter what, if there was a way. I got very upset but, see, I go in there, without a knife, alone, I'm going to get my brains knocked out. Even that, I wouldn't mind so bad, if I knew the girls were going to come out all right. But I knew they were still going to be played around with.

And there was nobody else who wanted to come with me. I don't think the guys I was with, they cared at all. Nobody would help me, not old people or kids. On that whole train, nobody, nobody. I was alone.

I feel lousy about it. I mean, even now, sometimes I look at a girl and I think, "Suppose that happened again? What would I do *this* time?" And I promise myself I'll go in, no matter what. But I couldn't do anything about it that time. I'm not afraid to fight, I've been fighting all my life. But nobody would help me start a little riot and get them off those girls.

There are some times, though, when everybody in the neighborhood does get together, agrees on one thing. Like the time there was one policeman who used to tease and bother everybody around the block. It got so bad that we had to fix that policeman. So everybody got together. Nobody was on the street that day except one boy, up on a stoop. The policeman said, "Get off. Get off that stoop. You don't belong here." Well, the boy stepped quickly back and the cop came up on the stoop. Up above there on the roof, they had a garbage can and they sent it right on his head. He was in the hospital for about three or four months, something wrong with his head. And the next policeman they sent wasn't so bad; he was just bad like a regular policeman.

The police are the most crooked, the most evil. I've never seen a policeman that was fair or that was even good. All the policemen I've ever known are hanging around in the liquor store or taking money from Jim on the corner, or in the store on the avenue. They're just out to make a buck no matter how they can do it. O.K., maybe if you gave them more money they wouldn't be so crooked, but what do you need to qualify for a policeman? I mean, if you have an ounce of brain and you have sturdy shoulders and you're about six feet one, you can be a policeman. That's all.

I mean, you've got to fight them all the time. A policeman is supposed to be somebody that protects people. You're supposed to be able to count on them. You're supposed to look up to policemen and know that if anything goes wrong, if any boys jumped me, I can just yell and the policeman will come running and save me. Around my block, you get jumped, the police will say, "Well, that's just too bad." He just sits there.

Even the sergeants are crooked. It's the whole police force is rotten. There was a man, I don't know who he was, way out in Brooklyn somewhere. He broke down a whole police station, a whole police force, the detectives, the policemen, the rookies. Everybody that was on that police force was crooked. Everybody in the precinct was crooked. He had to tell them all to go home.

Like take the Negro cop. The police towards discrimination are the same as anybody else. You have colored policemen, Italian policemen, every kind. But, you know, a Negro policeman will tend to beat up another Negro more than he would beat up anybody else, because he says to himself, "I'm a cop, and this guy is going to expect special privileges. I've got to show the other people it doesn't mean anything to me, that I'm really not going to treat them different." I think the Puerto Ricans would be just the same as the Negroes. He would tend to beat up Puerto Rican people more than he would a Negro or anybody else. Maybe you think he'd feel the Puerto Ricans were somebody he should help and he should try to solve some of their problems. But that's not the way it works.

And like I said, you think they protect you? When I lived downtown, it was a terrible neighborhood. There were so many killings, and people were being raped and murdered and all. Guys, you could see them, guys you could see jumping out of windows, running away from a robber, using a needle or something. I worked in a grocery there and I was afraid to go to work, but I guess I was lucky anyhow. I mean, I never got in any kind of real cop trouble or anything. They'd pick me up only in sort of like routine. They picked up everybody once in a while to make sure, you know, that nobody is carrying weapons and there is not going to be a fight that day. Of course, as soon as the police left, everything was the same all over again, anyhow.

That time they picked me up, I was halfway home from the grocery store where I worked and—well—I'll tell you how I felt like. I felt like the policeman was the rottenest person in the world. What would happen, see, is that I was always tall, and being tall, they think that I'm older. Then, no matter what you tell them, they believe that you're older. They were looking for a draft card and I didn't have one. I was too young and I told them I didn't have a draft card. Man, I was only twelve, thirteen or so, you know. Then they'd take me on the side and hit me a couple of times and I'd go home black and blue.

You wouldn't get picked up alone, even now. A person alone they never bother with, unless he's looking at cars or something. Whenever I get picked up, it's with a group. Like if I'm walking along and there's a group here and at the same time I'm walking, even though I don't know them, a policeman comes. They take all of us. Once I got picked up when there was a poker game going on or a crap game. They picked us up and they wanted to find out who had the money, who had the dice. They hit everybody. I think I even got hit the worst because I was a little taller than the rest of them. It happens right out on the street.

They tell you to get up against the wall of a building, and then they start searching you. And you can't talk to the policeman. Never say a word when they have you against the wall. Say anything and he thinks that you are making a false move and then he has the right to shoot you. So I would stand there and he asked my name, and I'd tell. And then he'd ask for my age and when I'd tell him twelve, thirteen, fourteen, he wouldn't believe me. They didn't think a Puerto Rican kid could be so young, so tall. Then they'd take me over the side and hit me a couple of times.

I'd be scared. Half the time I was petrified from being hit and because I was thinking of what my mother would say, you know, if I was taken down to the station. That I didn't do anything didn't make any difference to the police because I was still picked up. But I guess I was lucky because every time I was picked up I got sent home. There were a couple of boys that time that were Spanish and they didn't understand the language too well. When they tried to tell the policeman something, they got black and blue marks all over. Well, they didn't like it too much and they started trying to run away and talking back and pushing around, you know. The policeman just grabbed them, got them in the car and took them away.

PETER QUINN

I've always lived in this neighborhood. My parents moved to a house up the street a few years after they got married and they lived there until we moved to this building about eleven years ago. We've lived in this same building ever since, and my aunt and uncle and cousins have lived here even longer. My grandfather still lives a few blocks away, so we Quinns really are settled in here.

The apartment house we live in has run down lately like other parts of the neighborhood. My family is afraid it's going to turn into a high-class slum. There is always something being repaired with the plumbing or the electricity, since the building is pretty old now. You have to wait a longer time to get some repairs done and my mother says the service is not nearly as good as it used to be. For example, there was always a doorman at each entrance all day and all night. Now they've taken off the doorman at the back door for a few hours during the night. Another problem is that the elevators are now self-service and it's not nearly as convenient as it used to be, when there were elevator men.

We're lucky though. There's a very funny man in the house who really does a good job about all these complaints. He organizes meetings, and gets the lawyers who live here to advise him, and the tenants to pay a yearly fee for his committee, and I don't know what else. He's really a scream. I *love* him. I think he's great when meetings are held, and he really does accomplish things. The landlord has learned by now that he can't get away with anything because we're always alert to our rights.

I don't have any complaints about our own apartment though. It's spacious and has a great view of the park and my mother and sister are really great at interior decorating. I have my own room now. I used to share it with my brother, but since he's away it's exclusively for me. His bed is still there, though, and I wouldn't be sorry to have him back using it.

Aside from my sister's room and my parent's bedroom, there's a living room, dining room, kitchen and three bathrooms. My own room is really neat, the best room I know of in the world. It's got dark brown walls and orange bedspreads. I've got a guitar on the wall, a wine bottle, my school athletic letter. I love to hang things on the wall. There are two bachelor chests in the room, one for my brother, one for myself, bookcases, and trophies on a shelf, and my own desk. My brother and I each have our own closet and we fitted them very nicely with places for shoes and athletic equipment. Then there's a great big comfortable chair in my room which is the best thing to get into when you want to be off by yourself.

Sometimes, of course, my family thinks about moving because the neighborhood, in the side streets, and over in the projects, isn't what it used to be. You hear about people being mugged now and problems with gangs and all the rest.

When I was small, I knew everybody around our street; everybody was my friend. Every day all the kids would meet out at the park—we used to call it the big park. And every day we played skully bones with bottle tops and games like that and maybe threw a ball a little bit. I had no worries then. That is, I've never fought between my own friends and there weren't so many Puerto Rican or colored kids around. Now, sometimes, when I leave the house at night or have to meet off in the park somewhere, I am afraid. Or when I walk down the street and I see four Puerto Ricans—and I could tell them a mile away, not that they're Puerto Rican, but that they're that type that looks like they're going to kill anybody that steps in front of them—I am really terrified. I steer clear, I cross the street.

My friends never, never look for trouble. We don't like it. If we're coming head on to one of those gangs, we cross. I'll give them the right of way anytime if they think that makes them big. There've been a few incidents like that where these guys think that by being tough they really are getting something when it's really a laugh. Once, when I was a lot younger, a colored kid stopped me and asked me if I had any money on me. I told him I had two cents and I said, "You want it?" He answered that he did want it and that he would buy some lunch with it. I said, "Go ahead, buy all the lunch you can get with that."

Of course, not all Puerto Rican kids are like that or all colored, I guess. One guy, Fernando Gutierrez, is in our group and even he once got into trouble with them. One day we were all playing ball in the big park and he had a beautiful glove that cost his father about twenty dollars. A bunch of Puerto Rican and colored kids came out and they grabbed his glove and told him that they wouldn't give it back unless we gave them some money. Well, we chipped in and we got about fifty cents together and they sold the glove back to us for the fifty cents. They didn't even know what it was worth.

The trouble is that, living as they do, there wouldn't be much else for them to look forward to besides picking up a name for being tough. All they're looking for is a reputation, since they don't have much else to look for. I saw on a TV show once a story about a Puerto Rican boy who was really typical. That boy said that during the school year the one thing he looked forward to was lunch in the school cafeteria because it was the biggest meal he had. He kind of liked school because there isn't much for him to do otherwise except sit outside on the stoop.

Of course, they're not all like that. Two Puerto Rican boys who are with our group from our church—well, they're on our side. Because they've always gone where we've gone, they know how we think and what we like to do, and that we don't like to fight. They both go to good schools and don't have anything to do with the others. When . . . if ever there is an emergency, they're with us.

The one time we've had serious problems with those gangs was a few months ago. A group of us, about fifteen, had been up at a private pool swimming and when we came out, we were standing around saying good night. One real big kid, a friend of mine, had a soda which he was drinking and a bunch of Puerto Rican kids came along. They asked him to give them a drink out of his bottle and he wouldn't. He said that he'd just bought it and that everybody was taking a sip and that he wouldn't have anything left for himself. Well, one thing led to another, but my friend wasn't going to stand for being pushed around. He said, "I'm not going to let anyone push me or my friends around." Well, that did it. They left, but the next day the same boys came up to us, this time when we were standing in front of the gym. They gave us an ultimatum. They said that they would give us three choices: either we fight them; we back down; or we never go over onto their block. They left then and we were very worried.

Of course, there's quite a large group of us, too, who go to church, club meetings and play ball together and maybe go to dances together or date. But we are not any kind of fighting group. Nobody among us likes to fight, and we'll do anything we can to stop one. That time, it was a Saturday, and we went down to the gym in the cellar of the church and we set up chairs for the next morning's Mass. All the fellows got together there and we had a democratic meeting and a few suggestions were made. We decided that if we ever fought those boys everyone of us would be killed, really. Those Puerto Rican and colored kids from the projects can get so many others of their own kind in such a short time, it's really unbelievable. They get them from all over the city within a few hours by telephone, telling what's going on. It's sort of a chain. They're called War Lords or something like that, and they even have treaties.

We knew that, once we set up a fight, perhaps three or four hundred of them would show up. Another thing is, they'd all be armed. They have knives and chains and probably even pistols. I've never seen a Puerto Rican or a colored kid use a weapon on a white boy, though I've heard of it. What I did see was one Puerto Rican kid beat another one with a chain. That's a vicious weapon.

Well, we talked about how the incident had started, how we might have avoided it, what was going to happen that night, what the odds would be. We worked it out that it was fifteen to one against us, at the very least. The solution seemed simple. We decided to back down by saying, as we backed down, that we would not go as a group into their block. We met with one or two of them and we told them that when we saw them in a gang, on the street, we wouldn't say anything, wouldn't look at them. We would just ignore them as they would ignore us. That night, a meeting was arranged, with all of us on one side of the street and all of them on the other. One of our boys went out into the middle of the street. He says he felt very frightened and could see that they had weapons with them. Well, the two leaders met in the middle and discussed the matter and it all broke up. My friend was a fast talker and got us out of this by brains and not by muscle.

The thing is that we don't have to look for reputations, we don't have to pick up a name for being good fighters. We had decided all that in our strategic meeting and we all knew that it was a stupid move to fight. All we did was to provide those fools with another notch to their guns without losing anything ourselves. When you're dealing with that type, there's nothing to be ashamed of for having more brains. I'm not sure how to say it, but I think they felt a little bigger by showing us that they could put us down, because that's how they interpreted it.

The truth of the matter is that they don't like us and we don't like them. We come from Holy Family and we're white. They either don't go to church at all or go to the other parish, and they're colored—or Puerto Rican. According to their rules, making whites ashamed, as they thought they did, was real important. Then, the next time, when they see us using the private pool, or going off to the club to play ball, or driving by in our parents' car, they could feel that they were superior. The truth is that we were smart enough not to lose our heads.

There were two policemen around that night, but they didn't do anything. The policemen just told us to walk around and go home, but they didn't interfere because there was nothing really happening. The police do step in when there's any trouble, though. For example, there's one boy who lives in the project, but he hangs around most of the time with us. One night he was cutting across the playground of the project and a bunch of kids jumped him and were beating him up pretty badly. The police came along at just the right moment and got all those kids.

In general, the police in New York do a very good job. I think all this fuss about police discrimination and so forth is not true. Perhaps, once in a while, you can get a policeman who will be too rough or dishonest, but it's that way in any large group. Another problem is that if I were a policeman and I were offered $100,000 to forget about a gambling syndicate or something like that, I'd find it very hard to refuse. And I know there must be some policemen who are weaker than I am. Even with traffic violations, if they don't jeopardize anyone's life, I think it must be very hard to resist if someone gives you some money. It doesn't matter that much.

The police are just trying to do their job and if you know your rights, you're all right. For example, a bunch of us often meet up at the luncheonette at the corner and have Cokes in the evening when there's no school. Well, the proprietor doesn't like one of my friends and one night he just pushed him out. He was buddies with the policeman on the beat and he called him. When the policeman put his hand on my friend, my friend really began shouting. He told him, "I know just who you are and what you can do to me and what you can't. If you touch me again, my father will bring suit against the whole city government. I will not be discriminated against." Well, my friend was making such a fuss and drawing such a crowd, the policeman just slunk away and we went back to drinking our Cokes.

Another time something like that happened to my best friend. He goes to Europe with his family every summer, and last year he brought back a BB gun. We went into the park to a secluded place and he was trying out his gun on some pigeons—not that he could hit them, anyhow. Well, someone must have seen us and reported us to the police. The police came into the park and as soon as my friend saw them he put the gun into his pocket. The police shouted "Stop," but when John turned around and saw them he got scared and he began to run. He ran for many blocks until finally there was a policeman in front of him and policemen on both sides and they all had their guns drawn. They shouted, "Stop, or we'll shoot." Well, John stopped and fell to the ground so he wouldn't get hit and they put handcuffs on him and took him to the police station.

By the time I saw him next day there wasn't a clean place on him. He was black and blue all over, both arms were bruised, and he was really in bad shape.

I know he shouldn't have run, but he didn't want to get caught. He knew that police regularly beat people and I know for myself that I wouldn't want to be picked up by a policeman either. If I thought I had done something wrong, I would run away as far as I could.

Well, my friend's father was out of town on business, but his mother went down to the precinct as soon as she heard. The police told her that luckily all this had taken place during the day because otherwise he might have been really hurt. They said the ballistics report showed that the gun had only been used for BB's and so he was safe. Well, when my friend's mother saw the condition he was in, she was very angry and I think she threatened to sue. But nothing ever came of it that I heard.

The police took his gun, I guess took it home for their own kids. But, really, it was a good job they did. They didn't know what he was doing with that gun and it taught him a lesson. I'm on the law's side. After all, he could have seriously hurt somebody with those BB's which are very powerful. This way, he really learned his lesson.

In a way, it's funny that this particular boy was the one who got into trouble. He's really very smart and has very strong opinions about everything. He won a medal for the German language and I consider him one of my intellectual friends. You know, out of a large group, there are a few who are more serious-minded and perhaps who use a better vocabulary and that sort of thing.

Actually, most of my friends, my really close ones, come from the neighborhood. I know some boys at school very well, but it's not the same. Most of the kids I still see are the kids I graduated from Holy Family with. They're from this immediate area, and even though most of them are in different schools now, we still see each other. I guess you could say I belong to sort of a clique . . .

(Juan Gonzales)

What do you think?

1. In general, does Juan's present living situation seem better than the "old law tenements" that were demolished to make room for the housing project? Explain in detail.
2. How could a landlord who owns a slum building win cases in court? Do tenants and landlords have equal rights and privileges? See exercise #3 below for a detailed project on this question.
3. Is the tradition of being "introduced" to someone by fighting him a universal one or is it characteristic of certain social or economic classes? Certain sexes? Ages? Races? Is it a tradition in your community? Comment on why it is or is not.
4. Make the same kinds of comments and considerations about the tradition of belonging to a gang.
5. What do you think is an individual's responsibility for attempting to help a stranger who is in trouble? Explain in detail.
6. What does Juan mean when he says that the next policeman in the neighborhood was, ". . . just bad like a regular policeman?" Do you agree with this estimation of the "regular policeman"? Account for the similarity or difference of opinion in terms of the character of community-police relations in your neighborhood and in Juan's.

Suggestions for reading, writing, research, and viewing

1. In the library look in a specialized reference book such as *The Encyclopedia of the Social Sciences* for an explanation of the term, "the melting pot." What does it mean? Is it a fact or a fancy about the American experience?
2. Based on the kinds of information you find in exercise #1, write a brief paper (200-300 words) in which you explain whether the experience of you and your family conflicts with or reflects the "melting pot" theory. Be as concrete as possible.
3. Work with 2 or 3 other students on the project of examining an apartment lease. Determine the rights of the tenant relative to those of the landlord. Report to the class as to whether leases appear to be "fair" documents.
4. In some states there is a *Good Samaritan Law* which protects a doctor who responds in an emergency. Do research in the library in order to find out exactly what this law does and why it was designed. Do you approve of it?
5. Students who are interested in further reading in some of the subjects which Juan touches on in this article are invited to read any of the following paperbacks:

   Down These Mean Streets by Piri Thomas is a gripping novel about a young Puerto Rican becoming a man in New York City and his experiences as a gang member.

   West Side Story by Irving Shulman is an exciting novel about conflicts between Polish and Puerto Rican gangs in New York City and how they influence the lives of certain individuals.

   Beyond the Melting Pot by Nathan Glazer and Daniel Moynihan is a readable book that examines the group characteristics of ethnic groups in New York City, including Jews, Afro-Americans, and Puerto Ricans and the fact that they have not been assimilated into the mainstream of this country.

The City as Man's Home (National Film Board of Canada, 1963; 28 min.). This film takes the viewer into a wide variety of kinds of housing in the city: tenements, public housing units, luxury housing, and mass suburbs. The theme of the film is that communal standards of living have dropped, partly because of the kinds of buildings that are being erected.

(Peter Quinn)

What do you think?

1. How would you express the difference between the *kinds* of problems that Mrs. Quinn and Mrs. Gonzalez face insofar as their living conditions are concerned?
2. Do you have the impression that Peter's apartment affects his attitude toward himself? His family? His world? How is it affected? Why would he want to be off by himself in his "great big comfortable chair"? Does Juan have a comparable opportunity to be alone in his home?
3. Argue for or against Peter's contention that ". . . living as they (Puerto Rican and colored kids) do, there wouldn't be much else for them to look forward to besides picking up a name for being tough."
4. If you were Peter would you have backed down and agreed not to come into the gang's block? Why or why not? In your opinion, is he being cowardly?
5. Imagine that you were that policeman offered $100,000 to forget about a gambling syndicate. Would you accept the money? Would you rationalize your behavior? How?
6. Argue for or against Peter's contention that the policemen did "a good job" in capturing and beating his friend who had the BB gun.
7. Interpret Peter's statement, "I'm on the law's side." Would you think Juan would describe himself in the same way? Would you describe yourself in the same way? Explain your responses.

Suggestion for writing

1. Peter calls his close group of friends a "clique"; Juan calls his close group of friends a "gang." The words describe things that are approximately the same, but the associations of the words are quite different. What other examples can you find where two or more words have the same approximate meaning but different associations. Make a list like this:

Positive	*Negative*
generous	spendthrift

STORERONT CHURCH

Olga Cabral

Sad on a ghetto Monday
morning in winter
a storefront church with prayers
shut up for weekday:
old door with blisters, sealed
like a deaf mute's mouth,
windows like beggar's cataracts—
and peeping through worn blinds
a lonesome company
of Saints with plaster eyes:
an amputee angel
that will never take off for heaven
a chipped Madonna, shopworn
Christ with no nose:
the gods of the poor, themselves
so shabby, it is plain
they could not pay the landlord
and were evicted from heaven.

The blue of the painted robe
of the Madonna reveals
the shoddy clay beneath,
and is not the blinding
blue breathless spangled
folds of galactic
hosts, but the faded
old scrubrag of hope;
and her Son, compassionate
for all the trouble poured
in his private ear
is himself so beat
by misfortune, you might think
he had spent the night
in a flophouse;
and as for the Angel
of the Lord, whose name
only trumpets can rightfully
utter, with zithers
and cymbals and saxophones—he
left his wings in a pawnshop
and became a beggar.

It is not myrrh and frankincense
sweetens the gelid air within,
but oil of wintergreen—and groans
of wintry pain laid at their feet
above the dusty blooms of wax
makes the sad Saints but sadder:
they too are aching, old
and know their impotence.

"Storefront Church" by Olga Cabral Kurtz, from *Cities and Deserts,* 1959. Used by permission of author.

What do you think?

1. Is the poet insulting the parishioners by pointing out that their statues (the Saints, the Madonna, and Christ) are shopworn and broken? Explain. On the basis of your first answer, what do you think she feels about the congregation?
2. Why is the phrase "the scrubrag of hope" probably an appropriate description of the blue of the Madonna's robe? Who would use a scrubrag? For what?
3. Does it make sense for the poet to assume that a person would be "beat" if he spent the night in a flophouse? What is a flophouse? What kinds of people live in it?
4. What do you associate the combination "myrrh and frankincense" with? Would it be more appropriate in this church than oil of wintergreen? Explain why or why not.
5. In the last stanza the poet writes, "they *too*"; who is she referring to? Why would she call the parishioners "impotent"?

WHAT EVER HAPPENED TO NEIGHBORS?

Arlene and Howard Eisenberg

Are neighbors in America, like gray hair and home-made ice cream, becoming obsolete?

There is growing evidence that neighboring as our grandparents knew it is becoming a lost art. Whether we live in a teeming city or in a suburb separated by hedgerows, too many of us live side by side as strangers, tight little family islands in a sea of mutual disinterest.

Today we seem more concerned with good neighborhoods than good neighbors. In the new semantics of neighboring, a good neighbor drives the right car and increases our status. A bad neighbor neglects his garbage and devalues our property. The best neighbor keeps his distance except in times of crisis. We drive past him with a hurried wave en route to Somewhere, and he, in turn, brakes briefly en route to Somewhere Else.

Where have all the neighbors gone?

Consider this report from a transplanted Southerner, who described, in accents rich as Louisiana gumbo, his attempts to go right on being neighborly up North. "At Christmas, my wife baked up a batch of mincemeat pies, and my little girl and I took them around to our new neighbors. They opened the door, took one look, said, 'We don't need any,' and closed it in our faces."

Or take the rueful testimony of a young Chicago kindergarten teacher with her first apartment. "I guess my generation just isn't as warm as my mother's. I grew up in a Molly Goldberg kind of neighborhood, where people were in and out of each other's apartments every day. If Mrs. Gordon had to go out and a repairman was coming, she gave my mother the key to let him in. If the butcher made a delivery and my mother was away, a neighbor would lay out the money. But I've lived in the same apartment house for almost two years, and I still don't know a soul to ask a favor or offer one."

But the most damning evidence of the decline and fall of neighboring was a recent meeting for new residents in a bedroom community some twenty miles from Manhattan. A pert, open-faced mother rose to suggest the formation of a Newcomers' Club—"like one we had in Kansas City, to help people get to know their neighbors." The chairman passed around a paper to collect names and phone numbers of those interested. The sheet moved rapidly from row to row. When it was returned, it was blank.

Are we becoming, in the phrase of psychiatrist Joseph T. English, " a nation of strangers"? A hundred years ago, or even fifty, neighbors gathered to help a friend build his house, raise his barn, harvest his

Elihu M. Williams

crops, press—and drink—his cider. Today a contractor builds our homes, and we harvest our crops and cider at the supermarket.

Modern conveniences have made neighboring inconvenient. The home freezer, the automatic ice maker, and the second car have made neighbors less necessary. Suddenly, invisible technological walls separate us. Where Grandmother met her neighbor while hanging out the wash, the automatic dryer keeps her granddaughter inside, hermetically sealed off from the people next door. Our fathers exchanged pleasantries over the whisper of a lawn mower; the thunder of a power mower makes conversation impossible.

Where once we had to learn to accept and live with the people next door, the car and the plane now let us choose our friends without regard to geography. And the telephone has made, as one perceptive lady put it, "anyone within two message units a close neighbor."

Television has contributed to the demise by producing the ideal neighbors. Chet and David, the Smothers brothers, the ladies of Peyton Place, Johnny Carson are often more interesting than the people next door, you don't have to tidy the house for them, and they vanish the instant we weary of their company.

Neighbors come today, as they always have, in all sizes, shapes, and complaints: Noisy, Nasty, Compulsively Neat, Classically Nosy (also, happily, Nice, as well). Author Jane Jacobs believes that the nosy neighbors are actually a community asset: Neighborhoods where people peek through the curtains and take constant note of their neighbors' activities tend to have lower crime rates.

But for people who insist on privacy, all neighbors are too nosy. One writer who moved his family to the suburbs to escape the city escaped back within two years. "Suburbanites are dependable and kindhearted, but they should all be CIA agents. They want to know your salary, your kids' IQs, your golf score. One night I hit a rock with our lawn mower, and three guys came racing over to give me a lecture on how to mow my grass. So we moved back, where the only kind, dependable person I know well is my wife. Now I'm anonymous—and my own man again."

His wife also prefers the isolation of city life. "In the suburbs I had to be friendly with neighbors I would never have picked as friends, for the sake of my children. Here I've got only three friends—but we *chose* each other."

However, less sophisticated young women who push carriages in the courtyards of huge housing developments speak wistfully of the neighbors they left behind them. "I've got five hundred neighbors," said a young mother from a small university town, "and I've never been so lonely in my life. One girl let me use her phone before ours was connected, and she said to drop by for coffee someday. But I never got up the courage, and I suppose she never gave it a second thought."

Corporate uprooting of young families makes countless such women both cause and victim of the decline and fall of neighboring. The young executive wife ping-ponging from one area to another ("I sold the same house three times in three years to families from the same corporation," a real-estate saleswoman exulted) can hardly be faulted for lacking the urge for more than token friendship.

Crisply impersonal institutions now pay people to do what the folks next door once cheerfully did for nothing. But Red Cross, Blue Cross, welfare-department, visiting-nurse, and homemaker services notwithstanding, neighbors are still the first line of defense in a crisis.

One young mother said: "We put an ad in the paper to sell some things, and one man who called got lewd and abusive after I'd given him the address. I grabbed my child's hand and dashed over to a neighbor I'd barely said hello to in seven years. She wouldn't let me leave until my husband came home. And yet, the next day we went right back to nodding."

Crises keep neighboring alive, but reciprocity is a vital element. One-way neighboring lasts no longer than one-way love. A young wife in a vast housing project summed it up: "Neighboring is like a seesaw, and I've been on it since the week we moved here. I was pregnant when we moved in, and I stupidly started moving furniture around. I felt a sharp pain, so in desperation I phoned the name on the mailbox next to ours. She put me to bed and took over entirely for the next few days. A few months later, she came down with a fever of a hundred and four degrees, and it was my turn. Thanksgiving I had the flu, and she did our turkey."

Psychiatrist Alexander Gralnick regrets the decline of neighboring for neighboring's sake. "We miss a great deal if we call on our neighbors only in time of trouble. A mother can buy Doctor Spock in paperback for only seventy-five cents at the corner drugstore. But how much better it is to be reassured by someone who once went through the same worry with a slow walker. Young mothers who can rely on neighbors for advice or simply for the therapy of conversation are less likely to need me or my colleagues."

Fortunately, neighbors still represent security—and instant groceries. Borrowing relationships flourish in many neighborhoods in direct proportion to the distance to the nearest shopping center. One cliff dweller, a refugee from a small town, sees borrowing as a vital social epoxy binding her to her neighbors. "We're constantly shopping each other's shelves," she said. "A box of spaghetti, a couple of onions, a stick of butter, a lemon. It wards off loneliness without your having to admit you are lonely."

"The thing I miss most that I used to borrow back home," said a homesick young mother in a large housing project, "is time. Now when I send Chris to play in the next apartment, I feel I'm borrowing a cup of tranquility."

She's right. Somebody else's time—the basic currency of old-fashioned neighborliness—is the single commodity people seem increasingly hesitant to borrow. Said a candid Connecticut householder, "I'd rather call the plumber to unstop my drain than ask a neighbor for help. I tell my wife I just don't want to disturb him. But the truth is that I know if I call on him tonight, I've got to be willing to return the favor at *his* convenience. Frankly, I'd rather pay than get involved."

"It's better not to get involved" represents the majority sentiment—and may account for the decline of neighboring. Fear of rebuff, of commitment, of the responsibilities of involvement makes most of us hesitate to step into the lives and problems of people our parents would have helped without question.

The need for privacy, time to unwind in an increasingly complex world are most often offered as the standard excuses for being unneighborly. A sales executive put it simply: "I'm with people all day long. When I get home, the only people I want to see are my wife and kids, and sometimes I'm not so sure about them."

But social analysts suggest that the reasons for withdrawing into the family castle and pulling the drawbridge up behind us run broader and deeper. All around us society is nibbling away at our privacy—bugging our telephones, eavesdropping on us electronically, computerizing our credit records. We are megalopolizing our homes, our cities, our relationships. Anthropologist Robert Ardrey has pointed out that as elbowroom diminishes, irritability increases—and neighborliness falls victim to the process.

Studies of living in housing developments show that close neighboring enforces competitive conformity rather than closeness and distorts the values of children, who quickly learn the rules of the status game from their elders. Said one seven-year-old resident of a row-on-row suburb, in inspecting a young neighbor's new playroom, "A *playroom?* This is just an unfinished basement!"

Suburban court calendars are increasingly clogged with feuding-neighbor cases, most of which never come to trial. "What usually happens," one attorney said, "is that the sued neighbor thinks up a reason to cross-file, and the judge throws both cases out of court, with a warning that if he sees them again, he'll slap them both in jail for wasting the court's time." As a result, most people find it simpler and less expensive just to look the other way.

But those of us troubled by feelings that we are perhaps not quite the neighbors our grandparents were—in small favors offered and accepted with affection and without question—take refuge in the fact that we live in a world whose complexity allows no time for being neighborly.

Today it takes a national catastrophe to return us to the kind of neighbors we once were. A power blackout and a blizzard made New York, the coldest city in the world, into a small community of eight and a quarter million neighbors. And the deaths of two Kennedys and one King made total strangers turn to one another in the streets for sustenance and comfort.

Perhaps the real malaise of our time lies in the fact that neighborliness has gone out of it. Many of us who grew up in small towns believed that we had to get away from the neighbors in order to find ourselves. Yet somewhere along the way we miss the reassurance of a small community in which we call and are called by name.

And our children miss much more. Neighbors instruct children in the gentle arts of compassion, of respect for differences in people, in the sharing of the good times and the bad.

We do not have to love our neighbor, but we must be prepared to offer each other a cup of kindness, a stick of compassion, if we are both to survive. The neighbors of Kitty Genovese, the girl in Queens, New York, whose cries for help went unheeded, have learned their terrible lesson. And who knows what might have happened if the neighbors of the man called Sirhan had offered him a little warmth in an alien land in which he felt worthless?

A man must first like himself before he can love his neighbor. But it is quite possible to do both without destroying the fabric of family life. Privacy and compassion can exist side by side, and in the end the old-fashioned, neighborly virtues may best protect our privacy rather than invade it.

The time has come for the return to neighboring.

What do you think?

1. The gist of this article is that modern technological changes have interfered with the impulse to be neighborly. Is this accurate? Are there other circumstances that account for the decline of neighborliness? Or do you perhaps feel that there has been no significant decline?
2. The authors name certain categories of neighbors, such as Noisy, Nosy, Nice, and so on. Extend that list with other one- or two-word descriptions of other types you're familiar with or have heard of.
3. How would you describe yourself as a neighbor?
4. Interpret the following terms and statements that are used in the article. Let the context guide you in your interpretations.
   (a) "a bedroom community"
   (b) "Now I'm anonymous—and my own man again."
   (c) ". . . close neighboring enforces competitive conformity."
   Do statements (b) and (c) reflect or conflict with your own point of view? Explain.
5. Are the authors accurate in their assumption that our grandparents actually were more neighborly? Or is that merely another fantasy about "The Good Old Days"? You might have to ask someone older than yourself in order to get reliable answers.
6. Does your city or town compare favorably or not to the description of general unneighborliness offered in this article? Do you like it that way? Explain why or why not.

Suggestions for discussion and reading

1. Observe your own classroom and the campus you're attending. Is it a close-knit community where most people know one another by their first names? What explanations can you give for the state of affairs that you observe? Discuss your findings and conclusions with a small group of your classmates.
2. Jane Jacobs' book, *The Death and Life of Great American Cities,* has some interesting nontechnical chapters on the problems of large metropolitan areas in the United States.

STYLE: SECURITY IS A PLAYGROUND IN ACAPULCO

Jane Gregory

"Style: Security is a Playground in Acapulco" by Jane Gregory. From the *Chicago Sun-Times,* June 22, 1970. Reprinted with permission from the *Chicago Sun-Times.*

Ask Sloan Simpson if you want to catch up on what's the last word in chic in Acapulco, Mexico. Sloan knows all and has made a thriving business of answering visitors' questions about the tropic paradise she calls home.

The ultimate in Acapulco currently and as far into the future as anyone can peer, says Sloan, is Tres Vidas. It's Texas multimillionaire Troy Post's new private luxury development playground 20 minutes and a universe away from the resort's pedestrian old lush life. Tres Vidas has an initiation fee of $8,000, confided Sloan the other day when she passed through to whet local appetites for getting away from it all. The board of directors which bristles with international titles, is so illustrious it is ridiculous. The members, super achievers all, are the sort who value their privacy and can afford the security to maintain it.

"If your name isn't on the list for the guard at the gate, you don't get in," says Sloan. "Lyndon B. Johnson's wasn't and they kept him out."

If it's that tight now, heaven knows how brittle-nosed the guards will be when the complex of colonial white villas (each with its own pool, natch) and private homes opens formally next year. Cutoff point for the membership is 800. In the unlikely event they should all turn up at once, they'll have ample room. Tres Vidas has six miles of its own beach, 36 holes of championship golf courses and a central clubhouse to rattle around in. Of course, they'll never show en masse. In that set somebody is always off someplace else.

Sloan passed along the briefing on the development as incidental information re the current situation in Acapulco. Her primary reason for coming to Chicago was to stir up interest in her own new project. She has concocted a tour directed at the young active crowd who want to vacation in the resort on a less expansive scale. An extension of her present role as Braniff International Airways' special representative on the scene, her personalized package includes discounts on water-skiing lessons, a chance to have a go at fighting a baby bull in a miniature ring and masses of free time. "It is a completely nonorganized tour," says Sloan proudly. "The only touristy thing we will do is go to La Perla to see the divers. That is a must for anyone visiting Acapulco, especially for the first time."

Wardrobe is no problem, says Sloan. Bikinis and beach jackets are the universal uniform of the sunlight hours. At night anything goes as long as it is costume kicky. "There's something about the atmosphere," she maintains. "When Andrew Goodman, you know the Bergdorf Goodman man, came the winter before last, he said he wouldn't be caught dead in a shirt with a little eyelet ruffling. By the time he left he was in cotton velvet slacks printed in the wildest colors, a pleated shirt and chains."

What do you think?

1. Who is this column written for? A particular sex? Age? Economic group? Race? Do you read such columns regularly? Why or why not?
2. Is Tres Vidas appealing to you as a place to live? Explain.
3. What does the writer mean by the term "super achiever"? Do you know persons who would fit that description? Explain why this is true in the broadest terms possible.
4. What connection is there between these people being "super achievers" and their living in such luxury? Is there a direct relationship between the amount of money a person makes and the quality of his immediate surroundings? Always? Sometimes? What impression would the average observer get of you and your income if he looked at your house?
5. What is the writer's point in stating that Lyndon B. Johnson couldn't get in Tres Vidas? That Andrew Goodman left Tres Vidas wearing the clothes he did?
6. What does the term "Tres Vidas" mean? Why is it appropriate for this particular living development? Explain why it is appropriate, in view of the tight restrictions on who can live there. Does that feature seem fair or not? Explain.
7. Explain how the concept of what a good neighbor is in this article contrasts with the dominant concept in "Whatever Happened to Neighbors?"

Suggestions for reading and writing

1. Write a column modeled on this one in which you report on a type of housing that is *not* considered generally desirable such as a public housing unit, a slum tenement, a migrant camp, or the like. Be consistent in tone and details as you point out the *unlovely* features.
2. Write a description of a typical Sunday afternoon in the life of an occupant of Tres Vidas based on the information provided in the column. Highlight the person's attitude toward his neighbors and his property in your description.
3. Thorstein Veblen's well-known book *The Theory of the Leisure Class* has a chapter on the activity he calls "conspicuous consumption." After carefully reading that chapter, determine whether the residents of Tres Vidas can fairly be called "conspicuous consumers."

ASK ANN LANDERS

WILL THE REAL SLOB PLEASE STAND UP

Dear Ann Landers: I know you'll never print this because it's a slam against your city, Chicago, but here it is anyway.

We moved here from Montana—where folks treat each other with consideration. Chicagoans have the lousiest manners in the world. For example on the buses, people who don't have seats think nothing of asking a stranger who is seated to hold their packages, purses and what have you. I've gotten spots on my coat from leaky lunch bags and a rip in my sweater from a child's toy. This morning was the last straw—a woman asked me to hold her baby. You can guess what happened. What I handed her back the sopping wet child all she could say was, "Oh, my goodness!"

If you have any explanation for such slobbish behavior on the part of your fellow citizens, I'd like to hear it.

IRATE MAN FROM MONTANA

DEAR IRATE MAN?: I thought until I read your signature that you were a woman! I can offer no defense for people with such gall that they would ask strangers to hold their lunches and parcels. But the last incident is another ball of wax, my friend. A man who would remain seated on a bus and let a woman stand with a baby in her arms deserves whatever he gets.

Reprinted by permission of Ann Landers, Publishers-Hall Syndicate, Chicago Sun-Times, Daily News Building, Chicago, Illinois 60611.

What do you think?

1. Is any generalization, such as "Chicagoans have the lousiest manners in the world," true? What are such comments probably based on?
2. To what extent does environment affect a person's behavior? Would you act differently if you lived in a small town or a large city?
3. Which of these two seems most influential on a person's behavior and outlook: the immediate environment such as Peter Quinn's apartment and the building it is in (page 213) *or* the larger environment of a city such as Chicago? Explain how you arrived at your answer.
4. Is it an imposition to ask a stranger who is seated to hold something (or someone) for you while you stand on a public conveyance? If the seated person *volunteered* to hold the item or person would he show good manners? On a broader scale, is the exercise of good manners often a way of imposing on someone else's life-style? Such as a woman *having to wait* for a reluctant man to open a door?
5. Did Ann Landers really respond to the writer's chief complaint? Is her advice worthwhile in this case?

Suggestions for writing and viewing

1. New York City, the largest city in this country, is called many things by many different people. Some call it "Fun City," which suggests certain impressions of its residents and their activities. What other nicknames can you discover for New York City? For other places? What are the connotations of those names? Are they accurate? Write a short (500 words) paper on either one of the nicknames for New York City or that of another city or town. Comment on the accuracy of the nickname.
2. "Third Avenue El" is a short (15 min. color) film that shows the diversity of residential and commercial neighborhoods in New York City. New Yorkers, ranging from old stumblebums to a young child, add additional life to this fast-moving film. Harpsichord music in the background lends an additional dimension of interest.
3. "New York, New York" is a short (10 min., color) film that uses multiple images and other photographic tricks to catch the pace and feeling of this city. There is only the barest of structure, so this film could make an interesting companion to "Third Avenue El," which is conventional and literal in its approach to New York City. (This film is not recommended for students who have no familiarity with large cities.)

NAVAJO LAND

Olga Cabral

Time can be measured in hotrod horsepower
of the tin superheated thunderbirds
along the road that crosses the desert floor:
fleeing the hell's-afire cliffs
of an improbable land where they are aliens,
virgin as the moon's wilderness
and bare of billboard to reassure
the traveller the jet age did not end
in this time-trap.

Or time can be measured in cliffs
that long antedate the human:
eternity of canyon walls
that contain this frying-pan
country of the reservation lands:
cinerama of weathered runes
recording geological wars
of water and wind and rock
and seas long dried into sand.

Ester Henderson/Rapho Guillumette

The scenery's terrifying in monotony:
mud huts, stone age leftovers—
hogans and wickiups
at the great rock paws of the cliffs;
lava chunks like discontinued beasts,
leviathans on a sterile ocean of dust;
the bones of scrambled ages
regurgitated from time's orderly graveyard:
a place like the fiery womb of creation,
inhospitable to humans—yet
to a tribe, to a people
this is home,
the concentration camp we deeded to them
forever.

Motorists stranded report them unfriendly,
not willing to pose for kodachromes;
shooing their children indoors; proud
and quietly hating.
The past lies all about, the bones
of ancestors buried in back yards,
the populous white flocks
you might mistake for sheep, but are bleached stones
and are all their shepherds have.
Their black domed huts are dismal as caves,
tenanted by all the coughing, wasting ancestral
devils of poverty and disease—
yet here and there
a hogan may have a chimney
instead of a smokehole, even a door
with hinges.
Yes, and sometimes
beside a hut on a brutal clay field
there stands an old tin car
precious in all its rust.
It is strange how these people endure
on these pitiful farmsteads: this race
in velvet and azure stones
and silver of biblical kings,
dressed in blue magenta yellow violet green,
all the colors of their rainbow cliffs:
a people once rich in flocks of wool,
once splendid in calico herds:
a land reduced to clay and crumbling rock.
Day long and night long
the idiot thunderbirds
roar under the silent cliffs that can afford to wait
for seas to swallow sands,
for deserts to return in centuries
victorious over seas.
We too step on the gas,
cursing our tin-can culture,
fleeing the accusing want
of a people too proud to die.

But suddenly on the road we meet
our own century:
a rickety-rackety old truck
with a load of bouncing Indians:
a work crew in dirty khakis
going home to their hogans at the day's end, singing
some wild, incomprehensible song of their fathers
or was it "Casey Jones"?

What do you think?

1. Why does the poetess say the following things about the area?
   (a) That it is improbable.
   (b) That the thunderbirds are alien.
   (c) That this area is a time trap.
2. The poetess calls the Navajo land a "concentration camp." Do you agree with that label? Enumerate the features of a concentration camp and those of the desert. Are there more similarities or differences?
3. Does the picture on page 229 mirror this poem physically? How is it different? Does it communicate the same feeling that the poem does?
4. What is meant by the expression "tin-can culture"? Why are the thunderbirds "idiots"? Can you relate your answers to each question so that they complement one another?
5. Is it necessarily an *unfriendly* act to decline to have a stranger take your picture? What are some other reasons that a person might refuse to pose?
6. If the work crew in the truck is singing "Casey Jones," what is probably true about their contacts outside the community?
7. Time, heat, poverty, and starkness are concepts which run throughout the poem. What are the different ways in which the poetess expresses or dramatizes these four?

Suggestions for reading and writing

1. One of these books written about the Indian in the Southwestern part of the United States will familiarize the reader with the culture and country of particular tribes:
   The Tewa World: Space, Time, Being, and Becoming in a Pueblo Society, by Alfonso Ortiz, is a difficult book that describes and interprets the rituals of the Tewa.
   Miracle Hill: The Story of a Navajo Boy, by Emerson Blackhorse Mitchell, is an autobiographical account of a young Navajo's life.
   The Autobiography of Delphina Cuero: A Diegueno Indian, by Delphina Cuero, tells much about the traditional life of California Indians.
2. The word "thunderbird" might refer to actual birds or to automobiles. Because we cannot be sure, this is a case of deliberate ambiguity. Check the term "ambiguity" in a collegiate dictionary and write a very brief paper (150 words) explaining in what ways ambiguity can be useful to a poet.

Suggestions for viewing

1. "The Tree is Dead" is a short (12 min.) film which was made at the Red Lake Reservation in Minnesota. It presents a provocative picture of the poor and dismal aspects of life on the reservation, one which does not fit the relatively optimistic view of the narrator.

LONG NIGHT'S JOURNEY

Dan Wakefield

It is no good to be poor.
—Ricardo Sánchez, a Puerto Rican migrant

I

Ricardo Sánchez came from where the sugar cane is higher than a man to the plaza in old San Juan where the buses marked *Aeropuerto* stop. He came with his wife and two daughters and three suitcases and a paper bag and the promise from a brother in Harlem, New York, that there was work to be found in *fábrica*. The work in the sugar cane was over for the season and Ricardo had found nothing else. The government would pay him $7 every two weeks for thirteen weeks before the season began again, and then with the season he would get $3.60 a day for eight hours in the sun. He had done it before, as his fathers had done it, but this time he told himself he wanted something more. "It is," he said, "no good to be poor." His lean brown face was twisted in a grimace of disgust as he said the words, and remained that way, in the memory of poverty, slowly relaxing as he fingered the three fountain pens neatly clipped to the pocket of his new brown suit, and turned to face the dark from where the buses come.

Christopher Columbus, migrant by trade, stood by frozen in the stone of a statue, the accidental patron saint of the plaza that serves as a boarding place for those who go away. Even more practically, Columbus' weathered figure serves those who stay, for around it sit the old men who sit around the statues of the plazas of the world; these by the chance of Columbus' mistaken discoveries (and Ponce de León's mistaken hopes) speaking the language of his creditor the Queen. But the Queen is four centuries dead, and the island's highest ruler is a president from Kansas—a place whose name and language are totally foreign to the old men who sit by the statue.

Their fathers before them were Indians here, called Borinqueños, and Spanish followers of Ponce de Léon, seeker after gold and youth and captor of neither. His body is buried up the street. Their fathers were Negro slaves from Africa, brought here to fill the vacuum left when the Indians painfully vanished, by death and escape, from the Spaniards' rule. The Spaniards built great forts and repulsed the futile attacks of the French and the Dutch and Sir Francis Drake and ruled until 1898. It was then, a year after Spain had finally granted the people of the island a form of self-government, that Admiral Sampson bombarded San Juan and General Nelson Miles led his troops to the island soil with the news that he had brought "the advantages and blessings of enlightened civilization from the United States of America" and the island again was a colony without self-rule. The old Spanish walls of the city were broken at last, and to the east of the plaza of Christopher Columbus there stands today a building of the YMCA where there once stood one of the four city gates. The only gate remaining is used now not to keep enemies out but to draw tourists in. Across from the *Alcaldia*—the City Hall—constructed by the Spanish in 1604, is the New York Department Store, proclaiming in Spanish a sale in which "Everything Goes." Below the iron grillwork balconies of the Old San Juan Bar and Grill a sign in the window reads "Real Italian Pizza." A taxicab crawls through the narrow stone streets like an insect caught in a maze, turning the high-walled corners with painstaking care. The city is quiet, and the old men who sit in the plaza seem unconcerned. Their fathers are gone and their sons are free to go.

For more than a century the sons have left the plazas and the dust-and-green towns of the interior to come to New York. Ricardo Sánchez is young, but his journey is old. The first Puerto Ricans came to New York in the early 1800's, along with other men of good hope from the underfed islands of the Caribbean who decided that "it is no good to be poor." From Cuba and Santo Domingo they came, from San Juan and Haiti and Jamaica. Some survived and others were lost, and in 1838 the men from Puerto Rico who had managed to make themselves merchants of New York City formed a Spanish Benevolent Society for those of their brothers who had failed and were hungry.

Others went west, and by 1910 there were Puerto Ricans living in thirty-nine states of the Union. Twenty years later the people of the island were in every state, though the great majority were still in New York City. The journey north from the Caribbean became a regular route for those seeking something better (and having the money to make the search), and for most of the first half of the twentieth century an average of 4000 came from Puerto Rico to the mainland every year.

No one seemed to notice. It was not until near the end of the Second World War that the quiet, steady migration became the great migration—the promise of the mainland suddenly expanding with more new jobs than ever before and the word passing on from relative to relative, friend to friend, employment recruiter to unemployed. During the war there was little transportation available for Puerto Ricans who wanted to leave the island, but toward the end of it the U.S. War Manpower Commission brought workers up in army transports to help fill the booming job market. In the first year after the war 39,900 Puerto Ricans came to the mainland, and the annual stream reached an average of roughly 50,000 in the postwar decade. As it has throughout its history, the Puerto Rican migration curve followed the business curve on the mainland, and the start of the greatest postwar recession in 1957 was reflected by a 28 per cent decrease in migration from the year before. Downturns in the volume of business on the continent have always meant downturns in migration from the island, and during the worst depression years of the thirties the flow of migrants actually reversed itself, with more returning annually to the island than came from it. But barring an extreme and prolonged depression, the total of 600,000 first- or second-generation Puerto Ricans in New York City in 1958 was expected to rise to a million by the early 1970's. And, for the first time, the great migration had begun to spread more heavily in cities and towns throughout the country. In 1950, 85 per cent of the entering migrants settled in New York City, but by 1956 and 1957 the average was down to 65 per cent, with others going to expanding Puerto Rican settlements in cities such as Philadelphia (New York's largest Spanish-language newspaper now carries a special column of Puerto Rican news from Philadelphia), Chicago, Cleveland, Ashtabula, Bridgeport, Milwaukee, and others farther west.

The journey from the island had become not only more promising because of the market for jobs after World War II but also much easier to make because of the airplanes that rose from San Juan and landed at Idlewild, New York City, 1600 miles up the ocean, in only eight hours and for only $75 on regular airlines instead of the former price of $180. Besides the approved commercial lines that opened up regular service after the war there were secondhand planes making unscheduled flights for $35—they could charge that price because they were paid off later by men from the states who came to Puerto Rico and charged "employment agent" fees that often consumed life savings sweated from sugar cane as payment for nonexistent jobs in New York City. Some of the victims never found out because they first became the victims of ill-equipped planes that crashed in the ocean. After several such tragedies the government outlawed the small, unscheduled airlines from making the San Juan–New York run.

But the regular, legal air travel flourished—not only giving a boost to the old migration to the mainland cities but also opening up a new migration. Cheap and fast plane travel made it possible to transport idle agricultural workers from Puerto Rico during the heavy harvesting season on the mainland in the spring, and back again to the island when the sugar-cane season began in the fall. A new seasonal migration began on that basis after the war and has grown to an annual flow of about 30,000 workers (not counted in the regular migration figures of those who come and plan to stay). Contrary to popular belief, the great majority of Puerto Ricans who come to New York, and other U.S. cities, are not laborers but city people who have held city jobs on the island.

Ricardo Sánchez, who waited in the dark for the bus marked *Aeropuerto,* was one of the small but slowly growing number of Puerto Ricans who have left the sugar-cane fields for the city. The desire to escape from the backbreaking work of the cane cutting is still not easily fulfilled, but the dream has become much more widespread since many young men saw the world in service with the U.S. Army in Korea, and returned home with higher aspirations. Frank Ruiz, the secretary-treasurer of the *Sindicato Azucarero* (Sugar Workers Union) in Puerto Rico says that it is harder now to get the young men to work in the cane fields because "the army has refined them."

Ricardo Sánchez was able to make at least a partial transition in his work before the drastic change from the island fields to the New York fabric shops. During the idle season a year before, he had found a job doing piecework in a garment shop in the small town of Vega Baja. But the work didn't last, and after another season in the fields he decided to try his luck—and his brother's help—in the *fábrica* shops of New York City.

Ricardo held for himself and his family tickets on the $52.50 night coach Thrift Flight to Idlewild airport. It leaves six nights a week from San Juan at eleven o'clock and arrives the next morning at Idlewild at seven. The adjective "thrift" is the only term of distinction between this flight and the other night coach flight, which costs $64, leaves a half hour later, and arrives in New York City two hours earlier. The Thrift Flight is not recommended—or even suggested at the ticket counters—to non-Puerto Rican travelers. English-speaking people who ask about it are told that it is better to spend the extra money and go on the eleven-thirty flight.

There were only Puerto Ricans on the *Aeropuerto* bus that Ricardo Sánchez boarded in the plaza of Christopher Columbus. They stayed together when they reached the San Juan airport, checking in baggage and then joining friends and relatives and watchers in the crowd on the observation deck. When the flight was called, it was as if a troop plane were leaving for a war, or a group of refugees being shipped of necessity out of their native country. It is that way every night around eleven o'clock at the San Juan airport—the women crying and the men embracing them; the old people staring out of wrinkled, unperceiving faces and the young engrossed with the wonder, rather than the pain of it, pressing up against the iron rail of the observation deck and squinting through the dark to watch the line of human travelers move as if drawn by a spell through the gate below and into the still, silver plane that swallows them, closing silver on silver to complete itself, and then slowly moves toward the dark and disappears.

Inside the airplane Ricardo Sánchez had seated his wife and one of his daughters on the left-hand, two-seat aisle, and taken his other daughter and himself across to the right in the three-seat row with a stranger. The flight was full, as these flights are nearly always full. The $52.50 night flights run by both Eastern and Pan American airlines from San Juan to New York are booked for days in advance.

The plane was hot—hotter than the 75° weather outside—and many of the men already sweating, had taken off their coats. A young, dark-skinned woman in an aqua silk dress was crying softly and fanning herself with the plastic *Occupado* sign from the pocket of the seat in front of her. The stewardess appeared at the head of the aisle when the door was closed and gave a demonstration while the steward explained on the loudspeaker, first in Spanish and then in English, the instructions for putting on life jackets in case of an emergency.

The engines began, swelled, and the plane crept forward. The woman in the aqua dress pressed her face against the porthole-style window, crying much louder now. The balcony of watchers grew smaller and darker; became a few white handkerchiefs waved in the night, and then was gone. Babies began to cry as the plane rose, moving above the red, white, and green pinpoints strung geometrically and sparkling in the pattern of the city and suburbs of San Juan. In several minutes the dark had covered it. The no-smoking and safety-belt signs in the plane blinked off, the overhead lights went out, and only the small, individual reading lights above the seats were on. The babies stopped crying, and the temperature of the plane began to cool. Seats were pushed back, and soon the thin beams of light from the few remaining reading lights were thickened with cigarette smoke. The stewardess came by and asked Ricardo Sánchez if he wanted her to hang up his suit coat. The stewardess did not speak Spanish and Ricardo, looking at her quizzically and smiling politely, clutched his coat when she reached for it and held it folded on his lap. He leaned his head back against the seat, folding his hands on his lap, and stared straight ahead, the view slightly tilted with the angle of the seat; his mouth in a tight, tentative smile. After a while he closed his eyes.

The dull, steady roar of the engine was the single sound, growing louder and fuller as other sounds stopped, until, in its constant drone and throb, the sound of the engine became no sound at all, but a part of the plane's suspended life. It became a sound again several hours later when the screams woke Ricardo Sánchez from his tilted sleep:

"Ay, ay, *ayyyy!*"

The women screamed as the plane fell forward through the dark. The sound of the two engines heightened and throbbed. The plane leveled off from the drop, leaving the stomachs of the passengers with the sickening, overturned sensation that comes on a roller coaster during the sudden, steep descent. The steward hurried down the aisle with smelling salts.

Ricardo Sánchez leaned forward to look across the aisle at his wife. Her head was leaning across on her daughter, who sat in silence, her eyes widening to watch the steward stop by the seat and wave the smelling salts. Ricardo's mouth opened and his white teeth were clenched together as if he were being struck. He started up, but the safety belt was fastened on his waist. He looked at it a moment, then leaned back into his seat. The plane dipped again.

The steward stopped and explained to the only non-Puerto Rican passenger that the plane had hit a storm.

"We felt it quite a bit," he said. "The planes for this flight aren't pressurized. If you take the eleven-thirty flight—the $64 one—you fly above all this."

There was no announcement in Spanish about the storm. Ricardo Sánchez's wife, revived, pulled the white bag for vomiting out of the pocket of the seat and leaned into it. Lightning flashed as the plane pitched again in the dark—the tiny green light on the end of the wing was the only thing visible. Ricardo Sánchez tightened the safety belt of his daughter who sat next to him. She clutched at the arm of the seat, in silence, and pressed against the back of it, her thin legs sticking out with the shiny black patent leather shoes not touching the floor. Her father stroked her hair, then leaned back himself and touched the palms of his hands together, pointing upward, in his lap. Through the crack of the seat in front, the brown, large-veined hands of a woman twisted and knotted and pulled on a rainbow-colored silk handkerchief.

The dips became slighter and the screams lower, several becoming soft, continual moans that rose with the fall of the plane. A man walked back to the stewardess who sat reading a copy of the *Saturday Evening Post* and asked her in English if the worst of the storm was over. She looked up annoyed and said, "*I'm* not the pilot," touched her forefinger to her tongue, and flipped the page of the magazine.

A little after five o'clock in the morning the silver wings of the plane became visible, and then a layer of clouds below the plane. A pink strip grew at the end of the layer of clouds in the east, and an orange streak grew from the pink. The billowed layers of clouds below became blue-gray, then lighter blue. Ricardo Sánchez tapped his daughter's shoulder and told her to look. She leaned across on his lap and he explained, "It is dawn. Look—it is beautiful."

About six o'clock the stewardess came by with a tray of steaming paper cups and asked each passenger, in English, "Would you like some coffee?" Some didn't seem to understand so the stewardess repeated the question in more distinct tones, "Would you like some coffee?" There were those who still did not understand and the stewardess, seemingly annoyed, passed on. Some people nodded, or held out their hands, and were given coffee.

The woman in the aqua silk dress stood up in the aisle and pulled up her stockings. She sat back down, pulled a small bottle from her purse, turned it on her finger, and dabbed at her neck. The strong, sweet smell of perfume spread across the aisle. The plane had broken through the clouds and there was water below. Soon there was land—another island; this one, too, striped and set with rows of white lights and green lights, fewer lights in the growing gray dawn than were seen in the night above San Juan. The island that the plane approached seemed not so much larger than the island it had left. Lower, the land turned brown and barren, with a swamplike series of protrusions in the water, and the plane moved closer till the brown high grass on the land and the wind-ruffled waves of the water were clearly visible. The plane seemed about to touch the water and suddenly touched on land—the end of the Idlewild airstrip. The babies again were crying.

The plane stopped, and the passengers looked out the window at the quiet runways, the long, low buildings, and the high, silver lampposts that arched in a long and graceful curve like the neck of some thin and watchful animal, repeated row on row. The women stepped out of the silver door, clutching at their flimsy, bright-colored dresses, into the morning chill of New York and the gray, surrealistic landscape of Idlewild.

Friends and relatives waited at the gate with scarves and coats and kisses and handclasps and took the passengers out of the airport and into cars and buses to the Bronx and the lower East Side and the upper West Side of Manhattan and also to New York's first large Puerto Rican neighborhood, known as Spanish Harlem.

The landscape of Harlem is dark and loud. The sky and the land do not lie in sheets of pale, unbroken color as they do at Idlewild airport. There is no room. Sky and land are everywhere blocked and blemished by stone—old, smoke-and-weather-stained tenements grafted together in grassless blocks; raw, new walls of housing projects rising in brown, identical forms that stand together in arbitrary clusters like squads of dumb and paralyzed giants stuck in the mud they grow from. At 96th Street the long, fenced-in plots of lawn that run through the center of Park Avenue disappear, and in their place the New York Central Railroad rises from underground onto an elevated track that stretches north on Park, making a straight, black spine through Spanish Harlem. In its shadow to the west from 109th and 116th Streets is *La*

Marqueta—the open market place of fruits and fish and shirts and shoes and dresses and vegetables, owned mainly by Italians and Jews, sold mainly to Puerto Ricans. Goods are displayed on tables outside the store, some in the open, some underneath the awnings like the one that reads "Harry Schwartz Infants' and Children's Wear—*Se habla español.*" Growing out of the shadows of the soot-covered railroad bridge, west to Fifth Avenue, east to the East River, is the world of Spanish Harlem.

In winter the children build bonfires in vacant lots, and the tropics is only a memory, preserved by signs and language. The past on the island and the promise of New York are intermingled, and flow out of separate identities into a single experience, a single mixture, that is neither one thing nor the other. In old San Juan was the New York Department Store; in Harlem, New York, is the San Juan Restaurant. The wall of a coffee shop in old San Juan bore a sign advertising the flight to New York; the sign in a barbershop on Lexington Avenue advertises *La Isla Encantada.* "The Enchanted Island" was supposed to be New York, but it turns out to be Puerto Rico. . . .

II

. . . Before the local migration that created Spanish Harlem, the Puerto Ricans had existed literally on the fringe of New York. Their two small settlements were located close to where they got off the boat from the island, and they huddled there, balancing on the outer rim of the life of the city, never presuming to penetrate farther. The first of the colonies was begun by a group of cigarmakers who stopped at the entry point and place of first settlement of so many streams of immigrants, the lower East Side. The other was the Navy Yard section of Brooklyn, where a group of Puerto Rican seamen settled within sight of the docks they departed from.

The sea route provided the only means of entry from Puerto Rico in those days, and the sea route was largely responsible for the original choice of New York as the place for Puerto Ricans to settle in the United States. New York was the destination of the great majority of Puerto Ricans who wanted to come to the mainland. The only other regular continental stops that were made by ships from San Juan were the Gulf Coast ports, and they were less frequently run and more expensive than the $40, three- to five-day voyages to New York City. It has sometimes been questioned why the Puerto Rican migrants, who have to adjust to a new, cold climate in New York City, didn't take the Gulf coast route and settle in the South, where living and working conditions were more familiar. Aside from the obstacles of money and accessibility, the Puerto Ricans had to face the question of color. The Spanish-Negro-Indian heritage of the island has produced a variety of skin color, ranging from Negro to white with all shades in between, and an estimated one-fourth of the Puerto Ricans are of Negro complexion. The point of migration was—and is—to find a better life, and the South was obviously not the answer for workers of dark complexion.

New York was at least a workable answer, though not without its problems for people of color. But the darker-skinned migrants did not face the new discrimination of the mainland with all the innocence that often is believed. Because there is no legal discrimination based on color in Puerto Rico, it is commonly simply stated that "there is no discrimination." But the darker-skinned people on the island are seldom found in office or professional positions, or in the top hotels, night clubs, or social activities. When the Puerto Ricans meet discrimination on the mainland, it is not altogether a new experience. . . .

. . . Life on the mainland has, if anything, heightened the Puerto Ricans' color consciousness, for they are anxious not to be identified as American Negroes. It doesn't take long to learn that the Negroes are lowest on the scale in American life, and in order not to be like them the darker Puerto Ricans are often the most reluctant to learn English. Speaking only Spanish identifies them as foreign and therefore not just a Negro. The Puerto Ricans in New York City have learned the consciousness of color from both their old home and their new home, and that accumulated knowledge has brought them to the awful moments of fear and hope when the pregnant women in Spanish Harlem rub their stomachs with talcum powder to make the baby turn out light.

Like a shadow of their own dark fear, the Puerto Ricans are followed by American Negroes. The Negroes followed them into East Harlem, which had been a white neighborhood, and later into other places where the Puerto Ricans broke the color barrier in housing and automatically enabled Negroes to cross the line afterwards. The Jews of the neighborhood said that East Harlem was no longer desirable because the Puerto Ricans were moving in. Later on many Puerto Ricans said the neighborhood was no longer desirable because the Negroes were moving in. But the Puerto Ricans were not as easily able to move somewhere else. Those who were able moved to the Puerto Rican settlement in the Morrisania section of the Bronx; and the Puerto Rican community in East Harlem soon became known as a home for the poor. By 1927 the Puerto Rican Brotherhood of New York City was publishing an appeal for their brothers not to discredit the Puerto Ricans who lived in East Harlem. The Brotherhood sadly observed that many times Puerto Ricans in the city discredited *El Barrio* and that some of the most hateful remarks and rumors about that neighborhood came from other Puerto Ricans "who live on salaries in offices who think themselves superior."

The Bronx became known as *El Barrio de los adaptos;* Harlem was the home of the unadapted. But Harlem was hard to escape, not only because of financial reasons, but also because of housing discrimination in other areas. In the thirties the New York Spanish newspaper *La Prensa* printed a cartoon that embodied this frustration. One half of the cartoon pictured a fat, cigar-smoking American in a Spanish country, saying that he had *muchos pesos* and wanted to find a place to live. Two small Spaniards bowed before him, and bade him welcome to a fine house. The other side of the cartoon, marked "Washington Heights," showed an American woman waving a broom at a prospective tenant and saying "Get out! No Spanish people are allowed here."

Since that time many Puerto Ricans managed to penetrate the white lines of Washington Heights, and sections all over the city that were formerly barred to them. In 1958 there were Puerto Ricans living in all the health districts (the smallest city district breakdown) of New York, and heavy settlements on the upper West Side, the lower East Side, and the Bronx. But there still was East Harlem—more crowded than ever, more "Spanish" than ever, and still just as poor. The older groups who once were newcomers mostly had managed to move up the ladder, out of this slum. Italian groceries became *Bodegas.* Synagogues became Pentecostal churches with signs of services printed in Spanish.

On East 100th Street a storefront synagogue had to be sold to a Negro–Puerto Rican church because the old congregation was no longer large enough. The sale was in the summer, and the few remaining families of the synagogue asked the new owners if they might hold services on the sidewalk in front on Sabbath evenings. The request was granted, and the dozen or so members of the departed synagogue gathered on Fridays at dusk on folding chairs on 100th Street in front of their former temple. The weather grew colder and the crowd grew smaller on each succeeding Friday and then the first snow came, and after that the services were no longer held. When the good weather came again there were no more requests for the sidewalk synagogue meeting. The synagogue had died on the street, which is finally appropriate in Spanish Harlem, where so much has its birth and death on the street and the street holds so much life; and is, at times, alive itself.

When the good weather comes the chairs and tables come out to the sidewalk for checkers games and dominoes and sometimes cards, and the kids come out, the young ones playing in the vacant lots, the older ones huddled by candy stores and late at night in hallways of tenements, harmonizing. But the street comes most alive in the late afternoon when the men return home from work and the kids are home from school.

At five o'clock one hot June day on 100th Street that life began to grow. The women hung from the hundred faces of the windows, their breasts pressed against the sills, their eyes on the living street. In the vacant lot that looked like a bombed-out building site the small children romped across the dirt that glittered with broken glass, beneath the long-strung flags of washing—white, green, yellow, and red. Down the block the Pentecostal Church of *Espíritu Sanctu* beat its bass drum and made its call that comes whenever there are two or three to gather together in morning or afternoon or night. The men in slacks and sport shirts and open-neck white shirts sat, waiting on doorsteps, and stood beside doorways, leaning on buildings. The afternoon was hot and bright, and the sun made yellow shafts on the dark of the tenements.

A tall, dark man in a white shirt, a rust-colored cap on his head and a light brown jacket flung over one arm, stepped out of a doorway, looked each way down the street, and drew a large black wrench from under his jacket. He fitted it onto the top of the fire hydrant in the middle of the block, and twisted it. A silver stream came out of the hydrant, first in an arc, then thickened and straightened and shot across the street. The hissing sound it made grew as it widened and reached across the street, and was joined by the voices of the kids that grew around it. They ran from the vacant lot and out of doorways, dancing and yelling, and the man who had made the miracle—the silver water in a dry, dark land—stepped back into a knot of men and women, a smile across his face, his eyes fixed on the children. He slipped the wrench back under his jacket. Farther down the street the cry came to look—*"Mira, mira!"* The man with the wrench walked past the gusher, across the street to another doorway, watching the street from a different angle, smiling still, an artist appraising his work and finding it satisfactory.

A group of T-shirted boys had gathered at the hydrant, and one come running with an empty beer can whose ends were pushed out. The biggest of the boys knelt down behind the hydrant like a trapper of animals kneeling behind his prey, and fitted the can over the hydrant, over the silver stream, funneling it into the air, raising it to rain on the storefront window of the Baptist church across the street. The stream turned, writhed, and twisted, rose higher, the voices of the children rising with it, until the boy no longer had control and the can flew out of his hands and sailed through the air across to the other sidewalk.

A bony, tan boy in a skintight yellow bathing suit ran from a doorway and into the stream where the water hit the opposite curb and sprayed into white foam that flowed away in a small torrent that blackened with the street. The boy danced in the small spray, raising his feet as if the street were on fire. A boy on a bicycle sped toward the stream and streaked through it, and two more boys on bicycles followed. A barefoot girl tossed a tin can into the growing torrent at the curb. A new boy trapped the stream with a can and turned it skyward and a group of boys and girls ran under the high-falling spray, the hands and faces of the girls uplifted to catch it as it fell and cooled them. A boy lifted his pants above bright-striped socks and ran through the stream, his shoes sopping wet but his pants cuffs dry.

The yells of peoples' names and the exclamation of *"Mira!"* was suddenly interrupted by a different shout—*"Policía, policía!"* A boy from a window pointed toward First Avenue and a slowly striding, tall policeman, his face blank, his club swinging idly at his side. The kids dropped cans and ran and the stranger in blue brought his own wrench out and tightened the top of the hydrant. The gushing grew quiet, fizzed, drew in from its powerful stream across the street, became a small silver fountain poured on the curb, and died. The kids rushed around it and knelt below the mouth of the hydrant, holding up hands to catch the last drops of water. The stranger gave the final twist and the kids moved back, staring at where the life was, slowly scattering again to where they had been—marbles and baseball and doorsteps and glass-sprinkled empty lots of dust and garbage. Three bicycles returned, circling through the black surface of water still remaining, then they too moved on, pumping slowly, out of sight.

In several more hours the street will be dark, and the long, hot night of Harlem will begin. Within it, before it is broken with dawn, someone perhaps will remember the promise that made him come here and now has a different more hopeless significance. This is New York and the long night's journey is not yet over and it still is no good to be poor.

What do you think?

Part I

1. What explanation can you provide for the fact that quotations surround the phrase, ". . . the advantages and blessings of enlightened civilization from the United States of America"? (Page 233.)
2. Is the airline exploiting the mostly Puerto Rican passengers who take the "thrift" flight to New York City or is the airline being considerate by providing them with a bargain? Give reasons for your answer.
3. Why does the writer say that "The Enchanted Island" turns out to be Puerto Rico, not New York City, as the migrants had originally thought.
4. Describe the dominant tone of this first section.

Part II

5. Explain what is meant by the statement that "Negroes are lowest on the scale in American life." (Page 239.)
6. What explanations can you provide for the amount of time spent on and the number of activities that go on in the streets of this neighborhood? How does this compare with a typical hot summer day and night in your community? Why do you prefer any one style of streetlife?
7. Give reasons why the spontaneous manner in which the Pentecostal Church of *Espirítu Sanctu* begins its services seems like a reasonable or unreasonable one.
8. On page 240, men in open-neck white shirts are described as "waiting on doorstoops." What are they waiting for? Have reasons to support your response.
9. Describe the different tones of this section. How does the tone change when the fire hydrant is turned on? And how does the overall tone compare with that of section I?
10. Summarize the conditions that the Puerto Ricans in this essay are living in, which have made the promises of New York City hopeless ones.

Suggestions for writing and reading

1. Imagine a conversation between the *policía* who turns the fire hydrant off and the man who turned it on. What reasons would each offer for his action? Write the conversation, in strict dialogue form, in a short paper (500 words). Give each man an appropriate name.
2. Write a short paper (500 words) in which you explain why the description in the poem, "Storefront Church" (Page 219), would or would not fit with the impression of this neighborhood in Spanish Harlem.
3. *La Vida,* by Oscar Lewis, describes the life-styles of selected Puerto Ricans in both San Juan, Puerto Rico, and in New York City. The selection about Fernanda is especially lively and informative. Available in paperback.
4. *Down These Mean Streets,* by Piri Thomas, is a novel about a teen-aged dark-skinned Puerto Rican boy growing up in New York City. In paperback.

17

BROOKLYN ROADS

Words and Music by
NEIL DIAMOND

Brooklyn Roads

19
D7
Gm
C7
Two floors a-bove the butch-er, first door on the right,
I built me a cas-tle, with drag-ons and kings,
Does some oth-er young boy come home to my room?
F
Fmaj7
F7
F6
And life filled to the brim, as I stood by my win-dow and looked out on
And I'd ride off with them, as I stood by my win-dow and looked out on
Does he dream what I did, as he stands by my win-dow and looks out on
rall.
C
D
G
D7
to Coda
1
2
D.S. al Coda
those Brook-lyn Roads.
a tempo
CODA
G
D
G
D7
G
D
Brook-lyn Roads.
rit.
Brooklyn Roads

Elihu M. Williams

Brooklyn Roads
by Neil Diamond

If I close my eyes I can almost hear
My mother callin', "Neil,
Go find your brother, Daddy's home
And it's time for supper, hurry on."
And I see two boys racin' up
Two flights of staircase,
Squirmin' into Papa's embrace,
And his whiskers warm on their face.
Where's it gone? Oh, where's it gone?
Two floors above the butcher,
First door on the right,
And life filled to the brim, as I
Stood by my window and looked
Out on those Brooklyn Roads.
I can still recall the smell of cookin'
In the hallways, rubbers dryin'
In the doorways, and report cards
I was always afraid to show.
Mama'd come to school, and
As I'd sit there softly cryin',
Teacher'd say, "He's just not tryin'.
He's got a good head if he'd apply it,
But you know yourself,
It's always somewhere else."
I built me a castle, with dragons and kings,
And I'd ride off with them, as I stood
By my window and looked out
On those Brooklyn Roads.
Thought of goin' back, but all I'd see
Are strangers' faces, and all
The scars that love erases,
But as my mind walks thru those places,
I'm wonderin' what's come of them.
Does some other young boy
Come home to my room?
Does he dream what I did, as he stands
By my window and looks out
On those Brooklyn Roads. Brooklyn Roads.

What do you think?

1. Describe the dominant mood of the speaker as he remembers his childhood.
2. The description of his home sounds as if it might resemble the kind of place Juan Gonzalez (see page 209) lived in before it was torn down to make way for the public housing units. Does the speaker appear to have loved, liked, or disliked his home? Support your answer with references to the lyrics.
3. In general, what are the benefits and drawbacks to daydreaming? In this particular case, which are greater? Explain.
4. Interpret the expression, ". . . all the scars that love erases." Have you ever had experiences that reflect or conflict with this idea?
5. In the last stanza, the writer refers to the room as his own. How do you account for this? What is the implication about the nature of existence in this stanza when the writer assumes another boy is now living there? Is this in concert with your own view of human existence? Explain in some detail.

Suggestions for listening and writing

1. "Brooklyn Roads" is available on a 45-rpm record sung by the writer, Neil Diamond. Listening to it will enhance the mood hinted at in the lyrics. It's on UNI Label No. 55065.
2. In these song lyrics the writer singles out certain sensory experiences—cooking smells, clothes drying, his father's warm whiskers—to flesh out a picture of his homelife. Write a very brief paper (200 words) or a short poem in which you single out the sights, smells, sounds, and activities that have most impressed you—negatively or positively—about your home.

BIOGRAPHICAL INFORMATION

W. H. Auden (1907–) is thought to be a major figure in American and British poetry. He was born in England and was, for a short time, a schoolmaster there. He sees himself "in open rebellion against the morés and opinions of the upper bourgeoisie into which he was born." Other books by him include: *For the Time Being* (1944) and *Collected Shorter Poems, 1930–1944* (1950).

Michael S. Bell attended school in Chicago, Illinois, before moving to California where he is teaching/learning in the school of Critical Studies at the California Institute of the Arts. He has a wife, a daughter, a dog, a kitten, and a car.

Sally Benson (1900–) has worked as a bank teller, feature writer on a newspaper, book reviewer and film critic. She contributes stories to *The New Yorker* and has written numerous film scripts, among them, "Anna and the King of Siam" and "The Singing Nun."

Gwendolyn Brooks (1917–) is an American poet and novelist whose early poems were published in the Afro-American newspaper, *The Chicago Defender.* She has won a Pulitzer Prize for poetry and in 1968 was appointed poet-laureate of Illinois. Books by her include: *Annie Allen* (1949) and *In the Mecca* (1968).

Olga Cabral has authored three books of poetry. The first, *Cities and Deserts* was published in 1959. She is the widow of the Yiddish poet, Aaron Kurtz, whose poems she has helped translate. Of Portuguese ancestry, she has lived most of her life in New York City.

Ben Caldwell is a Harlem essayist-playwright-artist. His plays have been presented at Newark's Spirit House and on the West Coast by the Black Arts Alliance. Two of his plays are included in the anthology, *New Plays From the Black Theatre,* edited by Ed Bullins (1969).

E. Simms Campbell (1908–) is one of the most successful Afro-American commercial artists. His success dates back to the thirties and forties. He has illustrated children's books; his cartoons regularly appear in *Esquire* and *Playboy* magazines.

Pedro Contreras is a young Chicano whose writings have appeared in several periodicals.

Gregory Corso (1930–) is a poet who was born in New York City. His achievements include winning the Longview Foundation award. Books of poetry include: *The Happy Birthday of Death* (1960) and *Long Live Man* (1962).

Victor Hernandez Cruz (1949–) was born in Agus Buenas, Puerto Rico and has been associated with the Gut Theater in New York City having moved there in 1954. His poems have appeared in several small magazines including *Ramparts* and *Evergreen Review.*

E. E. Cummings (1894–) is an American poet who is considered by many to be in the vanguard of the ultra-moderns for he was experimental, radical, and eccentric in both his poetic technique and typography. His works of poetry include: *Seventy-One Poems* (1950) and *Poems, 1923–1954* (1954).

Joan Dash has written fiction for *Seventeen* and for literary magazines such as the *Minnesota Review.* Her nonfiction has appeared in several publications, including the *Manchester Guardian.* Presently she is working on a book that grows out of the article, "Gifted Women, and the Men They Marry."

Vine Deloria, Jr. is a Standing Rock Sioux who was formerly Executive Director of the National Congress of American Indians. His books include *Custer Died for Your Sins* (1969) and *We Talk, You Listen* (1970).

Neil Diamond records on the West Coast where much of the New Sounds in popular music originates. He has recorded several albums. Among his hit records are: "Kentucky Woman" and "Thank the Lord for the Night-time."

Arlene and Howard Eisenberg have shared bylines for at least 100 articles published in such magazines as *Saturday Evening Post, McCall's, Reader's Digest,* and *Ladies Home Journal.* Their favorite assignment was "Memories of a Monster" written with Boris Karloff.

Erich Fromm (1900–) is a German-born psychoanalyst, social philosopher, and author. His special field is the application of psychoanalytic theory to problems of society and culture. Other books by him include: *Escape From Freedom* (1941) and *Man for Himself* (1947).

Hoyt Fuller (1927–) has worked for many newspapers and magazines including *Ebony, Michigan Chronicle,* and *Detroit Tribune.* His articles have appeared in *The New Yorker, The Nation, Southwest Review,* and other publications. Presently he is managing editor of the monthly magazine, *Black World.*

Jane Gregory is a writer for one of Chicago's newspapers, the Chicago *Sun-Times.*

Ernest Havemann (1912–) was born in and attended school in St. Louis, Missouri. He was a reporter and rewrite man for two St. Louis newspapers, has been an associate editor of *Time* and *Life* magazines and a freelance writer. Books by him include: *I Never Thought We'd Make It* and *The Age of Psychology.*

Barbara Howard was a student in New York City at the time she wrote the poem appearing in this volume. She was a participant in the Teachers and Writers Collaborative of New York, a group which volunteers its time and talents to work with and learn from young New Yorkers.

Everett C. Hughes is an American sociologist who studied under the late Robert E. Park, noted sociologist. Mr. Hughes has done extensive research and other writing in the area of the relationship between professions and power.

Ted Joans (1928–) has been described by Andre Breton, a founder of the surrealist movement, as the only Afro-American surrealist. In addition to painting, he is a trumpet player and jazz poet. His works in progress are *Spadework: An Autobiography of a Hipster* and *Niggers from Outer Space,* a novel.

Oliver LaFarge (1901–1964) was born and educated in the East and South. His first novel, *Laughing Boy* won the Pulitzer Prize for fiction in 1929. He wrote short stories and anthropological books in addition to contributing articles on Indian conditions and culture to various magazines.

Ann Landers (1918–) has been a syndicated newspaper columnist since 1955. She is the author of several books: *Since You Asked Me* (1962); *Teen-agers and Sex* (1964) and *Truth is Stranger* (1968).

Mell Lazarus lives with his wife and three daughters in Scarsdale, New York. He created "Miss Peach" in 1957 and since then has compiled several anthologies of the strip: *Miss Peach* and *Miss Peach, Are These Your Children?* He has also written a novel, *The Boss is Crazy, Too.*

Carson McCullers (1917–1967) is an American novelist and short story writer who has been writing since she was sixteen. Her works are set in the South, many of them are about persons isolated in the lonely world which she creates in her fiction. Books by her include: *The Heart is a Lonely Hunter* (1940) and *The Member of the Wedding* (1946).

Claude McKay (1891–1948) was a prominent figure in the Harlem Renaissance of the 1920's. In 1912 he was the first Afro-American awarded the medal of the Institute of Arts and Sciences in Jamaica. His first novel, *Home to Harlem* (1928), was a best seller. He wrote two additional novels, *Banjo* and *Banana Bottom,* and published collections of short stories and poetry.

Albert Maltz (1908–) is an American novelist who has also written successful screenplays. In 1947, he, along with nine other prominent Hollywood writers, was indicted for contempt of Congress for refusing to tell the House Un-American Activities Committee whether or not he was a Communist. Other books by him include: *The Cross and the Arrow* (1944) and *The Journey of Simon McKeever* (1949).

Charlotte Mayerson is a general book editor with Holt, Rinehart and Winston, publishers. She has written, *Shadow and Light: The Life, Friends and Opinions of Maurice Sterne* (1965).

Marion Montgomery (1925–) has taught at the University of Georgia and been associated with the University of Georgia Press, the *Western Review,* and the *Georgia Review.* He received a Eugene Saxton Fellowship for work on his first novel, *The Wandering of Desire* (1962) and has published two collections of poetry.

David Murray, a native of Boston, is an editorial writer for the Chicago *Sun-Times* and author of the book, *Charles Percy of Illinois.*

Carl Rogers (1902–) has been a professor in departments of psychology and psychiatry at several U.S. universities. Among books he has written are: *On Becoming a Person* (1961) and *The Freedom to Learn* (1969). He continues to contribute articles to professional journals.

Ricardo Sanchez is a Chicano writer whose poetry appears in a collection entitled *Poeta.* In addition to writing, he has worked with the Colorado Migrant Council in Denver.

John Sharnik, in addition to writing articles and short stories which have appeared in magazines such as *Vogue* and *The New Yorker,* has worked on newspapers in positions ranging from reporter to editor. He has also written and produced several television documentaries.

Bob Teague has been a "Big Ten" halfback at the University of Wisconsin and a sports reporter for both the Milwaukee *Journal* and the *New York Times.* Presently he's the NBC-TV anchorman for weekend news broadcasts. Excerpts from his best-selling book, *Letters to a Black Boy* have been recorded with special music and songs.

John Updike is an American writer who received a degree from Harvard. He has worked on *The New Yorker* magazine and was the recipient of the

O'Henry Prize Story award (1967–68). Titles of others of his novels are *Rabbit, Run* (1960) and *Couples* (1968).

Dan Wakefield (1932–) has written nonfiction books, including *Between the Lines* and *Supernation at Peace and War.* His novel, published in July 1970, was entitled *Going All the Way.*

Marvin Weinstein (1937–) joined the Chicago *Sun-Times* in 1955 as a copy boy. Since that time he was appointed auto racing writer. He has done freelance writing for several publications.

Robert C. Wood is Professor of Political Science at the Massachusetts Institute of Technology. His other works in urban politics include *1400 Governments; Metropolis Against Itself,* and contributions to *The Suburban Community* and *Area and Power.*

John Yount (1935–) was born in North Carolina. He teaches at the University of New Hampshire. His first novel is entitled *Wolf at the Door.*